MY BROTHER'S KEEPER

MY BROTHER'S KEEPER

CHRISTIANS WHO RISKED ALL
TO PROTECT JEWISH TARGETS
OF THE HOLOCAUST

ROD GRAGG

CENTER
STREET

NEW YORK BOSTON NASHVILLE

Center Street
Hachette Book Group
1290 Avenue of the Americas, New York, NY 10104
centerstreet.com
twitter.com/centerstreet

First Edition: October 2016

Center Street is a division of Hachette Book Group, Inc. The Center Street name and logo are trademarks of Hachette Book Group, Inc.

The publisher is not responsible for websites (or their content) that are not owned by the publisher.

The Hachette Speakers Bureau provides a wide range of authors for speaking events. To find out more, go to www.HachetteSpeakersBureau.com or call (866) 376-6591.

Unless otherwise noted, Scripture quotations are taken from the King James Version of the Holy Bible.

LCCN: 2016912971

ISBNs: 978-1-4555-6629-7 (hardcover), 978-1-4555-6630-3 (ebook)

Printed in the United States of America

LSC-C

10 9 8 7 6 5 4 3 2 1

For my dear friends the Künstlers

CONTENTS

חסידי אומות העולם

"The Righteous Among the Nations"

A new commandment I give to you, that you love one another, even as I have loved you, that you also love one another. By this all men will know that you are My disciples. —John 13:34–35 ASV

It would be an honor, for me, to give my life for God's ancient people. —Casper ten Boom, 1944

They are perhaps the sole rays of light in this dark era, the few whose consciences prevented them from being indifferent. —Yad Vashem

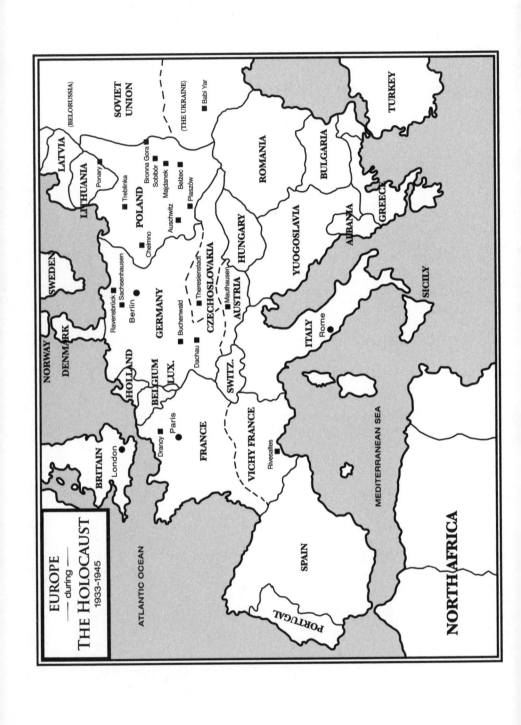

EUROPE
— during —
THE HOLOCAUST
1933-1945

ATLANTIC OCEAN

BRITAIN
London

NORWAY
DENMARK
SWEDEN

HOLLAND
BELGIUM
LUX.
Ravensbrück
Berlin
Sachsenhausen
GERMANY
Buchenwald
Dachau

Paris
Drancy
FRANCE

VICHY FRANCE
Rivesaltes

SWITZ.

LATVIA
LITHUANIA
Ponary
(BELORUSSIA)
SOVIET UNION

POLAND
Treblinka
Bronna Gora
Sobibór
Majdanek
Chelmno
Auschwitz
Belzec
Plaszów
(THE UKRAINE)
Babi Yar

Theresienstadt
CZECHOSLOVAKIA
Mauthausen
AUSTRIA
HUNGARY

ROMANIA

BULGARIA

YUOGOSLAVIA

ALBANIA
GREECE

TURKEY

ITALY
Rome

SICILY

MEDITERRANEAN SEA

SPAIN

PORTUGAL

NORTH AFRICA

INTRODUCTION

*Then the LORD said to Cain, "Where is Abel your
    brother?"
And he said, "I do not know. Am I my brother's
    keeper?"* —Genesis 4:9 NASB

MANY DID NOTHING—EVEN though they called themselves
Christians. Others joined the Nazis and supported the Shoah, or
Holocaust—the dark, deadly storm that swept over Europe with
the rise of Nazi Germany. In it more than six million Jewish men,
women, and children perished, killed by starvation or illness,
fatally tortured or beaten, shot by Nazi death squads, or executed
in concentration camp gas chambers. Contrary to popular mis-
conception, in many ways the Jews of Europe resisted the evil
that befell them. Many Jewish leaders courageously protested the
persecution before they were silenced. Countless numbers tried
desperately to escape captivity. Others became resistance fighters
or joined partisan bands. Some even tried to fight their way out
of the gas chambers. Most, however, were women and children,
often rendered helpless before the mighty force that overwhelmed
them—but even they tried to resist. Every Jewish mother who
gave her food ration to her child or shielded her infant's eyes from

looming destruction was a resister. And as the unimaginable horror of the Holocaust descended upon Europe, countless people who professed the name of Christ also refused to remain silent or inactive. Many risked everything to help rescue Jewish targets of Nazi tyranny. Some even made the ultimate sacrifice, faithfully fulfilling the words of Jesus: "Greater love hath no man than this, that a man lay down his life for his friends."

They ranged in personal faith from nominal believers to the devout. *My Brother's Keeper* records the stories of thirty of them, all of whom have been honored by the State of Israel as "the Righteous Among the Nations." In 1953 the Knesset—the Israeli national legislature—established Yad Vashem, Israel's official memorial to the victims of the Holocaust, which is located on the Mount of Remembrance in Jerusalem. There people of diverse nationalities, races, and religions are memorialized by Yad Vashem for a common cause: they risked all to assist the Jews who were victims of the Shoah or Holocaust. Within their ranks were the Christians whose sacrifices are chronicled in this work, and whose lives personify Yad Vashem's description of the Righteous Among the Nations: "In a world of total moral collapse there was a small minority who mustered extraordinary courage to uphold human values.... They are perhaps the sole rays of light in this dark era, the few whose consciences prevented them from being indifferent to the fate of the Jews." One of the Christians whose story is recounted in this work likely spoke for all herein when he explained why he chose to risk everything to save a single Jewish life. "I know that when I stand before God on Judgment Day," he said, "I shall not be asked the question posed to Cain—where were you when your brother's blood was crying out to God?"

MY BROTHER'S KEEPER

CHAPTER I

FENG SHAN HO

Riding triumphantly at the head of his motorcade, German Führer Adolf Hitler is saluted by crowds of admirers as he arrives in Vienna to claim Austria for Nazi Germany.   (CREDIT: DEUTSCHES BUNDESARCHIV)

"He saved us. It was a miracle."

ADOLF HITLER STOOD erect in a gleaming convertible limousine as it rolled steadily through the broad, tree-lined avenues of Vienna, Austria. It was Monday, March 14, 1938. On both sides of Hitler's parade route, held in check by helmeted German troops, exultant crowds of Austrian civilians packed the sidewalks, cheering, *"Heil Hitler! Heil Hitler!"* In the Austrian countryside far to the west, meanwhile, convoys of German tanks and trucks advanced deep into Austria from the German border. After scheming for years to engineer a German annexation or *Anschluss* of neighboring Austria, Hitler—the German Führer or dictator—had ordered a military invasion of Austria on the pretext of maintaining order—and had managed to conquer Austria without firing a shot. Now—with the joyful approval of many pro-German Austrians—Hitler had come to the capital city to claim his prize—the nation of Austria.[1]

At Vienna's Heldenplatz—Heroes' Square—more than two hundred thousand Austrians greeted the Führer as a triumphant conqueror, shouting their allegiance to the expanded Nazi state and waving miniature red-white-and-black flags bearing the spiderlike Nazi swastika. Attired in a khaki-colored German army uniform and an officer's cap, Hitler dismounted from his limousine, responded to the ecstatic masses with a well-practiced salute, and strode confidently toward Hofburg Palace to deliver a victorious balcony speech beneath huge Nazi banners. As he proclaimed the benefits of wiping Austria off the map and converting it to a German province, the excited masses in Heroes' Square roared their approval.[2]

One who did not cheer, and who watched the spectacle with silent disapproval, was a Chinese diplomat, Dr. Feng Shan Ho, the first secretary of the Chinese embassy in Vienna. Ho had joined China's diplomatic mission to Austria less than a year earlier, representing the Republic of China under Nationalist leader Generalissimo Chiang Kai-shek. To Ho's dismay the generalissimo admired Hitler, purchased arms for China from Nazi Germany, and had even sent one of his sons to Germany, where he had joined the Nazi army and was serving as a junior officer in the Austrian occupation. Despite China's official friendship with Nazi Germany, Ho privately considered the Nazis to be "devils" and deeply distrusted Adolf Hitler. Observing the German Führer in person, Ho was unimpressed: Hitler, he concluded, was a "short little man" with a "ridiculous moustache" who behaved like "an unspeakable martinet."[3]

Feng Shan Ho was a Chinese Christian. He was born in China's Hunan Province in 1901. When he was seven years old his father died, leaving the family in desperate poverty. Lutheran missionaries from Norway who were ministering in Hunan Province provided critical assistance to Ho's family and befriended the young boy. Eventually Ho professed faith in Jesus Christ as Lord and Savior, and began what would become a lifetime association with the Chinese Lutheran Church. Bright, determined, and compassionate, he attended Lutheran schools as a boy, and received a Western-style college education in China, graduating from Yale University through a Chinese extension program. Afterward he managed to travel to Germany to do postgraduate work at the University of Munich. In 1932 he graduated magna cum laude with a doctorate in political economics. It was while studying in Germany that Ho became a witness to Adolf Hitler's remarkable rise to power.[4]

In the opening decade of the twentieth century, Hitler was a high school dropout and teenage loafer—a self-styled artist who evaded ordinary jobs to peddle his mediocre artworks on the streets of Vienna. Even though he was Austrian, he idolized neighboring Germany, and joined the German army in the First World War. As a German infantryman and corporal, he finally found a purpose in life—a fanatical devotion to Germany's war effort. His zeal earned him an Iron Cross medal for boldly carrying military dispatches under fire, and he was deeply distressed when the war ended in a German surrender. Afterward, he joined a radical nationalistic workers' party—and quickly displayed an extraordinary talent for political intrigue, mesmerizing speech-making, and ruthless leadership. He renamed the fledgling organization the National Socialist German Workers' Party—the Nazis—organized a thuggish gang of storm troopers, and adopted the ancient swastika as the symbol of an anti–Semitic, Germanic master race.[5]

In 1923, amid the political turmoil of postwar Germany, Hitler bungled an attempt to transform a Munich beer hall rally into a fascist revolution and was convicted of treason. He spent eight months in prison, but it proved to be the experience that catapulted him to power. Incarcerated by the government in a comfortable prison suite, he had ample time to write a laborious autobiographical rant entitled *Mein Kampf* (My Struggle). It blamed Germany's desperate postwar conditions on the war's victors, the Communist Party, and Germany's Jews. Unexpectedly it became a German best seller, and elevated Hitler to the national stage. It also became the bible for the Nazi Party.[6]

In the early 1930s, while Feng Shan Ho was studying in Munich, Hitler surprised Europe by emerging as dictator of a powerful, resurgent Germany. Except for his peculiar, riveting pale-blue eyes, Hitler was physically unimpressive, with a pallid complexion, slicked-down dark hair, and a faddish toothbrush mustache. He had developed his dramatic oratorical skills to a fever pitch, however, and could incite German audiences to ecstatic or angry frenzy. Funded by opportunistic industrialists and fueled by a diabolical but effective propaganda machine, Hitler's Nazi Party won increasingly large blocs of seats in Germany's parliament, the Reichstag, until Hitler attained the post of German chancellor. In 1933, when a suspicious fire ravaged the building housing the German national legislature, Hitler exploited public fears to obtain legislation granting him unprecedented power as chancellor. He then quickly and ruthlessly outlawed all other political parties, raised up a brown-shirted paramilitary force called the Sturmabteilung, or "storm troopers," and jailed, exiled, or murdered more than two hundred political opponents. In 1934, with no one left to seriously challenge him, Adolf Hitler combined the offices of chancellor and president to become the dictator, or Führer, of Nazi Germany.[7]

By then Dr. Ho was pursuing a career in the Chinese diplomatic corps, and in 1937 he was promoted to the post of first secretary at the Chinese embassy in Vienna. Personally energetic and capable, Ho was good-humored, witty, and gifted with a diplomat's skills, but was also known as a man of character who was committed to defending what he believed was right. In appearance he was distinguished-looking: dark-haired, mannerly, well-groomed, and given to European attire. He and his wife were well received within the Austrian capital's diplomatic community and by the city's intelligentsia. Among their numerous friends were respected members of Vienna's large Jewish community. Partially because of his concern for the welfare of the nation's Jews, Ho was alarmed and appalled at the outpouring of public support for Hitler and the Nazi takeover of Austria. Hitler had openly expressed his anti-Semitic racism in *Mein Kampf*, describing a Jew as the "parasite of the nations" and "a vampire" who "drags everything that is truly great into the gutter." By 1938 Hitler and the Nazis dominated all of German life. Even elementary school children were taught to say of the Führer: "I shall always obey you, like father and mother."[8]

With their country now a province of Germany, Austria's 185,000 Jews were in obvious peril. German laws denying citizenship to Jews and restricting their freedom were now applied to the Jews of Austria. Hitler's storm troopers and his secret police force, the Gestapo, stopped Jewish men and women on the street in Vienna and put them to work scrubbing sidewalks and cleaning street gutters. Jewish children were ordered to sweep the city's wide avenues. Jewish society matrons and business leaders were ordered to clean Vienna's public toilets and the latrines in the Gestapo barracks. At a park in Vienna, Nazi storm troopers pulled Jews from the streets and forced them to eat grass until they became ill. Influenced by Nazi law and propaganda, non-Jews who had been friends, neighbors, and business associates for decades now stopped on the streets to jeer and taunt the Jews. Thousands of Jews were jailed and their property was looted by Nazi officials, troops, and police. "I myself," recalled a foreign journalist, "watched squads of [storm troopers] carting off silver, tapestries, paintings and other loot."[9]

Ominously, a hundred miles west of Vienna at Mauthausen, the Nazis began building a concentration camp like those rumored to exist in Germany. Since 1933 Nazi Germany had pursued a policy of *judenrein*—a "cleansing" of Jews from Germany—and almost one-fourth of Germany's Jewish population had fled the nation. The Nazis' euphemistically named Central Office for Jewish Emigration would reportedly allow "noncriminal" Jews to leave the country if they transferred all their property and finances to the German government—and if they were issued an official entry visa by a foreign nation. Many nations would not accept Jewish refugees, and even Western nations such as Great Britain and the United States severely limited Jewish immigration. In July 1938, delegates from thirty-two countries assembled at the French resort city of Évian-les-Bains to discuss the status of immigrant refugees. Among the countries of the Western world represented at

the Évian Conference, only the Dominican Republic and Costa
Rica offered to increase immigration quotas to accept Jewish refugees. Influenced by worries about the Great Depression and the
US State Department's diplomatic concerns, President Franklin
D. Roosevelt and the US Congress rejected pleas to allow signifi-
cant numbers of Jewish refugees to enter the United States. Other
major Western nations also refused.[10]

**"If I had never knocked on that door in Vienna, I would have been in
a concentration camp."**

Meanwhile, when Austria was absorbed into Germany, most staffers at the Chinese embassy in Vienna were transferred to China's
Berlin embassy. The former Austrian embassy was designated as a
consulate, and thirty-seven-year-old Feng Shan Ho was officially
appointed as its consul-general. Although he was left with a single
trusted associate, Dr. Ho saw the change as an opportunity to save
Austria's persecuted Jews. Courageously, he began issuing visas
that allowed Austrian and German Jews to resettle in the Chinese city of Shanghai. Officially, the Chinese government did not
require a visa to immigrate to Shanghai, but Ho figured the Nazis
did not know that—and Germany required a visa for Jews to leave
the country. He also knew that most of the Jewish refugees would
not go to Shanghai—they would use the visas to flee Germany
and seek asylum wherever they could find it. So Ho began signing
and issuing visas—a few at first. Then dozens. And hundreds. And
eventually thousands.[11]

He contacted American Christian ministries in Austria, which
helped him notify the country's Jewish community. Austria's
Jews spread the word: If you can get to the Chinese consulate in
Vienna, you can get exit visas for yourself and your family—even
dozens at a time. Ho understood the risks. Generalissimo Chiang
Kai-shek and China's foreign service office were cultivating Hitler as a friend and Nazi Germany as an ally. Issuing a flood of

visas to Austrian and German Jews so they could escape Hitler and the Nazis would potentially infuriate Ho's superiors, threaten his diplomatic career, and even endanger his life. It was a risk Ho was willing to take. Quietly, he sent his wife and their eleven-year-old son safely out of the country, then began working day and night to issue visas to Jews. Why was he willing to risk so much? "He knew he had received many gifts from God," Ho's Lutheran pastor would later observe. "He felt that they were not given to him solely for his own benefit, but to do for others."[12]

Long, winding lines of Austrian Jews formed at the entrance to Vienna's Chinese consulate. Thugs from the SS and the Gestapo harassed those who were waiting, sometimes dragging Jewish men aside and beating them. But day after day, the lines continued to form, and one after another, Austria's Jews were issued lifesaving Chinese visas. One of them was Hans Kraus, a Jewish surgeon, who lined up with the throng outside the Chinese consulate for almost a week. The crowd was so large and the wait so long that he feared he would be arrested before he and his family could obtain visas. Then one day he saw Ho's official car pull up to the consulate gate. The automobile's windows were down, so Kraus desperately tossed his completed visa application form inside the vehicle. A few days later, he received a telephone call from the Chinese consulate notifying him that his visa was in the mail. Soon, the lifesaving documents arrived, enabling Kraus and his family to escape from Nazi Germany.[13]

Ho's dangerous attempt to thwart Nazi persecution of Austrian Jews was not confined to his consulate office. Several times he confronted Gestapo agents as they attempted to arrest his Jewish friends. He also made regular visits to the homes of Jewish families he knew in the hope that a relationship with a foreign diplomat would protect them. Once, Gestapo agents attempted to arrest one of his Jewish friends while Ho was visiting his home, but backed down when Ho boldly presented his diplomatic credentials and insisted they leave. In another case Ho learned that his Jewish friend Karl Doron had been arrested and imprisoned at the notorious Dachau concentration camp. Ho issued a visa for Doron and officially demanded that he be freed. Surprisingly, Nazi officials complied with the request, and Doron became one of the few Jewish inmates released from Dachau.[14]

One of the Jews helped by Ho, Eric Goldstaub of Vienna, had visited dozens of foreign consulates in search of a visa, only to be turned away. Then he heard about Feng Shan Ho and the Chinese consulate, where he received visas for himself and his entire extended family, which numbered twenty. Before the family could leave, however, Goldstaub and his father were arrested by Nazi agents. But when they saw the Goldstaubs' Chinese visas, the Nazis let the family go. "If I had never knocked on that door in Vienna, I would have been in a concentration camp," Goldstaub later concluded. "And I would have died.... Our whole family would have died. We needed Feng Shan Ho. He saved us. It was a miracle."[15]

For almost two years, Feng Shan Ho issued an average of five hundred visas every month. At least once he issued more than a hundred in a single day. Eventually the Chinese government learned of the flood of Jewish visas being issued by China's Vienna consulate, and Ho received an angry telephone call from the Chinese ambassador to Germany. Ho's actions threatened China's official relationship with Nazi Germany, the ambassador warned him, and he ordered him to close down his visa mill. Realizing that his rescue operation might soon be shut down, Ho ignored the order and sped up his activities. Soon an official from Berlin appeared unannounced at the Vienna consulate and informed Ho that he was suspected of selling visas. Ho forcefully denied the charges, and the official left. Ho waited for another reprimand or a recall to China, but he heard nothing—so he continued to issue visas at a frantic pace. Eventually Nazi officials became suspicious and confiscated the consulate building, claiming it was Jewish property. When the Chinese government refused to lease a replacement, Ho used personal funds to rent a new office and continued to issue visas. Finally, in the spring of 1939, the Chinese government officially censured him, and soon afterward ordered his transfer to a different diplomatic post. By then, however, Japan had invaded China, and as Japan's Axis partner, Germany was no longer viewed as a Chinese ally. Ho had no choice: he had to leave—but he continued to issue Jewish visas until the end.[16]

Ho held other diplomatic posts during World War II, and continued to serve Nationalist China even after Mao Zedong's Communists won the Chinese Civil War and forced Chiang Kai-shek's government to flee to Taiwan. Ho's campaign to save Austria's Jews left a shadow over his career, however, and after forty years of dedicated service, he was censured and dismissed by his government. He moved to the United States, where he continued to be active in the Chinese Lutheran Church. In 1997 he died at age ninety-six. His dangerous, heroic efforts to assist the Jews of Austria were known to but a few, and the humble former diplomat seldom told others about his deadly drama in Vienna. "I thought it was only natural to feel compassion, and want to help," he said simply. Some who escaped Nazi terror with Ho's help eventually made a remarkable calculation: thanks to Dr. Feng Shan Ho's courageous actions, more than twelve thousand Jews escaped the Holocaust.[17]

CHAPTER 2
OTTO AND GERTRUD MÖRIKE

A Nazi storm trooper strikes a threatening pose outside a Jewish business in Berlin. The sign reads: "Germans! Defend yourselves! Do not buy from Jews!" (CREDIT: NATIONAL ARCHIVES)

"As a Christian, I must reject National Socialism."

PASTOR OTTO MÖRIKE was dragged from his bed in the middle of the night by Nazi storm troopers. They hauled him into the street, threw him down before a mob of cheering Nazis, and then savagely beat him until he was bruised and bloody. His crime? He had voiced his opposition to Adolf Hitler's policies on what was supposed to be a secret election ballot. Ironically, Mörike was a veteran of the German cavalry in the First World War and had once enthusiastically supported the Führer. Like most Germans after the war, he was distressed that the Treaty of Versailles had officially forced Germany to accept full blame for the Great War, which had resulted in the loss of seventeen million lives. Overburdened by the huge reparations payments required by the treaty, Germany's economy plummeted following the war. Inflation and unemployment soared, and the German people lived in desperation and rising resentment well into the 1930s. Amid such harsh conditions, Mörike initially viewed Hitler as a reformer whose strong leadership might heal Germany. He soon changed his mind, however, as Hitler's true intentions became apparent.[1]

"Soon, the ideology revealed itself in an ominous manner," Mörike later recalled. "I knew I had been deceived." When Hitler came to power in 1933, Mörike—a tall, lanky, bespectacled thirty-six-year-old—was a minister in Germany's Evangelical Church. His wife, Gertrud Löcher Mörike, a twenty-nine-year-old pastor's daughter, was a mother of three and a fearless believer. Theirs was a joyful home, marked by frequent laughter, daily family devotions, and Christ-centered optimism. Both Otto and Gertrud grew increasingly concerned, however, as they saw Hitler persecute Germany's Jews and any Christians who objected.[2]

In April 1933, Hitler ordered a national boycott of Jewish-owned businesses, which was followed by the dismissal of Jewish employees from government positions, including public schools and universities. Jewish doctors, pharmacists, and attorneys were placed under severe restrictions. Jews were banned from holding positions as judges, lawyers, journalists, broadcasters, artists, musicians, actors, and farmers, and were prohibited from serving in the military. Jewish schoolchildren were barred from classes. At universities throughout Germany, Nazi professors and students made huge bonfires of books by Jewish authors, including an estimated twenty thousand volumes set afire at Berlin's Humboldt University. Increasing numbers of Jews and others deemed to be enemies of the state were hauled off to newly constructed concentration camps, which, in the words of one horrified observer, "sprang up like mushrooms." By year's end there were at least fifty camps in Germany, the most notorious being outside the town of Dachau. An estimated thirty-seven thousand Jews fled the country in 1933; the rest hoped the persecution would pass. Instead it worsened.[3]

On June 30, 1934, on what would become infamous as the Night of the Long Knives, Hitler purged the Nazi elite of everyone he considered a threat to his leadership. More than two hundred prominent or high-ranking Nazis were executed in a single night. Hitler also replaced his brown-shirted quasi-military storm troopers with a brutal elite force of black-uniformed troops called the Schutzstaffel, or SS. As he consolidated power, he also brazenly defied the Versailles Treaty by ordering a massive buildup of the German military. From the lowliest enlisted man to the highest-ranking officer, every member of the German armed forces had to take a new oath of allegiance: "I swear by God this sacred oath, that I will render unconditional obedience to Adolf Hitler, the Führer of the German Reich."[4]

As Hitler moved against the Jews and others he considered enemies of the Nazi state, he also took action to repress opposition by

Christian leaders and church members. In the summer of 1933, the Nazi government signed a treaty with Pope Pius XI that guaranteed religious freedom for Germany's Catholics and the right of the Catholic Church to "regulate her own affairs" within the Third Reich. However, Hitler used the treaty to try to legitimize the Nazi government, which was drawing international scorn for human rights abuses, and ignored it when German Catholics opposed his rule. He ordered the arrest of Catholic priests and nuns who criticized Nazi actions, shut down Catholic publications, and moved to replace the Catholic Youth League with the newly formed Hitler Youth.[5]

Hitler's persecution of Germany's Protestant churches was even harsher. A majority of Germans were professing Protestants, and Hitler aggressively moved to Nazify the nation's Protestant denominations. His ultimate goal was promotion of the Nazi *Deutsche Evangelische Kirche*, commonly called the "National Reich Church," which was intended to replace Christianity with worship of pagan tribal gods from ancient Germanic history and the occult practices popular among some Nazi leaders. The doctrinal statement of Hitler's Nazi denomination specified that "the Christian Cross must be removed from all churches, cathedrals and chapels...and it must be superseded by the only unconquerable symbol, the swastika." Hitler's trusted top aide Martin Bormann no doubt spoke for the Führer when he said, "National Socialism and Christianity are irreconcilable."[6]

In an attempt to justify its persecution of Germany's Jews, the Nazi government quoted obscure sixteenth-century anti-Semitic writings by the revered Protestant reformer Martin Luther, while simultaneously using terror tactics to silence Protestants who criticized Nazi policy. German Protestants who considered defending the Jewish people knew that they would likely suffer harm for doing so. The renewed prosperity that Hitler had brought to Germany also made it easy for professing Christians, Protestant and Catholic alike, to look the other way. They now had jobs, an improved quality of life, and pride in a resurgent nation, all of which encouraged silence as Hitler progressively stripped them of their individual freedoms and savagely assaulted everyone he denounced as enemies—especially the Jews. Recalled a German Protestant pastor, "Some people said then, 'No, that's not what we wanted.' But it was too late. No one dared anymore, really, to open his mouth."[7]

Some Christians, however, did resist, and Pastor Otto Mörike was one of them. In 1933 he pastored an Evangelical Church congregation in Oppelsbohm, which was located near Stuttgart in southern Germany. Alarmed by Nazi actions against Christianity and mistreatment of Germany's Jews, Mörike shifted his allegiance to the newly formed Confessing Church, which had been founded by Lutheran pastor Martin Niemöller to counter Nazi attacks on the church and Germany's Jewish population. In 1934, at a Confessing Church synod assembly in Barmen, Niemöller and pastors such as Dietrich Bonhoeffer publicly denounced as "false doctrine" any notion that the state "should and could become the single and totalitarian order of human life," and reaffirmed the Jewish connection to Christianity through the Old Testament or Hebrew Bible. They also boldly encouraged Germany's Christians to "let no fear or temptation keep you from treading with us the path of faith and obedience to the Word of God." The stand by the Confessing Church was a rare expression of solidarity against the Nazi regime by an organized denomination, and Hitler's initial reaction was to back away from attacks on the Confessing Church.[8]

He recovered, however, and launched a brutal assault on the church and its resisting pastors. Pastor Niemöller was arrested and imprisoned, was eventually placed in the Dachau concentration camp, and remained incarcerated until the end of World War II. Although he had made statements critical of Judaism as the Nazi intimidation intensified, in his final sermon before his arrest,

Niemöller exhorted German Christians to resist Nazi tyranny as Hitler persecuted the Jews and others. "No more are we ready to keep silent at man's behest when God commands us to speak," he said. "For it is, and must remain, the case that we must obey God rather than man." Some protesting ministers in the Confessing Church were murdered, and more than eight hundred were forced from their pastorates and imprisoned. Even as the resistance of the Confessing Church was reduced by the Nazi crackdown, however, some members—and even entire congregations—became stronger under persecution, and continued to resist Nazi oppression and the mistreatment of the Jews. On more than one occasion, when Gestapo agents raided church services to confiscate collections for Nazi victims, church members spontaneously broke into Martin Luther's Reformation hymn of faith, "A Mighty Fortress Is Our God." Instead of submitting to Nazi intimidation, some Christians redoubled their efforts to assist Jewish targets of Nazi persecution. Otto and Gertrud Mörike were among them.[9]

One day in 1933, Pastor Mörike arrived at his church to find a Nazi flag flying from the church steeple. With the help of a neighbor boy he pulled down the flag, and then he drove into Stuttgart, where he calmly delivered it to Gestapo headquarters. "The swastika does not belong on the steeple of a church," he told Gestapo officials. They accepted the flag with little comment, and allowed him to leave unmolested—but soon Gestapo agents began trailing Mörike's movements and appearing at his Sunday worship services. As he watched Hitler's policies smother freedom in Germany and place the nation's Jews under increasing persecution, Mörike's protests became bolder. In August 1934, now a pastor in the Confessing Church, Mörike preached a Sunday sermon from the Old Testament book of Joshua, emphasizing how God destroyed the walled city of Jericho because of its wickedness—and concluded by comparing Jericho to the Nazi Party. A Gestapo agent sent to spy on Mörike furiously took notes during the pastor's sermon, and when the worship service ended, a Gestapo detachment appeared at the church parsonage to arrest Mörike. The agents retreated, however, when they found the parsonage surrounded by members of Mörike's congregation. The next day the Nazis returned and forcibly escorted Mörike to Gestapo headquarters in Stuttgart. There they demanded that he provide a written copy of the sermon, which Mörike cheerfully did, hoping that any Nazi who read it might be converted.[10]

He was allowed to return home unharmed, but from that point onward the Mörikes knew they were under constant Nazi surveillance. Even so, both believed their faith in Jesus Christ as Lord and Savior compelled them to resist Nazi tyranny and its persecution of the Jews. "I accepted the struggle against the system," Mörike would later write, "for I [feared] that democracy would eventually perish and, with it, freedom of speech." He watched grimly as Hitler's Nuremberg Laws were enacted in 1935, stripping Jews of their German citizenship and criminalizing marriage between Jews and non-Jews. Supervised by Nazi judges, the German courts ruled that Jews had no legal rights. Hitler meanwhile placed the Gestapo under the control of the SS, enlarged the powers of both, and transformed Germany into a Nazi police state. The concentration camps that were being built in increasing numbers were operated and guarded by the SS Totenkopfverbände, or Death's Head Units, whose members wore a skull-and-crossbones insignia. Hitler's ruthless rule of Greater Germany was now total. Recalled a foreigner living in Berlin, "No one—if he were not foolish—said or did anything that might be interpreted as anti-Nazi."[11]

In April 1938, a month after the annexation of Austria, Hitler ordered a plebiscite in which the German people were to approve the takeover after the fact, and also state their approval of Adolf Hitler's leadership. The ballot bore a large *Yes* and a tiny *No*, and voters everywhere were scrutinized by the Nazi secret police as they voted. Predictably, 99 percent of voters approved the annexation and gave Hitler and the Nazis a resounding vote of support—but Otto and Gertrud Mörike did not. Courageously, they recorded their disapproval of Hitler and the Nazis. On his ballot Pastor Mörike wrote, "I deplore the degradation of morality and justice in Germany and the destruction of the church by the de-Christianization of our people." Gertrud Mörike, who was pregnant at the time, penned an equally bold message on the ballot. "As a Christian," she wrote, "I must reject National Socialism as an ideology inasmuch as it leads to the curse and eternal damnation of our people."[12]

That night Nazi election observers examined Otto and Gertrud Mörike's ballots and read their criticisms of Hitler and the Nazis. Although the ballots were supposed to be anonymous, the Nazis knew they had been cast by the Mörikes. News of the couple's opinions spread to a beer garden not far from the Mörikes' home. There Nazi storm troopers and their supporters were celebrating the Nazi election victory, and they were enraged that the pastor and his wife dared to criticize the Führer and his Nazis. Led by approximately thirty storm troopers, an angry mob marched to the Mörike home. The storm troopers forced their way into the house, pulled Pastor Mörike from his bed, and—while his pregnant wife watched in horror—dragged him to the street outside and pounded him to the pavement as the surrounding mob cheered. Mörike was beaten almost to death, and was spared only because local city police officers decided to haul him to jail before he was killed. A Nazi judge sentenced him to ten months in prison for his opposition to Hitler, but commuted the sentence to probation when Confessing Church officials agreed to move Mörike to another parish more than forty miles away, in the town of Weissach-Flacht.[13]

The beating and punishment only strengthened the Mörikes' determination to resist the Nazis—and they decided the best way to do so was to secretly assist Germany's imperiled Jews. Hitler's initial solution to Germany's "Jewish problem" was to forcibly expel all Jews from Greater Germany, which was now composed of Germany and Austria. As they were processed for forced deportation, Jewish families were stripped of their property and bank accounts. "You put in a Jew at one end…," reported one Jewish survivor, "and [he] came out at the other end without property, without privileges, without rights, with nothing except a passport." Nazi persecution of the Jews was emboldened by the failure of Western diplomats at the Évian Conference to provide a safe haven for displaced Jewish refugees. Germany had tried to "get rid of our Jews," a top-ranking Nazi official gloated to Hitler, "but… no country wished to receive them." Soon afterward, Hitler began devising a new, more deadly plan to deal with Greater Germany's Jews.[14]

An individual act of Jewish resistance gave him the excuse to do so. In October 1938, the SS rounded up more than seventeen thousand Polish Jews who were living in Germany, forcibly loaded them onto railroad cars, and shipped them over the border into Poland—although Poland's government protested that more Jews were not wanted there. Hearing that his family had disappeared in the relocation, a distraught Jewish teenager in Paris shot and killed a German diplomat. It was the opportunity Hitler needed for a further crackdown on Germany's Jews. He secretly approved a nationwide Nazi attack on Jewish businesses, synagogues, hospitals, schools, and cemeteries on November 9, 1938. In what would become infamous as *Kristallnacht*—"Crystal Night," or the Night of Broken Glass—Nazi thugs wrecked and looted more than seven thousand Jewish shops, set fire to 119 synagogues, damaged unknown numbers of Jewish schools and hospitals, desecrated Jewish cemeteries, killed thirty-five Jews, and arrested thousands more. *Kristallnacht* spurred a wave of panic in Germany's Jewish community, prompting thousands of Jews to attempt to leave the country and sending untold numbers into hiding.[15]

"They were the good Samaritans of the Third Reich."

At their church in Weissach-Flacht, Otto and Gertrud Mörike courageously developed a secret plan to assist German Jews who were hiding from the Nazis. Working with other like-minded pastors in the Confessing Church, they devised an underground railroad that would pass Jewish refugees from one church to another, hiding them until they could escape the country. When World War II began in 1939, and escaping from Germany became almost impossible, the Mörikes arranged to hide endangered Jews in church parsonages in a secret rescue operation known to participants as the Parsonage Chain. Pastor Mörike served three churches in the Weissach-Flacht region, traveling among them on a motorcycle, which allowed him to keep the chain active. Enlisting some of the members of his churches, he eventually organized more than a dozen safe houses, where Christians secretly protected and supported Jews in hiding.[16]

To avoid alerting suspicious neighbors, Jewish refugees seldom stayed long in a single place, but were moved from one safe house to another. The Mörikes' teenage son Frieder was often seen casually riding his bicycle through the family's neighborhood, but in reality he was scouting for Gestapo raids called in by Nazi neighbors. More than once his warnings enabled Jews in the Mörike parsonage to escape only moments before Gestapo agents arrived. "My mother would stall them at the front door," one of the Mörike children later recalled, "and the Jews would go out the back door." Eventually the Mörikes decided to hide their Jewish escapees in plain sight. By then the war was under way, and Allied bombing raids on urban war industries had prompted many Germans to move in with relatives who lived far away from cities that were bombing targets. Otto Mörike casually mentioned to his neighbors that he had invited his friends from Berlin to visit the family as a reprieve from the bombing. The ploy allowed different Jewish families to be seen around the Mörike house without suspicion until they were eventually transferred to other locations. "We always seemed to have guests from Berlin," a Mörike daughter would remember. "I didn't know that they were Jews, of course; I was only 5 or 6 years old."[17]

In 1943 the Mörike parsonage received a Jewish couple who had survived an extraordinary odyssey. Max and Karoline Krakauer were Berliners who had been forced into slave labor by Nazis in the German capital. They had managed to escape and fled across Germany, moving from one Gentile safe house to another as they dodged the Gestapo. By the time the war ended, they would have stayed in sixty-six locations, and yet managed to survive. They were at the Mörike home for a month—the longest period that Germans escaping the Allied bombing raids could visit anywhere without registering with the Nazi government. According to Max Krakauer, Pastor Mörike "welcomed us with such a winning smile and found such kind words for us that without knowing why, I sensed he would play an important role in our lives." When it was time for the Krakauers to leave, Otto Mörike arranged for them to be carefully transferred to another safe house in the Parsonage Chain. Krakauer was deeply moved that the Mörikes would risk their lives and the lives of their five children to help persecuted Jews. "I know they wanted no gratitude and did not desire earthly rewards; but rather, they were motivated by human love and Christian compassion," he later observed. "They were the good Samaritans of the Third Reich."[18]

Miraculously, Otto and Gertrud Mörike survived the Holocaust without the Nazis finding their extensive safe-house network. While most professing Christians in Germany remained silent and inactive in the face of tyranny, untold numbers of Jewish refugees survived the Holocaust through the Parsonage Chain established by Otto and Gertrud Mörike, who never thought of themselves as heroes. Their faith, they believed, compelled them to demonstrate the love of Christ to people in desperate need—and to resist evil. As Gertrud Mörike had penned on her plebiscite ballot in 1938, "As a Christian, I must reject National Socialism." To those who came to know their story, it was an inspiring witness to their faith in Christ. Twenty-two years to the day after he was beaten by Nazi storm troopers, Otto Mörike received a telephone call from an anonymous caller, who promptly hung up after delivering a memorable message: "I was there on April 10, one of the key participants, and I'm sorry."[19]

CHAPTER 3
FRANCIS FOLEY

To most, Frank Foley was a low-level British bureaucrat serving in Berlin on the eve of World War II. In reality, he was a British army officer and intelligence agent who was credited with saving thousands of Jewish lives.

(CREDIT: YAD VASHEM)

"Tomorrow you will be freed."

FRANK FOLEY DID not look like a spy. He was a small man, bespectacled, quiet, and reserved in nature. But on the eve of World War II, he was considered by some to be the most important British intelligence agent in Nazi Germany, and by war's end he would be credited with saving the lives of more than ten thousand German Jews.

Few Britons understood the brutal nature of Nazism better than Francis Foley. He had distinguished himself in combat as a British infantry officer in the First World War, and at war's end he was recruited into MI6—the top-secret British intelligence service. He was posted to Germany in 1922, officially serving as Britain's passport control officer in Berlin. To the British diplomatic staff, he appeared to be an unimportant, middle-aged midlevel bureaucrat, but in reality he was a British master spy, focusing initially on the rise of German Communists and then on Adolf Hitler's campaign to reactivate and expand the German military. His most important intelligence coup occurred when he recruited a highly respected Austrian science journalist who provided British authorities with information on the development of Germany's V-2 rocket and on Hitler's top-secret program to build an atomic bomb.[1]

Foley's intelligence operation also revealed evidence that Jewish inmates imprisoned in the Nazi concentration camps being erected throughout Germany were suffering horrors far more shocking than anything British, French, or American leaders had imagined. Despite his protests, however, his London superiors waved away the accounts as ridiculous exaggerations. Foley then appealed to British immigration officials, asking them to expedite Jewish requests for asylum in Great Britain and its colonies, but encountered more bureaucratic apathy. Frustrated but determined, Foley decided to help Germany's Jews himself. Using his official cover as the British passport control officer in Berlin, he began issuing droves of passports to Jews seeking escape from Germany. Like Feng Shan Ho, his Chinese counterpart in Austria, Foley was motivated by more than just humanitarian concerns: his faith as a Christian compelled him to act, he believed—especially when so many of those who were persecuting the Jews claimed that they were Christians. Benno Cohn, a leader in Germany's prewar Jewish community, later credited Foley's Christianity as the force that drove him to help Germany's Jews: "He often told us that, as a Christian, he wanted to prove how little the 'Christians' then governing Germany had to do with real Christianity." To Foley, Nazism was evil—what he called "the realm of Satan"—and as a follower of Christ, he had no choice but to fight it.[2]

"I believe that God put Frank Foley in Berlin to do His work."

Born in Somerset in southwestern England, Foley had been raised in a devout Catholic home where faith in Jesus Christ reflected a surrendered heart rather than simply cultural identity. He had seriously considered entering the priesthood, but eventually came to believe that he had found his calling in the intelligence service. His nephew, an Anglican minister, agreed: "I believe that God put Frank Foley in Berlin to do His work," he said. Hard work, dangerous work—and a lot of it—is what Frank Foley encountered when he set out to oppose the Holocaust. "He worked without a break from 7 a.m. to 10 p.m., personally handling as many applications as he could," Foley's wife, Katherine, later recalled. "Some people were hysterical, many wept and all were desperate. For them, Frank's 'yes' or 'no' really meant the difference between a new life and the concentration camp."[3]

After *Kristallnacht* in 1938, the desperation increased within Germany's Jewish community. Determined to escape the Nazis and save their families, German Jews began showing up unannounced at Foley's Berlin apartment. As a passport officer, he did not have diplomatic immunity, and he knew what could happen to him if Nazi authorities learned he was issuing thousands of passports or personally harboring Jews. Despite the danger, he continued his mission. "Frank would slip down to the door late at night and let them in," said his wife. "I do not know what the Nazis would have done if they had discovered that we were sheltering people." Outside the British consulate on Berlin's Tiergartenstrasse, where Foley maintained his small office, frantic Jewish men, women, and children waited in long lines to petition Foley for a passport to some safehaven in the British Empire. "Foley saved my life," recalled Meriam Posner, then a sixteen-year-old Jewish girl who came to see Foley with her mother. "We heard that there was this man Foley who was kind to the Jews. My mother begged him. He just paced up and down a little, then asked for my passport and put the visa stamp on it. He was small and quiet. You would never have suspected that he was a spy."[4]

Every month hundreds of Jews came to Foley seeking escape from Nazi Germany. He realized that most of them would be hauled off to concentration camps before they could be processed by the ponderous, bureaucratic British immigration system—so he developed a streamlined process that severely stretched regulations but still complied with British law. The British government required immigrants to possess a huge sum of cash, for instance, but the Nazis confiscated the Jews' wealth when they emigrated, leaving them penniless. To circumvent the regulation, Foley accepted promissory notes from immigrants or letters from relatives and others promising to support the immigrants when they reached British soil. Many Jews wanted to escape to Palestine, the future site of the nation of Israel, which had been under British control since Britain captured the region from the Ottoman Empire in World War I. Others wanted to go to a British colony, while many sought refuge in the British Isles. Usually, Foley found a way. Using his espionage contacts and tradecraft, he even managed to bribe SS officers into allowing him to officially remove Jews from concentration camps.[5]

Gunter Powitzer was a Jewish inmate in the Sachsenhausen concentration camp when Foley's passport operation was working at its peak. Sachsenhausen was a state-of-the-art camp located north of Berlin. It operated under the direction of *Reichsführer* Heinrich Himmler, the leader of the SS, who had expanded the SS from a few hundred troops in 1929 to more than fifty thousand by 1938. Himmler had made Sachsenhausen the model for Germany's rapidly expanding concentration camp system, and just the mention of its name was enough to instill fear. But not in Frank Foley. When Powitzer was imprisoned at Sachsenhausen for having an Aryan girlfriend, his family turned to Foley, who agreed to help.[6]

Powitzer was working an exhausting shift of hard labor at the camp one day when an SS officer ordered him off the job and marched him into another section of the prison. Wondering what fate awaited him, Powitzer did as ordered—and was shocked when the officer handed him clean clothes and pointed him to a shower. When he emerged, showered and shaved, Powitzer found the officer waiting for him, holding a long gray coat. *Was ist los?* Powitzer asked, unable to control himself. "Shut up and put this on," the SS officer told him, handing him the coat. The Nazi herded the startled prisoner into a small room, then abruptly departed. "There sat a short man with eyeglasses," Powitzer later recounted, "who told me in English, 'My name is Foley, and I am from the British consulate in Berlin. Tomorrow you will be freed.'" A few weeks later, Powitzer was safe in Palestine. He never learned how Foley had managed to extricate him from Sachsenhausen, where more than fifty thousand prisoners eventually died.[7]

As relations deteriorated between Nazi Germany and Britain and France, Foley realized that war was imminent, and redoubled

his efforts to help Jews escape Germany. When warfare erupted in
September 1939, Foley disappeared—off on the first of many wartime espionage assignments in which he would distinguish himself
as one of the key Allied intelligence operatives of World War II. A
few days before the war began, Leo Baeck, a leading German rabbi
and one of Foley's chief Jewish contacts, received a message to pick
up a package from Foley's office in the British consulate. Foley was
gone when Baeck arrived, but the package awaited him. It was
Frank Foley's final outreach to the imperiled Jews of Germany.
Inside were more than eighty British passports officially stamped
and approved for travel outside Germany, each with the spaces
for name and address left blank—to be filled in by escaping Jews
whom Frank Foley had never met.[8]

CHAPTER 4

GEERTRUIDA WIJSMULLER

Jewish Kindertransport *children fleeing Nazi persecution in Germany arrive by ship in Great Britain in 1939.* (CREDIT: DEUTSCHES BUNDESARCHIV)

"I forgot to bring my husband. You'll have to deal with me."

IN THE WINTER of 1938, the last thing Truus Wijsmuller expected was to have a face-to-face encounter with one of Germany's most notorious Nazi leaders. At age forty-two, Wijsmuller was an attractive, fashionable, dark-eyed Dutch banker's wife living a comfortable life in Amsterdam. A Dutch Christian, she had been taught by her parents as a child to always be ready to help those in need, "no matter the color of their skin or their religion." Her parents had followed their own advice by caring for child refugees displaced by the First World War. So Truus—whose maiden name was Geertruida Meijer—developed a heart for those in need at an early age. At twenty-six, armed with a business school education, she was hired by a bank in Amsterdam, where she met her future husband, a successful young banker named Johannes "Joop" Wijsmuller. Eventually she quit work to have children, but was dismayed to learn that she was unable to become pregnant. Her physician suggested that she might instead become involved in social work. She did, and excelled at it.[1]

In the early 1930s, as Adolf Hitler increased the persecution of German Jews, she volunteered with a Dutch social agency, the Netherlands Children's Refugee Committee, which attempted to relocate Jewish families from Nazi Germany. Then, in November 1938, came the news of *Kristallnacht*. The reports of blazing synagogues, smashed and looted Jewish businesses, and the brutal mistreatment of Germany's Jews shocked and repulsed her. Unlike most Europeans, however, after learning of *Kristallnacht* she did not simply continue with life as usual. Instead she looked for more opportunities to help Germany's persecuted Jews. Initially Hitler intended to rid Germany of its Jews by terrorizing them into fleeing the country—after stripping them of their money and property. *Kristallnacht* raised the level of terror in Germany, and also increased public sympathy for the Jews in Western nations such as the United States, Holland, and Britain. There, new laws to accept Jewish refuges were proposed, but most would allow only Jewish children to immigrate, not their parents, and even those proposals failed to become law in most cases. In the United States, for example, a bill to accept twenty thousand child refugees was killed in Congress, buried in bureaucracy by lawmakers who feared that it would somehow worsen the Great Depression. The Dutch government also limited its response, agreeing to accept child refugees only if most traveled on to final destinations elsewhere.[2]

In Great Britain, however, Parliament voted to allow ten thousand children under age seventeen to enter the country for relocation in foster homes. It was understood that most of the child refugees would be Jewish. In response, British and Dutch relief agencies acted quickly to rescue Germany's Jewish children—and Truus Wijsmuller led the effort in Holland. She was the perfect choice. She had years of experience working with German refugees, including small groups of children. She and her husband had extensive international business contacts, and she spoke fluent German. She was also charming, resourceful, and relentless. Immediately she was tapped by relief agencies to organize a *Kindertransport*—a "children's transport"—to move Jewish children from Nazi Germany to safety. Her first assignment: to arrange for a *Kindertransport* that would take Jewish children by rail from Vienna to Holland, where they would then be ferried by ship to Britain. Austria had been absorbed into Greater Germany, so she had to fly to Vienna to negotiate with a high-ranking Nazi official. His name was Adolf Eichmann.[3]

Although he had been born in Germany, Eichmann—like Hitler—was raised in Austria. At the time Truus Wijsmuller met with him in Vienna, he was a smirking, cold-eyed thirty-two-year-old Nazi officer, who was rapidly rising in power as an expert on the "Jewish question." After drifting from job to job in his twenties, he had become an early and enthusiastic member of Austria's Nazi Party, and then joined the SS. His anti-Semitic fanaticism spurred his upward progress through the Nazi ranks. After the takeover of Austria in March 1938, he was placed in command of the Nazis' Central Office for Jewish Emigration in Vienna, and developed a plan for the forced emigration of Austria's Jews that would be followed as a model when Hitler conquered other countries. Eventually Hitler would order Europe's Jews incarcerated in concentration camps, and then would attempt to eliminate all of them through mass murder. Eichmann would be given the task of executing Hitler's orders, sending millions of Jewish men, women, and children to their deaths—an assignment, he once stated, that gave him "extraordinary satisfaction." At war's end he would escape to Argentina, but would be tracked down and apprehended by Israeli intelligence operatives in 1960. Brought to Israel, he would be tried and convicted of crimes against humanity and the Jewish people, and then hanged and cremated.[4]

In December 1938, however, *Untersturmführer* Adolf Eichmann was a fearsome figure in Vienna. A German contemporary described him as "a man who sat there like a block of ice or marble, not feeling anything at all." Truus Wijsmuller wanted to transport six hundred Jewish children from Austria to Holland, then on to Britain, and to do so she had to receive permission from Eichmann. She managed to stifle any fear and revulsion she felt in Eichmann's presence, confidently looked him in the eyes, and requested the approval necessary to transport the children. Although his goal was to banish Jews from Nazi Germany, Eichmann did not want to make the job easy for a Dutch outsider, especially a do-gooder woman. He parried and resisted, but he did not intimidate Wijsmuller; she wanted her children. Finally Eichmann snorted that he was not used to doing business with women. "I'm sorry," Wijsmuller retorted, "but I forgot to bring my husband. You'll have to deal with me." Eichmann dismissively gave his permission, but—perhaps simply as harassment—he demanded that she assemble the Jewish children and get them out of the country in four days. It seemed impossible, but Wijsmuller did it: within days six hundred Jewish children crossed the German border into Holland by train, bound for Britain and safety.[5]

Working with humanitarian agencies and volunteer groups from denominations such as the Swedish Lutheran Church, the Mennonites, and the Quakers, Wijsmuller organized a *Kindertransport* system that funneled train after train of endangered children out of Germany and occupied Austria. Most of them were Jewish and most went to foster homes in Great Britain. The children were recruited mainly through the Reich Representation of German Jews—an unofficial agency established by Jewish leaders in the early days of Nazi rule—and through a German Evangelical pastor named Heinrich Grüber. Every group of children had to be approved and processed by Nazi emigration officials.[6]

Staging points were at railway terminals in Berlin, Hamburg, Frankfurt, and, later, more remote places. Nazi officials insisted that the *Kindertransport* trains leave from secondary rail stations and at night, allegedly because German civilians would be enraged at seeing so many Jews in one place, but more likely to avoid arousing sympathy for the Jews among the German people. The tearful departures *were* heartrending to watch. "The people were behind gates, and the parents were telling the small children to get on the train," an observer later recalled. "The children didn't want to leave...and there was crying and it was bedlam."[7]

Each child was allowed to carry a single suitcase and ten reichsmarks—the same pitiful amount of money that the Nazis allowed a Jewish adult to take when emigrating. Typically a child's suitcase was crammed with clothes, family photographs, a picture book, and a favorite toy or beloved doll. Each child wore a card with his or her number on it, fastened to a string that was worn around the neck. Final good-byes and embraces were given in a rail station hallway, and many parents assured their children that the separation was to be only temporary. Most parents knew otherwise, however, and so did the older children. "Mama said that she thought she and papa would get to England in about six weeks, God willing...," one Jewish girl later recounted. "A thought kept coming into my head: what if we never see each other again?" Some Jewish children—displaced by the Nazi violence of *Kristallnacht*—were already orphaned. "I was sitting all by myself," one child, a teenager at the time, would later remember. "I had no parents—nobody...all I knew was that I was going away. I was going to England." Then, suddenly, in a crowded rush, the children and their train were gone, leaving grieving parents standing forlornly in the railway station.[8]

Gestapo agents accompanied the trains to the Dutch border, often treating the Jewish children and their escorts with disdain and sometimes slowing progress with needless harassment. Wijsmuller dealt with them with efficiency and creativity, charming some, disarming others with authoritative assertiveness, and placating some with gifts—all depending on what she deemed the most effective tactic at the moment. Dutch and British officials also sometimes hampered the *Kindertransport*. Once, a Dutch customs agent balked at the paperwork accompanying some of Wijsmuller's children, and announced that he was sending them all back to Germany. Knowing that a return to Germany would be a death sentence for the children, Wijsmuller responded boldly. She had heard passenger gossip that members of the Dutch royal family were aboard the train, and she used their presence to her advantage. *Let my children in*, she warned the stubborn official, or she would march down to the royal family's railway car and report his uncooperative attitude. The agent relented, and the children went on to safety in Britain. Such actions made Wijsmuller an overnight legend within Germany's endangered Jewish community, where she became known as "*Tante* Truus" ("Aunt Truus"). Every week, from December 1938 through the summer of 1939, she managed to dispatch trainloads of Jewish children out of Greater Germany to freedom and safety.[9]

"I could have saved a good many more people."

In September 1939, the outbreak of war shut down the *Kindertransport*—but Wijsmuller found other ways to help Europe's persecuted Jews, especially children. When Nazi troops invaded Holland and were approaching Amsterdam, she managed to round up a convoy of buses and drivers, loaded seventy-four Jewish children from an Amsterdam orphanage into them, and drove them to a Dutch seaport. There she went from ship to ship until she found a captain who agreed to take the children to Britain aboard his freighter. "If only I could have laid my hands on more vehicles," she later commented, "I could have saved a good many more people." When Holland was conquered and occupied by Nazi forces, she chose to remain in Amsterdam with her husband, but she did not stop working to help funnel Jews to safety. Initially, following their policy of ridding German-occupied areas of all Jews, the Nazis allowed Jewish families to leave Holland for a price—and Wijsmuller hastily organized a transport system that enabled untold numbers to escape to neutral Spain or Palestine.[10]

As the war continued, and Nazi scrutiny of her activities intensified, she focused on organizing shipments of food parcels to Jewish orphans at Westerbork, a refugee and transit camp in northern Holland. At one point a shipment of fifty food parcels was returned to her. When she inquired why, she was told that the camp's fifty Jewish orphans were being transferred to another camp—one that she secretly knew to be a Nazi death camp. Immediately Wijsmuller made her way to the Nazis' Bureau of Jewish Affairs in

Amsterdam, where she confronted its commander, a Dutch collaborator, with a wild accusation. Did he not know, she demanded, that the fifty orphans at Westerbork were actually the children of German soldiers and Dutch women? And how would Nazi officials back in Berlin respond if he allowed those children—who had German soldier fathers—to suffer possible harm? Wijsmuller could have been sent to a death camp herself for such a bold confrontation, but her ploy apparently worked: the Jewish orphans were routed to another transit camp and all fifty reportedly survived the Holocaust.[11]

Truus Wijsmuller also survived, although she narrowly escaped. Twice she was detained and brought to Gestapo headquarters for questioning about rumors that she was illegally aiding Dutch Jews. Each time, however, she was inexplicably released. At war's end she continued her good works, seeking no glory for her actions and the many Jewish children she saved—which were eventually calculated to number more than ten thousand. In 2011, decades after Wijsmuller's passing, a monument to the *Kindertransport* was unveiled in Amsterdam. Standing by the statue, gazing at the childlike bronze figures with suitcases in hand, a Jewish man softly commented, speaking for thousands of Jewish *Kinder*, "I was one of those children. If it wasn't for her, I wouldn't be alive today."[12]

CHAPTER 5
HEINRICH GRÜBER

With religious-like fervor, young trumpeters from the Hitler Youth signal a Nazi celebration. (CREDIT: NATIONAL ARCHIVES)

"The Lord whom I alone obey, tells me, 'Go thou and do likewise.' "

WHAT SHOULD HE do? Pastor Heinrich Grüber had struggled with
the question again and again. He was a forty-three-year-old Protestant minister in Germany when Hitler came to power in 1933.
Although his mother was Dutch, Grüber considered himself a
loyal German. He had served in the German army in the First
World War, and he loved his country. He had been hopeful when
Adolf Hitler was voted into office, believing that fresh leadership
was needed to rebuild Germany's economy and provide a better
life for its people. In a burst of patriotism, he had briefly joined
the Nazi Party, but he soon quit, unnerved and disillusioned when
the party's godless policies were revealed. He was headmaster of
a church-related school for learning-disabled children, and was
undoubtedly troubled by the Nazi goal of engineering a super race
that excluded the Jews, the Gypsies, the handicapped, the mentally
ill, and anyone else deemed imperfect by Nazi policy.[1]

But what should he do? Many other Germans, including
many professing Christians, embraced the Führer out of a sense
of patriotism. What was *his* duty as a Christian? Should he remain
patriotic and loyal to Germany, supporting his country whether
right or wrong? Many Germans did so, even as they saw the
nation rapidly abandoning the moral teachings of the Bible. But
Grüber could not. Despite his love of country, he concluded that
as a Christian he could not support a government that persecuted
Jews and others, and clearly violated the teachings of the Bible. He
joined the Confessing Church established by Martin Niemöller
and Dietrich Bonhoeffer, and openly expressed his concerns about
the direction in which the Nazis were leading the nation. As punishment, Nazi officials forced him out of his job.[2]

To Grüber the banishment proved to be a blessing. He became pastor of a Confessing Church congregation in a working-class suburb of Berlin that included a large population of Dutch immigrants. There, his pastoral influence grew his church and transformed the neighborhood into a Confessing Church stronghold that was also quietly anti-Nazi. Among the members of his church were numerous Jewish Christians who accepted Yeshua—Jesus—as the promised Messiah of the Hebrew Bible. As they and their relatives suffered increasing Nazi persecution, Grüber helped many of them to emigrate to Holland and Switzerland, using family contacts in Holland to persuade reluctant customs officials to take small groups of refugees. In response to the anti-Semitic violence of *Kristallnacht*, he publicly denounced Nazi policies from his pulpit. "I declare herewith solemnly and publicly," he stated, "that I do not want to have anything to do with this German nation."[3]

He was detained and questioned by the Gestapo, but was released—and his reputation as a friend of the Jews spread rapidly throughout Berlin's Jewish community. After *Kristallnacht*, scores of alarmed and endangered Jewish refugees appeared at his home, seeking his help in escaping from Nazi Germany. Many were Jewish Christians, who were also targets of Nazi persecution. The Confessing Church had been banned by the Nazis, but still unofficially operated, and its leaders asked Grüber to expand his efforts to rescue Jews into a nationwide network. Hitler was still trying to rid Greater Germany of its Jews by forced emigration, and with few countries willing to accept large numbers of Jewish refugees, church leaders believed, Grüber's experience and contacts could save many Jewish lives. Berlin's Jewish leaders, he was told, also believed that the Nazis would be more willing to resolve Jewish issues with a Protestant clergyman than with a Jewish leader. Grüber was a bespectacled, middle-aged pastor and theologian—a little old to lead a life-and-death rescue operation—but he accepted the opportunity as a call from God. He and his wife, Margarete, poured their lives and life savings into the cause. Soon Grüber had established an office in Berlin and a network of more than thirty assistants in Germany's major cities.[4]

His agency was not associated with any denomination or church, but in order to deal with Nazi immigration officials, Grüber named it what his Jewish clients were calling it: *das Büro Grüber*—"the Grüber Bureau." Soon after *Kristallnacht*, Grüber went to the Berlin State Police Office to discuss Jewish emigration with Nazi officials of the Judenreferat—the "Jewish Department." Accompanying him were three prominent Jewish leaders, including the revered rabbi Leo Baeck, who was Grüber's close personal friend. At police headquarters Grüber was offered a chair while Baeck and the other Jewish leaders were left standing. Grüber looked at the Nazi official seated before him and said, "If the three gentlemen are standing, I shall also stand." Despite such protests, Heinrich Grüber—the Christian pastor—became a principal negotiator with the Nazis on behalf of German Jews.[5]

"You are under arrest."

His negotiations with Nazi officials brought him repeated encounters with the steely-eyed Nazi leader whom Truus Wijsmuller had faced in Austria—Adolf Eichmann. Grüber came to view Eichmann as a *Landsknecht*—a "mercenary"—a heartless fanatic "who, as he dons his uniform, doffs his conscience and his reason." As a Christian, Grüber tried to understand what really motivated Nazis such as Eichmann, hoping to somehow appeal to their deeply buried sense of morality, but he concluded that many Nazis were simply evil.

"There was not the slightest stirring of emotion," he later explained, "but just an unfathomable hatred." Eventually Grüber decided that Adolf Eichmann was possessed. "It was always difficult for us to understand how someone could become entangled in hatred and intensify his hatred even more," Grüber admitted.

"And once someone is in the grip of this demonic possession, it gets stronger and holds the person more tightly."[6]

Once, as Grüber sat before Eichmann in his office, exhausted from a long day of lobbying on behalf of a group of Jews, he thought he detected a glimmer of sympathy in the "monster" of the Holocaust. "Why do you care about the Jews at all?" Eichmann suddenly asked him. "No one is going to thank you for your efforts." Always looking for an opportunity to share the truth of the Gospel and the love of Jesus Christ, Grüber turned to the Bible and Jesus's parable of the Good Samaritan. "You know the road from Jerusalem to Jericho," he said, aware that Eichmann had spent time in Palestine. "Once there lay on that road a Jew who had fallen amongst thieves. Then a man passed by, who was not a Jew, and helped him. The Lord whom I alone obey tells me, 'Go thou and do likewise.'" For once Adolf Eichmann had no reply.[7]

Despite Eichmann's indifference, Grüber believed that the Gospel of Jesus Christ was powerful enough to change the heart and mind of even the most ruthless Nazi. Therefore he tried to approach every Nazi he met as someone who needed redemption. "When you remonstrate with someone," he later explained, "that is not something you do by means of orders. A pastor who uses nothing but imperatives is not a good spiritual advisor." As the war overtook his rescue efforts and Nazi policy shifted from banishing the Jews to incarcerating them in concentration camps, his work acquired a deeper urgency—and his personal approach produced results. Some Nazis—even SS officers—secretly helped him and the Grüber Bureau protect the Jews.[8]

"If only I could get out of here," one Nazi official told Grüber in private, "but there is only one way out...and that is via a concentration camp." Another Nazi, a young SS officer, confided to Grüber that he had come to realize that his duties in the Schutzstaffel were nothing more than godless criminal activities. Would Grüber be willing, he asked, to visit him regularly? Grüber readily agreed, and in the privacy of the man's office the pastor tried to counsel the morally tormented young officer. Sitting at his desk, attired in his black SS uniform with its skull's head insignia, the officer would listen intently to Grüber's spiritual counsel, rising occasionally to stomp around the room and yell at Grüber in a mock outburst intended to reassure the Nazis working outside his office. The man never confessed his repentance, but he began leaving secret orders lying openly in front of Grüber—silently alerting the pastor of new impending regulations against the Jews. Other Nazis who were influenced by Grüber also gave him advance warning in their own ways, and on several occasions some actually delayed orders so Grüber could protect Jews.[9]

Pastor Grüber and his Grüber Bureau, with the assistance of Rabbi Baeck and others, found housing for homeless Jews with members of Grüber's church, assisted ill and elderly Jews, provided food and clothing for the displaced, and established a school for Jewish children in Grüber's office. Through his emigration efforts, Grüber also enabled more than two thousand Jewish men, women, and children to escape Nazi Germany. When the war began in September 1939, however, Grüber's job became even more difficult. At least two hundred thousand Jews remained in Germany, and to deal with his "Jewish problem," Hitler ordered more concentration camps built in Germany and regions newly conquered by his armies.[10]

In early 1940, the first mass deportation of German Jews began. Thousands were rounded up and shipped to concentration camps in German-occupied Poland. From the beginning, deported Jewish families were treated brutally. One night in February of 1940, for example, Nazi troops rousted more than a thousand Jews from their beds in the city of Stettin, in northeastern Germany. Men, women, children, the elderly, the infirm—all were ordered to pack one suitcase, leave behind their homes and belongings, and stumble through heavy snow in freezing weather to a distant railway station.

Even nursing homes were emptied of Jewish residents. Many died on the way. Those who survived were jammed into old cattle cars and shipped by rail to towns in Poland. There, they were ordered off the trains and left to fend for themselves. Most were taken in by local Jewish families, but many died before they could be housed.[11]

Later that year, in the autumn of 1940, Hitler ordered more than seven thousand Jews deported from Greater Germany and placed in concentration camps in Poland and elsewhere, and a year later forty-two thousand more were arrested and deported. From then onward, the deportations continued regularly and were expanded to include Jews in areas conquered by or aligned with Nazi Germany. When Jews were deported, their wealth and property were confiscated by the Nazi government under what Hitler called the Reich Citizenship Law. Initially, some were spared—military veterans, the elderly, those who were married to non-Jews—but soon anyone with any suspected Jewish connections was targeted for deportation. Nazi propaganda depicted the new concentration camps as humane centers where the Jews were well treated, received excellent medical care, and even enjoyed concerts and theatricals.[12]

Pastor Grüber and others knew better. Rumors circulating within Germany's Jewish community reported brutal treatment and deplorable conditions within the camps—and some accounts reported mistreatment too horrible to believe. When the deportations began in 1940, Grüber immediately filed a protest with Nazi officials, and was summoned to Gestapo headquarters in Berlin. There, a Nazi official ordered him to stop criticizing Nazi policy. "I replied," he later recalled, "that as long as I could speak, I would continue to speak out, and as long as I could work, I would carry on working." Eyeing him coldly, the Nazi replied, "One could always put an end to the machinations of men of your sort." Despite the threat, Grüber beseeched one Nazi official after another until he worked his way up the Nazi chain of command to the German Chancellery, where he tried to see Hitler's deputy, Hermann Göring. When turned away, he wrote a long protest letter to Göring, an early associate of Hitler who commanded the Luftwaffe—the German air force—and also supervised Nazi policy toward the Jews. His protest accomplished little, other than to raise his profile among the Nazi leadership, but Grüber would not give up. Unable to stop the deportations, he began to plan how to visit a concentration camp to determine conditions for himself. Instead, the Nazis did it for him.[13]

On December 19, 1940, he arrived at his Berlin office to find it surrounded by Gestapo agents. "You are under arrest," one of them told him. "You may no longer speak to anyone." The Grüber Bureau was shut down, and most of Grüber's associates throughout Germany were arrested and sent to concentration camps. So was Grüber, first to Sachsenhausen and then to Dachau. Constructed near Munich in 1933, Dachau originally housed political prisoners, then was expanded to incarcerate enslaved munitions workers, Jewish inmates, and more than seven hundred anti-Nazi clergymen. By war's end more than thirty-two thousand Dachau inmates would die of starvation, disease, and mistreatment, and more than one hundred thousand others would be shipped to Nazi death camps.[14]

Grüber survived, but barely. His teeth were knocked out, he suffered from near starvation, and his health deteriorated until he was close to death. Even so, he considered his torment minor compared to what befell countless Jews in Nazi captivity. "I can only say that what I suffered was a trifle compared to the sufferings of my Jewish friends," he would later state. "Millions have perished who could neither cry nor lament, who went through more than Dante's inferno." At one point while in Dachau, Grüber and other imprisoned clergymen were put to work sorting the clothing taken from Jews who had been executed in Nazi death camps. Grüber soon realized that he was viewing the mute evidence of mass murder on an unprecedented scale. "When in the first consign-ment we found a pair of tiny children's shoes, we were all shocked to our inner souls by this," he later remembered, "and we men, for all that we were used to terrible things, had to struggle with our tears, because it brought all the suffering of these children before us. Then more and more children's shoes arrived."[15]

Dachau was also the site of a Nazi medical "research center." Selected inmates were subjected to horrible experiments that were intended to determine how long a person could survive in freezing water, how quickly a man would die without oxygen, the effects of poison bullets on the human body, and how rapidly germ war-fare could kill a victim. Directing Dachau's chamber of horrors was an SS physician, Dr. Sigmund Rascher, whose behavior was so notorious that his Nazi superiors eventually executed him. While at Dachau, Pastor Grüber became a candidate for Dr. Rascher's diabolical experiments. It happened after Grüber collapsed one day from a near-fatal heart attack. Unconscious, he was mistaken for dead and tossed onto the day's pile of corpses. Lying among the dead, he revived—with a Bible verse on his mind: "God hath caused me to be fruitful in the land of my affliction." Maybe, he thought, God intended him to survive. A friend discovered that he was still alive, and he was carried to the camp hospital. There he was confronted by the fearsome Dr. Rascher. Address-ing him as "Pig"—the doctor's common salutation for prisoners—Rascher ordered Grüber to undress for an examination. Learning from his questions that Grüber was a pastor, Rascher commented matter-of-factly that his grandfather had been a minister.[16]

Instantly, Grüber recalled the New Testament passage that referred to "a cloud of witnesses" viewing human activity from heaven. If he was planning any medical mistreatment, Grüber warned the maniacal doctor, he needed to be aware that his clergyman grandfather in heaven knew "what his grandson is up to." Grüber then braced himself for the worst, but Rascher simply dismissed him. The next day he was escorted back to the hospital, where he expected to be punished by becoming the victim of some deadly experiment. Instead, Rascher addressed him as "Sir," gave him a thorough physical examination, and explained that he intended to recommend his release from Dachau for health reasons. Soon afterward Grüber was set free.[17]

Reunited with his wife back in Berlin, he slowly regained his health—and his mission. His Grüber Bureau was gone, but he was still determined to help rescue Jews from persecution. Soon afterward, a young Jewish brother and sister appeared at his home seeking protection. They had been rounded up in a deportation, they explained, and were being herded aboard a train bound for a concentration camp when an Allied air raid sent their Nazi captors scurrying for cover. In the resulting confusion, they escaped and made their way to the Christian pastor who was said to have a heart for the Jews. Would he help them? Despite the danger and his broken health, Grüber sheltered the two until war's end. After the war, he continued pastoring his church, again facing totalitarian rule as the Soviet Union imposed Communism on East Berlin. In 1961, more than forty years after confronting Adolf Eichmann, he again met the "monster" face-to-face—this time as a prosecution witness at Eichmann's trial in Israel. In the postwar era, Grüber worked tirelessly for peace between the East and the West and to provide relief for those in need. His deepest hope, he once stated, was that those who had survived the horrors of war would experience the grace of God through Jesus Christ. "My entreaty, my endeavor," he said, "is that there will be forgiving love and forgiven sin."[18]

CHAPTER 6
NICHOLAS WINTON

Nicholas Winton holds a Jewish Kindertransport *child.* (CREDIT: YAD VASHEM)

"The idea was to save children."

WHEN ADOLF HITLER told him face-to-face how he planned to invade his country, the president of Czechoslovakia fainted. His name was Emil Hácha, and for decades he had been a distinguished Czech judge. When he met with Hitler in March 1939, however, he was aged, timid, and suffering from a heart condition. He had become president of Czechoslovakia just months earlier, when the Czech government had collapsed under threats from Hitler and abandonment by its allies—France, Britain, and the Soviet Union. Created by the Versailles Treaty that ended the First World War, Czechoslovakia was the first democracy to be established in central Europe.[1]

After Hitler's takeover of Austria and its absorption into Nazi Germany in 1938, Czechoslovakia had become the Führer's next target. He demanded that the Czech government cede Germany an eleven-thousand-square-mile region of Czechoslovakia called the Sudetenland, which contained a large population of ethnic Germans. To justify a German invasion of the region, he unleashed a Nazi propaganda campaign to provoke unrest in the Sudetenland, then used the turmoil as an excuse to muster a German invasion force on the Czech border. Czechoslovakia boasted a powerful army, strongly fortified borders, and a mutual defense alliance with France and the Soviet Union, and Hitler privately feared Nazi forces could be defeated by combined Czech, French, and Soviet troops. As he had hoped, however, his threats of war prompted French premier Édouard Daladier, a former college professor, to back away from his nation's treaty with Czechoslovakia, as did the Soviet Union. Daladier appealed to British prime minister Neville Chamberlain for help, and Chamberlain—worried that

Britain was no longer a match for Germany's rebuilt military—engineered a conference with Hitler in Munich, Germany. Meanwhile prompted by Hitler's threats of war, the British government ordered workers to hastily dig air raid trenches in London, and in Paris panicky refugees clogged roads leading out of the city.[2]

On September 29, 1938, Prime Minister Chamberlain, Prime Minister Daladier, Czech officials, and Benito Mussolini—the fascist dictator of Italy—arrived at the Führerbau, an ornate government facility that the Nazis had recently constructed in Munich. A devoted ally of Hitler, Mussolini was purportedly present to help broker terms, but a compromise proposal he planned to present had been secretly dictated by Hitler, who had thus managed to rig the conference in advance. The Führer also insisted that the Czech representatives be excluded from the negotiations. Chamberlain and Daladier conceded, so the two Czech officials waited outside the conference room as the fate of their nation was decided by the others.[3]

As engineered by Hitler, Mussolini's compromise proposal stated that Nazi Germany would be allowed to seize the Czechoslovakian Sudetenland, but that Hitler would agree not to make any more territorial demands in Europe. Chamberlain and Daladier welcomed the proposal and pledged that Britain and France would abide by it. Hitler quickly signed the document, feigning satisfaction that war had been avoided. "The deluded British Prime Minister did not know, of course," an observer would later report, "that...Hitler and Mussolini had already agreed at this very meeting in Munich that in time they would have to fight 'side by side' against Great Britain." Daladier flew back to Paris, where—to his surprise—he was met at the airport by cheering supporters rather than the angry crowd he had expected. At the airport in London, Chamberlain was also welcomed home by enthusiastic supporters. He stood triumphantly before newsreel cameras and waved his copy of the Munich Agreement, which, he proudly proclaimed, would ensure "peace for our time."[4]

It was not to be. German troops promptly occupied the Sude-tenland as planned—but within months Hitler was demanding that Czech officials cede what remained of their nation to Germany or face immediate invasion. Amid rising tensions the Czech government dissolved, Judge Hácha was made president, and Hitler officially invited him to Berlin to discuss measures to avoid warfare. On March 14, 1939, Hácha arrived at the Berlin railway terminal amid blowing snow, and was saluted by an honor guard of German troops despite the weather. It was all for show: when Hácha met with Hitler, the respectful atmosphere disappeared. The Führer purposely set the meeting for one a.m. so the aging, ailing leader would be too exhausted to think clearly, then intimidated him with rage and threats. German troops and airpower would ruthlessly annihilate Czechoslovakia, Hitler warned the white-faced Czech president—or Hácha could order his nation to surrender and be absorbed into Nazi Germany. His ultimatum delivered, Hitler left the room—and President Hácha fainted. Nazi officials revived him, and after telephoning officials in the Czech capital of Prague, he signed an agreement surrendering his nation to Nazi Germany. Within hours, motorized columns of German troops and tanks were spreading out through Czechoslovakia, which was quickly overrun. Hitler meanwhile publicly announced that Czechoslovakia had ceased to exist and its former lands and citizens now belonged to Nazi Germany. The governments of Britain and France protested, but did nothing more.[5]

In early December 1938, twenty-nine-year-old Nicholas Winton, a London stockbroker, was getting ready for a skiing vacation on the European Continent when his telephone rang. It was his skiing buddy, Martin Blake, and he had some surprising news. "The skiing's off," Blake abruptly told Winton. "I am off to Prague instead…and I need your help." Blake was an English schoolteacher who volunteered with the British Committee for Refugees from Czechoslovakia, a rescue agency established after the takeover of the Sudetenland to help Jews and other Czechs targeted by the Nazis. Blake had been recruited to go to Czechoslovakia and help set up a *Kindertransport* program similar to those that had rescued so many Jewish children from Germany and Austria. It was a last-minute opportunity, Blake explained, surely more important than a skiing trip, and since he was taking off work anyway, why couldn't Winton come and help?[6]

Although insulated from the turmoil of Czechoslovakia in faraway London, Winton had probably been much more attentive to the news of the Sudetenland takeover than most Britons—and with good reason. He had been born Nicholas Wertheimer, and his ancestors were German Jews. His parents had become Anglicans when he was an infant, and he had been baptized into the Church of England as a child. Like many professing English Christians of his day, Winton considered himself a nominal Christian at best, but his friend's call for help interrupted Winton's everyday life and touched his heart. "Who's helping the children?" he found himself asking.

Blake's response: "Come as soon as you can. And don't bother bringing your skis."[7]

Slim, bespectacled, well dressed, and given to old school ties, young Winton typified the confident, successful London stockbroker—which he was. His father had been an affluent merchant banker in England, and Winton had grown up in a rambling London mansion, well educated, gifted in the sport of fencing, and fluent in French and German. While others of lesser and greater means looked the other way, Winton used his upscale connections and financial contacts as tools to rescue Jewish children of Czechoslovakia from Nazi tyranny—and he began as soon as he reached Prague. There he found a nation turned upside down, with Czechoslovakia's 118,000 Jews now on the Nazi target list.[8]

As soon as German troops rolled into the Sudetenland, Nazi forces began burning synagogues, confiscating Jewish property, and deporting Jews to concentration camps. Thousands of frantic Jewish families and other Nazi victims had fled to makeshift refugee camps. The governments of neighboring European countries—and the United States—had refused to accept large numbers of Czech refugees, but the British government had agreed to take several thousand. Winton settled into a hotel room in Prague and soon connected with humanitarian leader Doreen Warriner, also British, who had come to Czechoslovakia soon after the surrender of the Sudetenland. Warriner was directing assistance efforts for the British Committee for Refugees from Czechoslovakia. In Prague, Winton asked the same question: "Who's helping the children?" Warriner, who recognized Winton as "a really first class organizer," had an answer for him: *You are.* Instead of merely helping Czech refugees, Winton found himself organizing and directing a *Kindertransport* program similar to those that had saved Jewish children from the Nazis in Germany and Austria.[9]

"There is weeping when they can't go, and weeping again when they go."

It was an almost overwhelming task, even for a competent, well-connected businessman like Winton—and it became even more desperate when Hitler incorporated what was left of Czechoslovakia into Greater Germany in March 1939. Immediately all of Czechoslovakia's Jews found themselves targets of the Nazi policy of *judenrein*—designed to make what had formerly been Czechoslovakia "cleansed of Jews." Following the Nazi pattern, more synagogues were set afire, Jewish families were stripped of their wealth and income, and Jews were forbidden to visit city parks, use public transportation, attend school, or even shop except during designated hours. Throughout the country Czech Jews were pressured by the Nazis to leave the country—but they were stripped of the finances they needed to emigrate, and most had no place to go. Almost overnight Jewish life in Czechoslovakia changed from normal to desperate, and many Jewish parents were frantic about their children's safety.[10]

They turned to Nicholas Winton. Plunging into the pandemonium of the Czech relief effort, he arranged to put thirty Jewish children on an aircraft flight from Prague to London, even though he was warned that his contact—"the most beautiful girl in Prague"—was a Nazi mole seeking background on the newly arrived Briton. Winton waved away all objections, saying he didn't care who she was if she could really snare thirty seats on an airplane. She proved to be a legitimate supporter with good contacts, and Winton thus rescued his first thirty children. News quickly spread through the Czech Jewish community that a British businessman was rescuing Jewish children. Besieged by panicky Jewish parents at his hotel, Winton was forced to open an office in Prague—and outside, crowds of parents lined up to arrange safe passage for their children to foster homes in Britain.[11]

As if he were setting up a new business on a demanding deadline, Winton established a *Kindertransport* system to shuttle Jewish children from Prague by rail to the Netherlands, and then by ship to Britain. Back in London he enlisted the aid of influential family, friends, and business contacts to help lobby the British Home Office for the necessary emigration documents. With extraordinary zeal and efficiency, he recruited English sponsors for the children and raised funds to transport them. His competency amazed leaders of the participating relief organizations, but sometimes annoyed British government bureaucrats. "They just called me a bloody nuisance," he later recalled—but he persevered.[12]

Others were also frustrated by Winton's get-it-done attitude. Some humanitarians complained that they needed more time to properly match refugee children to foster parents. Likewise, some Jewish leaders were understandably concerned that Jewish children were being placed in non-Jewish foster homes. Winton was unmoved by complaints: Czechoslovakia was being swallowed whole by Nazi Germany, and he was determined to save the life of every Jewish child whom he could rescue. "I didn't mind if the children were Jewish or Communist or Catholic if they were endangered, and I didn't mind who they went to," he later explained. "At least they were in England. To my mind, that was the most important thing at that point...the worst that would happen to them in England was better than being in the fire."[13]

In the winter, spring, and summer of 1939, Winton managed to pack one train out of Prague after another with refugee children—most of them Jewish—heading for the Dutch coast and passage to Britain. Soon, Hitler's dark plans for Europe's Jews would become even more sinister—the Holocaust loomed ahead. But even as late as the summer of 1939, his plans were still developing and he was content to simply strip Greater Germany's Jews of their wealth and force them to flee. So the Nazis allowed the *Kindertransport* to continue in Czechoslovakia, at least for the time being. The numbers of Czech children that Winton rescued continued to mount: One hundred. Two hundred. Three hundred. Four, five, six hundred—all headed to safety in faraway Britain as their families back home were slowly cloaked in the darkness of Nazi brutality.[14]

The full horrors of the impending Holocaust were still unimagined in the summer of 1939, but many Jewish parents in Czechoslovakia could sense the evil that was closing around them. They were unable to escape, but they made the unselfish, unbearable decision to send their children to safety through Winton's *Kindertransport*. "By April 1939 my parents realized the game was up, and my father sat my brother and me down and told us we were going on a long journey," a *Kindertransport* child recounted as an adult. At the train station, his mother gave him a parting memento. "As it came time to leave," he said, "she took off her wristwatch and gave it to us. For us it was a mixture of fear and adventure—we didn't really understand." Another of "Winton's Children," a nine-year-old girl, was also left with vivid memories of a final farewell from her mother and father. "The parents were heroes," she recalled, "because none of them let on that this was in all probability the final goodbye. We sat in the carriage and held hands, saying together, 'We are not going to cry.'"[15]

For Winton, dealing with the parents was anguishing. As Jews left behind in Nazi Germany, they knew that they would probably never see their children again, but they were nonetheless desperate to place them on Winton's *Kindertransport*, knowing it would likely give them life. "And so," Winton later explained, "there is weeping when they can't go, and weeping again when they go." He steeled himself to go forward amid the anguish, forcing himself to ignore the agonizing circumstances, focusing instead on his goal of putting every Jewish child he could find on a train to survival. A slower anguish awaited the child refugees in Britain, as they gradually came to realize that they would probably never again see their mothers and fathers. Typically, after they were safely housed with English foster families, the children received letters from their parents for a while—and then the mail stopped. "We want to say farewell to you who were our dearest possession in the world," read a final letter sent to two young Jewish boys by their Czech parents. "[We] ask you to become good men and think of the years we were happy together. We are going into the unknown." Of the 118,000 Jews living in Czechoslovakia in 1939, more than 78,000 were killed by the Nazis. Most of the children rescued by Winton never saw their parents again.[16]

When the Nazis invaded Czechoslovakia, Winton could no longer travel to Prague, so he directed the *Kindertransport* from London, continuing to rescue Jewish children from occupied Czechoslovakia. When the war began in September 1939, however, the Nazis abruptly halted the *Kindertransport*. Even so, in the nine months since he had abandoned his skiing vacation to go to Czechoslovakia, Nicholas Winton had managed to rescue 669 children, most of whom were Jewish. A humble man, he took little comfort in thinking about the children he had saved, but instead mourned those he had not. His most sorrowful thought was the memory of the last train—the one that never left. The day the war began, the Nazis shut down rail service from Prague, leaving a trainload of 250 Jewish children sitting at the railway station, waiting for permission to depart. It never came; permission was denied—and most or all of the children aboard perished in Nazi concentration camps.[17]

Nicholas Winton, the stockbroker who could have put the Jews of Czechoslovakia out of his mind and gone on vacation, was transformed by his spontaneous decision to help rescue the perishing. For the rest of his life, he would continuously seek to help others, serving in Britain's Royal Air Force during the war, then pursuing a long career as a humanitarian. He would live to the extraordinary age of 106, and in his final decades he would be celebrated and honored as a hero of the Holocaust. With typical modesty he would wave away the accolades, giving credit to others and lamenting all the children who had not been saved. Although he would seldom speak of the *Kindertransport*, he would never forget it—nor the life lesson he had learned from it. "There is a difference between passive goodness and active goodness," he concluded in 1939. "It entails going out, finding and helping those in suffering and danger, and not merely in leading an exemplary life in a purely passive way."[18]

CHAPTER 7
JAN KARSKI

German SS troops in Poland round up Jewish families for deportation to a Nazi death camp.

"All the Jews who were slaughtered [have] become my family."

ON SEPTEMBER 1, 1939, lines of German panzer tanks roared across Germany's border with Poland and headed eastward, followed by advancing columns of German troops. Precise formations of high-level German bombers appeared in the skies over Polish air force bases, unleashing streams of falling bombs that destroyed Poland's air force while it was still on the ground. In numbers that seemed to fill the sky, they moved on to bomb the Polish army's staging areas, consuming men, trucks, tanks, and barracks in cauldrons of fire. Supporting the bomber formations were fast *Stuka* dive bombers that screamed out of the clouds, bombing and strafing any Polish military convoys that had somehow escaped the high-level bombers. It was a new kind of war—a *Blitzkrieg*, or "lightning war"—developed by Hitler's military high command to rapidly destroy the enemy with overwhelming airpower and ground forces. Unmatched by Nazi firepower, the Polish army melted away—but not without courage. In some places legions of splendidly mounted Polish cavalry charged German tanks and machine guns with lances, only to be utterly slaughtered.[1]

The Nazi war machine also launched a terror campaign against Polish civilians, bombing Poland's cities and using fighter aircraft to strafe roads packed with panicky, fleeing families. "We found the highways jammed with hundreds of thousands of refugees," recalled a defeated Polish soldier, "soldiers looking for their commands, others just drifting with the tide.... Frequent strafings [left] smoking, abandoned ruins of towns, railroad junctions, villages and cities." Within little more than two weeks, Nazi forces controlled the western half of Poland, and—beginning on September 17—the eastern side of the nation was invaded by troops from the Soviet Union. Although bitter enemies with Germany, the Russians had not come to help repel the German invasion, but to conquer and occupy the regions of Poland unclaimed by Nazi forces. One week before the Nazi invasion—in a feat of diplomacy that shocked the leaders of Britain and France—Hitler had achieved a nonaggression agreement with Soviet dictator Joseph Stalin. By dividing Poland with his archenemy, Hitler held back the huge Soviet army without having to sacrifice German blood or treasure. Polish patriots valiantly stalled Nazi forces outside the Polish capital of Warsaw, but within a few more weeks they were bombed and starved into surrender. On October 5, 1939, Hitler led a victory parade through Warsaw as he had done earlier in Vienna and Prague: this time, however, his parade route was lined by ruins and marred by the odor of dead bodies. Like Austria and Czechoslovakia, Poland as a nation had ceased to exist.[2]

This time France and Britain declared war on Nazi Germany, but they did nothing to save Poland. Hitler claimed that Germany needed neighboring Poland for *Lebensraum*—the "living space" necessary for Hitler to establish a thousand-year reign, or *Reich*, by Nazi Germany. He had rearmed the nation, reclaimed control of the Rhineland, occupied Austria, seized the Sudetenland, and conquered Czechoslovakia—all without firing a shot; but he was willing to go to war to conquer Poland. "Further successes are impossible without the shedding of blood," he had told his generals months earlier when planning Poland's downfall. The Polish people were inferior to the Nazi master race, Hitler believed, and he intended to make them "the slaves of the Greater German World Reich." Even deadlier were his plans for Poland's three million Jews—the largest Jewish population of any nation in Europe.[3]

Soon after Poland was conquered, two SS soldiers grew weary of guarding a work detail of fifty Polish Jews who had been ordered to clean up wreckage. The Jews were simply not working hard enough, the Nazis concluded. So they marched them inside a nearby synagogue and killed them. Shocked by the brutality, an officer from the Wehrmacht—the regular German army—ordered the two murderers court-martialed for atrocities, but the SS intervened and the soldiers went unpunished. It was just the beginning. On the eve of the invasion, Hitler had sanctioned SS chief Heinrich Himmler and his top officer, Reinhard Heydrich—who was also a brutal and fanatic Nazi—to unleash a new weapon against Poland's Jewish population. It was the Einsatzgruppen—highly mobile SS "death squads" that followed the Wehrmacht into conquered countries, beginning with Poland. Jews were to be "housecleaned"—a Nazi euphemism for annihilation—along with Polish intellectuals, political leaders, military officers, Communists, and others deemed unfit for the future Nazi age—even the mentally ill and handicapped. In Poland the Einsatzgruppen established a deadly pattern: Jews were rounded up by the thousands and confined to blocked-off neighborhoods deemed ghettos. Then at some point they were marched or transported to preselected killing fields and systematically executed in mass murder.[4]

After the war, when surviving Nazi leaders were put on trial for war crimes, General Otto Ohlendorf, who had commanded one of the Einsatzgruppen, was asked how many Jewish men, women, and children his unit had killed. Coldly he shrugged his shoulders and answered matter-of-factly, "Ninety thousand." By war's end the Einsatzgruppen had killed at least two million people, more than half of whom were Jewish. In his testimony Ohlendorf described the death squad tactics:

> The Einsatz unit would enter a village or town and order the prominent Jewish citizens to call together all Jews for the purpose of "resettlement." They were requested to hand over their valuables and shortly before execution to surrender their outer clothing. They were transported to the place of execution, usually an antitank ditch, in trucks—always

only as many as could be executed immediately.... Then they were shot, kneeling or standing, by firing squads in a military manner and the corpses thrown in a ditch.

The previous six years of Jewish persecution in Germany, Austria, and Czechoslovakia had merely been a prelude to Adolf Hitler's grand and sinister scheme to destroy the Jews of Europe. In a speech delivered several months before his Polish invasion, he had threatened to oversee "the annihilation of the Jewish race in Europe." In Poland the annihilation began.[5]

Somehow the world had to learn what the Nazis were doing to the Jews and others in Poland. That was Jan Karski's motivation when he accepted what amounted to a suicide mission: escape from Poland and report the mass murders to leaders in London and Washington, D.C. Success seemed impossible, but Karski was clearly the right man for the job. When Nazi forces invaded Poland, Karski was a twenty-five-year-old Polish army officer—a slender, athletic, well-educated young man who was gifted with a near-photographic memory. Karski was a practicing Catholic, the oldest of eight children, and—like countless other Poles—he had been instilled with what would prove to be a lifelong devotion to Christianity. He held a law degree and had served in the Polish diplomatic corps, posted to Paris and London, but had left it to become an army officer when Poland appeared threatened by Nazi Germany.[6]

His military career was short-lived: his regiment was captured by Soviet forces when Stalin's Russian army invaded Poland as Nazi Germany's partner. Determined to regain his freedom and fight for Poland, Karski disguised himself as a private and escaped Soviet captivity, thus avoiding the slaughter of more than twenty thousand Polish officers by Russian troops at the infamous Katyn

Forest Massacre. He was incarcerated by German forces as a prisoner of war, but escaped again—this time by jumping from a moving train. He made his way to Warsaw, which was occupied by Nazi troops, and managed to join the Polish Underground, a secret resistance movement, serving as a courier between Poland and the Polish government-in-exile in Paris. He repeatedly conducted dangerous secret missions, taking reports back and forth between the Underground in Poland and the Polish government-in-exile. Once, he was captured and tortured by the Gestapo, but Underground agents managed to rescue him.[7]

In 1942, as Karski prepared for another secret mission to the Polish government-in-exile, which had moved to London, he was visited in Warsaw by two Jewish leaders who had slipped out of Warsaw's Jewish ghetto with an urgent message for him. The Nazis were systematically slaughtering Poland's Jews, they reported, and they pleaded with him to take the story to British leaders in London and even to the American president in Washington, D.C. Karski was well aware of the Nazi capacity for brutality, but even he was shocked by the stories the Jewish leaders reported. He agreed to return with them to the ghetto—a sprawling Jewish neighborhood in Warsaw that Nazis had surrounded by barbed wire, brick walls, and armed guards. When occupied by the Germans in 1939, Warsaw had boasted a Jewish population of 350,000, which was more than in any other metropolitan area in Europe and second only to New York City. All of Warsaw's Jews had been forcibly relocated to the ghetto, along with thousands from nearby regions, giving the Warsaw Ghetto a population of more than 400,000. Fitted with ragged clothes and the Star of David armband all Jews were required to wear, Karski entered the ghetto with his escorts. He was stunned by what he witnessed.[8]

Dead bodies lay in the streets, felled by starvation, illness, and gunfire from Nazi guards. Intentionally starved by the Nazis, emaciated Jewish men, women, and children moved listlessly through the ghetto, looking like living skeletons. From an apartment window, Karski watched two chubby boy guards from the Hitler Youth, armed with rifles, as they randomly took potshots at Jewish civilians, laughing and cheering when a human target fell dead. "Remember this, remember this," one of Karski's Jewish guides urged him. More than two hundred thousand people—half of the ghetto's population—had already been deported, Karski was told, and by now were probably dead, executed in newly built Nazi death camps. By their count, Jewish leaders told him, the Nazis had already murdered almost two million Polish Jews—and they obviously intended to kill the rest.[9]

In order to see for himself, Karski sneaked into a transit camp, where deported Jews were assembled for final transfer to a nearby death camp. Outfitted in the uniform of a camp guard, he watched with grim self-control as railroad cattle cars rolled to a stop and were emptied of their human cargo—starved, frightened, and dazed Jewish men, women, and children. The victims were stripped of their suitcases, then herded to other cars on nearby tracks—on the route to the death camp. Those who moved too slowly were beaten or bayoneted to death by Nazi guards. Sometimes, Karski was told, the packed cars were left on rail sidings until all occupants died from dehydration, suffocation, or starvation. Most victims, however, wound up in death camps, where they were killed by poison gas. Afterward, their bodies were cremated. Even at a distance, Karski thought he could smell burning flesh.[10]

"They want to destroy the entire Jewish nation."

After what he had witnessed, Karski was determined to make his way to London and Washington—to tell the world what was happening to Poland's Jews. He would have to travel from Poland through Nazi Germany, make his way through France—which by then had been conquered by Germany—and then on to Spain, which was officially neutral. From there he could get passage to London. To avoid revealing his Polish accent to suspicious Nazis while traveling, he had a dentist pull several of his teeth, which swelled his face and gave him an excuse for not talking. Despite the perils, he made it to London. There he eventually obtained an audience with British foreign secretary Anthony Eden. Karski poured out his story, giving a gruesome report of the mass murder he had seen firsthand. It was a credible eyewitness account by a seasoned intelligence operative who was also a former diplomat and military officer. Great Britain had to do *something* to save Poland's Jews, Karski urged the foreign secretary.[11]

Eden's response shattered his hopes. By accepting one hundred thousand Jewish refugees, the foreign secretary told him, Great Britain had already done its share. British officials did agree to issue a joint public statement with American and other Allied leaders, which condemned Nazi Germany's "cold-blooded extermination" of the Jews. However, little else was done. Unwilling to give up, Karski turned to Szmul Zygielbojm, a high-ranking Jewish leader in the Polish government-in-exile who had also escaped from Poland. Zygielbojm believed Karski, but he feared the Nazi atrocities were so horrible and on such a massive scale that his report would be dismissed as propaganda. "It's impossible," he told Karski, "utterly impossible." Even so, he promised to do all in his power to convince Allied leaders of the truth. Soon afterward, however, after writing a public letter criticizing world leaders for "permitting the annihilation of the Jewish people," Zygielbojm committed suicide.[12]

His only hope, Karski decided, was to take his report to the president of the United States, Franklin D. Roosevelt. The United States had been officially neutral when Nazi Germany invaded

Poland and ignited World War II, but had been drawn into the war two years later. Surely, Karski reasoned, if President Roosevelt understood what Hitler was doing to the Jews, he could do *something* to help save them. He urged the Polish government-in-exile to intercede with American leaders, and in the summer of 1943, Karski found himself in the United States, sitting face-to-face with President Roosevelt in the private quarters of the White House. Karski tried to be concise in his report to the president—"Be exact and brief," the Polish ambassador had told him—but he was also intentionally pointed. Nazi oppression in Poland was brutal beyond belief, he explained—especially toward the Jews. "There is a difference between the terror used against the Poles and the Jews," he told Roosevelt. "The Germans want to destroy the Polish nation as a nation, but they want the Polish population in these territories deprived of their political, intellectual, religious and economic elites, [leaving] only farmers, workers and the city middle class. With the Jews, they want to destroy the entire Jewish nation." Without the intervention of the United States and the other Allies, Karski told the president, the Jews of Poland "would cease to exist."[13]

President Roosevelt listened intently and asked numerous questions—but nothing about the Jews. He even asked about the condition of Polish livestock, but according to Karski he failed to ask a single question about the mass murder of the Jewish people. Dejected, Karski left the White House believing that he had failed in his mission. He realized that his lobbying had surely alerted the Nazis to his identity, which meant he would never survive if he returned to Poland. So he decided to remain in the United States—and go public. He set up countless interviews with the news media, made speeches, even wrote a book about his experiences in the Polish Underground. His publicity campaign eventually produced an invitation to a private dinner with three high-ranking Jewish members of the Roosevelt administration. One of them was US Supreme Court Associate Justice Felix Frankfurter, a man who was known to be a trusted adviser to the president.[14]

This time Karski did not worry about being brief or restrained in his comments. With all the gruesome, shocking details, he recounted what he had personally witnessed in Poland: railway cars packed with victims left to die, corpses lying on the streets of the Warsaw Ghetto, Jewish families herded to mass executions in the Nazi death camps, where the odor of burning flesh wafted in the breeze. Frankfurter was unable to remain seated. He rose from the table and paced back and forth as Karski revealed the sensational horrors of the Holocaust. Finally Karski finished. Frankfurter stopped pacing and stood silently for a long moment. Then he spoke. "Mr. Karski...," he said. "I am unable to believe you." The Polish ambassador to the United States was present, and he exclaimed, "Felix, you don't mean it! How can you call him a liar to his face! The authority of my government is behind him." Frankfurter looked sad, and replied softly, "Mr. Ambassador, I did not say this young man is lying. I said I am *unable* to believe him. There is a difference."[15]

Finally Karski understood. Normal, rational, moral-minded people simply could not comprehend the grand scale of evil that Adolf Hitler had unleashed against the Jews of Europe. Without witnessing it firsthand, such horrors were beyond the ability of most people to imagine. British and American leaders had repeatedly told Karski that the best way to rescue Poland's Jews was to defeat Hitler and win the war. Now Karski told himself that he would have to settle for that—and that his mission to the Allied leaders on behalf of Poland and its Jews had been unsuccessful. In reality, he had not failed: public opinion and Allied policy *would* change because of his efforts. After weighing Karski's report, British foreign secretary Eden publicly unveiled Hitler's Holocaust to the world in a speech to the British Parliament. Poland had become a Nazi "slaughterhouse," he declared, and Adolf Hitler intended to murder every Jew in Europe. "The number of victims of these bloody cruelties," Eden proclaimed, "is reckoned in many hundreds of thousands of entirely innocent men, women and children." The British legislators received the shocking news in stunned silence.[16]

Karski's impact was even greater in the United States. Due in large measure to his efforts, rescuing Europe's Jews became an American war aim—one of the reasons for defeating Nazi Germany. Later the United States also took the lead in prosecuting surviving Nazi leaders at the postwar Nuremberg war crimes trials. Over the course of a dozen trials, 185 Nazi leaders were indicted. Four committed suicide before trial, four were declared unfit for trial, and of the 177 who were tried, 142 were convicted, with twenty-four sentenced to death and the remainder imprisoned. While the number caught and punished was small compared to the thousands guilty of abetting the Holocaust, the Nuremberg Trials put the horrors of the Holocaust on public record with testimony that could never be credibly denied. Karski's testimony also apparently motivated President Roosevelt to establish the War Refugee Board to assist Jewish survivors of the Holocaust. The board's director, John Pehle, stated that Karski's meeting with Roosevelt "changed U.S. policy overnight from indifference to affirmative action." According to research by the Holocaust Memorial Museum in Washington, D.C., the War Refugee Board rescued more than two hundred thousand Jewish refugees.[17]

Jan Karski's impact was in fact enormous—but he never seemed to fully appreciate what a difference he had made. After the war, when Soviet forces occupied Poland and imposed Communist totalitarian rule, Karski chose to remain in the United States. He became a revered professor at Georgetown University, and was eventually lauded for his efforts to save the Jewish people of Poland. Always he remained humble about his efforts, commenting once that his deepest regret was that he had not done more. "I hope God will forgive me," he tearfully stated. Before his death at age eighty-six, he was invited to address the US Congress. Looking upon the assembled lawmakers, the aging Catholic—by then renowned for his wartime heroism—summarized his feelings for all those he had been unable to save. "All the Jews who were slaughtered," he declared, "[have] become my family."[18]

CHAPTER 8

JÓZEF AND WIKTORIA ULMA

Devout believers and the parents of six children, Wiktoria and Józef Ulma pose for a self-portrait.

(CREDIT: YAD VASHEM)

"Saving the lives of others, they laid down their own lives."

Józef and Wiktoria Ulma understood the risk they were taking—what could happen to them if they were caught. When Nazi forces overran Poland and began executing the nation's Jews, the Polish people were warned that anyone found helping Jews would be killed too. Even so, when the Goldmans—a Jewish couple and their young daughter—turned up at their door seeking escape from the Nazis, the Ulmas believed they could not turn them away. Already Józef Ulma had constructed a makeshift shelter for a Jewish family hiding in a ravine near the Ulma family farm. The farm lay outside the village of Markowa, which was located in southern Poland and had a population of approximately four thousand. The village's isolated location spared it from being overrun by Nazi forces in 1939, but eventually a Nazi death squad reached Markowa, rounded up most of the town's hundred-plus Jews, and killed them. The death squads then spread out through the surrounding countryside and on to other villages, rounding up the Jewish population and either executing them on the spot or deporting them to death camps.[1]

In the fall of 1942, Nazi leaders in the Markowa area ordered members of the town's fire brigade to help track down Jewish families who had escaped Markowa's initial executions. As the hunt intensified, a Jewish father named Szall and his four sons appeared at the Ulmas' farm and asked the couple to hide them from the Nazis. They were from another town, but they had heard from other refugees that the Ulmas were devout Christians who cared for their Jewish neighbors. Both Józef and Wiktoria had been raised in serious Catholic families and were known locally as loving, cheerful believers. They had met seven years earlier as volunteer performers in a church play. In 1942 Józef was forty-two years old, Wiktoria was thirty, and they had six children. Although he had received limited formal education, Józef was known in Markowa for his talent and ingenuity. On the family farm he experimented with novel methods of beekeeping, cultivated silkworms, and had won several regional awards for innovative methods of farming. He also volunteered as the town librarian, and was an accomplished amateur photographer who enjoying documenting daily life around Markowa. Wiktoria was known to neighbors as a devoted wife and mother.[2]

"May their sacrifice be a call for respect and love."
Soon after the father and sons requested help, a Jewish couple— the Goldmans—appeared at the Ulmas' house with their young daughter, seeking sanctuary. Józef and Wiktoria decided to hide them too. All eight refugees slept in the Ulmas' attic at night, and during the day they helped with the farm chores. All hoped that the Ulma farm was so isolated that no one would know that Jews were hiding there. In early spring of 1944, however, Włodzimierz Leś, a Polish policeman in a nearby village, learned that Szall and his sons were hiding at the Ulmas' farm. Earlier Szall had paid the policeman to hide him and his sons from the Nazis, but they had fled when the arrangement began to unravel, leaving their valuables behind. After living in the Ulmas' attic for more than a year, Szall went back to Leś's home to retrieve some of his belongings, and the policeman turned on him, reporting him to Nazi officials.[3]

In the early-morning darkness of March 24, 1944, a squad of Polish policemen under the command of a Nazi officer, Lieutenant Eilert Dieken, arrived at the Ulma farm in two horse-drawn wagons. Most of the squad belonged to Poland's national police force—the Granatowa policja, or "Blue Police"—which had been forced to serve the Nazis after the invasion or suffer death. Lieutenant Dieken's second-in-command was a fanatical young

Czech-German Nazi named Joseph Kokott. He led the raid on the Ulma home, breaking into the house and rousting Józef and Wiktoria from their beds—even though Wiktoria was seven months pregnant with the Ulmas' seventh child. The couple was dragged outside, along with all their children, the oldest of whom was a first grader. The raiders quickly discovered the two Jewish families hiding in the attic, and hauled them outside also. All sixteen were lined up under the glare of police flashlights and executed—each shot in the back of the head, children included. Kokott forced the two Polish cart drivers to witness the executions, so they could tell others what would happen to other Poles who hid Jews. "Look how the Polish swine who have hidden Jews are dying," Kokott told the wide-eyed drivers. Afterward the raiders buried the sixteen bodies in shallow graves, then looted the Ulma home.[4]

Later some of their friends reinterred the Ulmas' bodies in a local cemetery. Upon learning of the massacre, members of the Polish Underground assassinated Włodzimierz Leś for betraying the Ulmas and the two Jewish families they were hiding. After the war Lieutenant Dieken was tracked down for prosecution as a war criminal for the murders, but he died before he could be brought to trial. In 1957 Joseph Kokott, the Nazi who had carried out the raid and the executions for Dieken, was discovered living in Czechoslovakia, and was arrested by Polish war crimes investigators. He was tried and convicted for the murders at the Ulma home, and spent the rest of his life in prison, where he died. In 1995 a stone memorial honoring Józef and Wiktoria Ulma and their children was erected at the village of Markowa. The inscription on it reads: "Saving the lives of others, they laid down their own lives.... May their sacrifice be a call for respect and love to every human being."[5]

CHAPTER 9

MAX LIEDTKE

Hands raised as ordered, Polish Jews are rounded up by SS troops for deportation to a concentration camp. In the Polish city of Przemyśl, Major Max Liedtke, a German army officer, tried to save local Jews from such a fate.

(CREDIT: NATIONAL ARCHIVES)

"The worst they can do to us is shoot us."

IT WAS STILL dark when Major Max Liedtke received the alert: the SS was coming for the Jews. Liedtke was a forty-eight-year-old officer in the German Wehrmacht, the regular German army, and just weeks earlier he had arrived from a post in Greece to take command of the German garrison in the Polish city of Przemyśl, which lay on the San River in southern Poland. A veteran of the First World War, Liedtke was a tall, distinguished-looking officer who carried himself with a proper military bearing. He was also a professing Christian, a Lutheran, the son of a vicar, and had spent his preacher's-son childhood in the German province of East Prussia. He did not like the Nazis, and privately opposed what they were doing to the Jews in Poland and elsewhere. Now, on the morning of July 26, 1942, he had to decide whether protecting the Jews was worth risking his own life.[1]

Liedtke was serious about his faith. After graduating from high school, he had entered a Christian university to study theology, but had been swept up into the German army when the First World War began. After the war he became a journalist and rose to the position of editor in chief at the *Greifswalder Zeitung*, a daily newspaper in the German city of Greifswald. He editorialized against the Nazi Party when it came to power in the late 1920s, and he became a Nazi target when Hitler became Führer in 1933. Two years later political pressure from Nazi officials cost Liedtke his job. Blacklisted by the Nazi Party, he had difficulty finding another position, and then in 1939 he was recalled into the German army with the rank of major. He was spared an active role in the barbaric invasion of Poland, and was posted to Belgium and Greece as German forces overran one country after another.[2]

He had come to Przemyśl in early July 1942 with the new Wehrmacht district commander, General Curt L. *Freiherr* von Gienanth, who had appointed him to command the city's Wehrmacht garrison. Liedtke had barely begun to learn his way around his new command when he was given the predawn notice that a column of SS troops—a large death squad—was approaching the bridge over the San River en route to round up Przemyśl's Jewish population. The city's eighteen thousand Jews had been cordoned off in a ghetto, and now the SS was on its way to enforce a "resettlement"—which meant, Liedtke knew, that the Jews were going to be shot or deported to a death camp. Hitler's top Nazi in Poland, Governor General Hans Frank, had recently revealed the Führer's plan for Poland's Jews: "As far as the Jews are concerned," Frank had told a Nazi gathering, "I want to tell you quite frankly that they must be done away with one way or another. . . . We must annihilate the Jews."[3]

Although many Wehrmacht officers were untroubled by SS brutality toward the Jews and other Poles, some detested the black-uniformed elite forces, which had grown from Hitler's bodyguard to a huge wing of the German armed forces. By war's end numerous Wehrmacht soldiers would be guilty of numerous atrocities themselves, but officers such as Major Liedtke considered members of the SS nothing more than thugs and mass murderers. His adjutant, *Oberleutnant* Albert Battel, shared his revulsion for the persecution of the Jews—even though Battel was a longtime member of the Nazi Party. His party membership was in anything but good standing, however—he had been reprimanded by Nazi officials for befriending Jews, a practice he had continued when he had been posted to Przemyśl. A middle-aged attorney in civilian life, Battel was also a German veteran of the First World War, who had been recalled from his law practice to serve as a Wehrmacht officer in the German invasion of Poland. Before Liedtke's arrival, Battel had been reprimanded by the Gestapo for his respectful treatment of Jewish leaders in the Przemyśl Ghetto. It was Battel who brought Liedtke the report that SS forces were coming for Przemyśl's Jews.[4]

In the few weeks that he had held command in Przemyśl, Major Liedtke had supported humane treatment of the Jews, and had even spoken of establishing a "model Jewish community in Przemyśl." General von Gienanth—a highly decorated career Wehrmacht officer—supported Liedtke's position, and had put more than four thousand of Przemyśl's Jews to work in local armaments factories. Although they were forced to work for the German war effort, their jobs protected them and their families from execution by the SS. Now, with an SS death squad approaching, Liedtke was determined to save as many Jewish lives as possible.[5]

Lieutenant Battel proposed a plan: Could they somehow delay the SS long enough to at least rescue the Jewish workers and their families? Major Liedtke agreed: "The worst they can do to us is shoot us," he replied, only half-joking. Then he issued an extraordinary order for a German officer: Barricade the bridge over the San River entering the Jewish ghetto, fortify it with regular army troops, set up machine guns—and warn the SS troops that they'll be fired on if they try to break through the roadblock. All of Przemyśl was currently under martial law—a sort of state of emergency, he reasoned—and he would use that as an excuse to halt the SS. Then he would officially argue that the city's Jews were needed for war-related labor. Maybe the tactic would give him enough time to enlist General von Gienanth's support; he hoped the general would agree that the Wehrmacht should not cooperate with SS death squads.[6]

Battel hurriedly directed the defense of the San River bridge. As Liedtke had ordered, Wehrmacht troops were rushed to defend the span, barricades were hastily erected, and heavy machine guns were mounted at the roadblock under the command of a tough regular army sergeant major. Somehow news of the approaching

SS column spread through the nearby Jewish ghetto, and its inhabitants were stunned to see German regular army troops in their gray-green uniforms setting up machine guns to stop the SS. Soon after daylight the rumble of engines signaled the approach of the SS column—truckloads of black-uniformed soldiers accompanied by trucks to haul away the ghetto's Jews to death camps. The motorcade rolled up to the bridge—then halted, facing a barricade manned by regular army troops and topped by machine guns.[7]

The SS commanding officer demanded to know why his route was blocked. Przemyśl was under a military emergency, he was informed, and no traffic would be admitted. The officer protested, fumed, and ordered the roadblock removed—but the Wehrmacht sergeant major commanding the bridge defenses replied that he had his orders: No one could pass. The SS officer angrily ordered the Wehrmacht troops to retreat, but no one moved. For a long moment, the SS commander appeared ready to order an assault against the bridge's defenders, but the sergeant major stuck to his orders. Attempt to break through the barricade, he told the incensed SS officer, and he would order his troops to open fire. Finally the SS commander backed down. "This is outrageous," he sputtered—then ordered his column to reverse course and leave.[8]

"I have ordered that ruthless steps be taken against all those who think that they can...protect the Jews."
Major Liedtke knew that the SS would immediately send an angry protest up the army chain of command. He hoped that General von Gienanth would back his actions, but he did not intend to waste the time his bold defiance had bought him. Move quickly, he ordered Battel: Use Wehrmacht troops to break into the Jewish ghetto, then load as many workers and their families as possible onto army trucks and bring them into the Wehrmacht garrison for protection. Battel managed to hastily relocate more than a hundred Jewish families before new orders arrived from Wehrmacht headquarters. As Major

Liedtke had hoped, General von Gienanth had tried to have the SS called off, arguing with the high command that the Jews in the Przemyśl Ghetto were needed for war labor. Soon, however, he had been overruled—by none other than Hitler's powerful top SS commander, *Reichsführer* Heinrich Himmler, who angrily declared, "I have ordered that ruthless steps be taken against all those who think that they can use the interest of war industry to cloak their real intentions to protect the Jews."[9]

The next day SS troops rolled into the Przemyśl Ghetto and forcibly deported more than fourteen thousand Jewish men, women, and children to death camps, where they were eventually executed. The Nazis' deportation tactics were described by a survivor of a similar raid in another Polish city. "They surrounded house after house," he reported. "The sick were shot in their beds. People jumped from the top stories in order to hasten their deaths and avoid being tortured. Jews were forced out of rooftop hiding places with clubs, and fell to their deaths.... Young, physically fit men were sent to the labor camps. The others were made to undress and [were] loaded on railway trucks, destined for the crematoria." The SS was delayed in rounding up the Jews that Liedtke had evacuated to the Wehrmacht garrison, but they too were eventually rounded up and shipped to death camps.[10]

Through his close association with Hitler, *Reichsführer* Himmler managed to fulfill his threat to punish the Wehrmacht officers who tried to protect Przemyśl's Jews. Despite his long and distinguished service in the German army, General von Gienanth was removed from his district command and forced into retirement. Lieutenant Battel was discharged from the Wehrmacht, allegedly for health problems, and was drafted into the Volkssturm—the German home guard. He survived the war, but was barred from practicing law by the Allied occupation government because he had once belonged to the Nazi Party. Targeted as the mastermind of the San River roadblock, Major Liedtke was dismissed from his command

and shipped to where no German soldier wanted to go: the dreaded Eastern Front, where the German army was engaged with Soviet troops in brutal conditions. In 1944, Major Liedtke was among the three million German troops captured by Soviet forces. Ironically, he was among the countless German officers declared war criminals by the Soviet Union's Communist government, and was banished to life imprisonment. He later was reported to have died in a Soviet labor camp. His valiant confrontation with the Schutzstaffel is believed to be the only instance of German regular army troops facing down the SS on behalf of Jews.[11]

CHAPTER 10
JULIUS MADRITSCH

SS troops "liquidate" the Warsaw Ghetto and deport its Jewish inhabitants to a death camp. The same fate befell Julius Madritsch's Jewish factory workers in Kraków.   (CREDIT: NATIONAL ARCHIVES/WIKIMEDIA)

"Through the work they would have a chance at survival."
AT FIRST JULIUS Madritsch was simply trying to save his own life. Then he realized that he had the opportunity to save hundreds of Jewish lives, maybe even more—if he was willing to risk death. And he was. When Adolf Hitler triggered World War II with the 1939 invasion of Poland, Julius Madritsch was a thirty-three-year-old Austrian businessman. He detested the Nazis and the way they had taken over his beloved country. He also watched with revulsion as they tormented Austrian Jews on the streets of Vienna, and then uprooted them from their homes and shipped them off to what was rumored to be a horrible end. Then, when the war began, it was his turn: He was drafted into the German army.[1]

He could not bear the thought of fighting for the Nazis, but what could he do? By the time the war began, everyone in Austria understood that resisting the Nazis meant imprisonment or death. Then he discovered an opportunity for survival. The Nazi war effort needed factory managers for war production. Qualified businessmen who had experience in manufacturing were exempted from the German military draft if they were engaged in war production. Madritsch had managed textile manufacturing operations in Austria, and he was good at it. To avoid fighting for the Nazis, he hastily applied for a license to manufacture uniforms for the German army—and got it. His new post would still require him to assist in the German war effort, but at least he would not be killing people for Adolf Hitler. Soon he received his orders from the Nazi government: He would travel to the Polish city of Kraków, where the Nazis had seized two factories after the invasion. There he would restart the factories and fulfill his contract. For a labor force, he was informed, he would select Jewish laborers from the newly established Kraków Ghetto, where the city's Jews had been forcibly resettled.[2]

In 1940, when Madritsch arrived in Kraków, it was a city of almost half a million people—and more than sixty thousand of them were Jewish. As in other Nazi-occupied countries, Polish Jews who survived the 1939 invasion were required to openly wear a Star of David at all times. They were tormented by Nazi troops and police, robbed of their possessions, and shot dead on the spot if they showed the slightest resistance. Soon the city's entire Jewish population was forced to live in a single closed and guarded neighborhood—the Kraków Ghetto. In reality, it was a giant prison. There, under the direction of a Jewish council that answered to the SS and Gestapo, the ghetto's residents were jammed into overcrowded living spaces, and forced to live on near-starvation rations. At first they tried to establish a quality of life, especially for their children, setting up health care facilities, children's activities, and day care for the children of workers. However, as Hitler's diabolical plan for Europe's Jews changed from isolation to elimination, increasing numbers of Jewish families were deported from the Kraków Ghetto—never to return. By late 1942, deportation came to mean a death sentence for every Jewish man, woman, and child who was marched out of the ghetto under Nazi guard. Even Jews who collaborated with the Nazis were shipped away to execution. The only Jews who were spared were those who worked as laborers in Julius Madritsch's uniform factories.[3]

When he set up his factories in Kraków and saw the severe persecution of the city's Jewish population, Madritsch was horrified. He had been raised in a devout family in Vienna, and his Christianity was central to his life. In Kraków he soon realized that for his workers and their families, a job in his factory meant the difference between life and death. "Through the work," he later explained, "they would have a chance at survival." Making a personal profit was not his goal. Neither was his own safety. He had been placed in a unique position, he believed, and his faith compelled him to save as many Jewish lives as he could. Arguing that he needed more workers—and healthy ones—he convinced the factory's SS overseers to allow him to add to his workforce and to obtain more food for them. At one point, he oversaw more than three thousand workers. "The main thing...," he later recalled, "the real aim, was to save lives and soothe the pain and injury."[4]

Madritsch was assisted by a like-minded operations manager named Raimund Titsch, a colleague from Vienna who was also a devout Christian. Together, using Madritsch's personal automobile, they smuggled in extra food, clothing, and other necessities for the workers and their families. "Madritsch was helpful in bringing in food [and] soap," recalled Lewis Fagen, who was one of Madritsch's factory workers. "I remember when my spectacles broke, he got me another pair of glasses. When we needed extra underwear or whatever, he was always smuggling it in." Even more important than food and clothing were the work permits issued by Madritsch to his Jewish workers. He had to pay the SS for each worker, but despite the expense, he was able to issue more lifesaving work permits by adding overnight shifts in his textile factories and assigning three workers to each sewing machine, even though the machines could be operated by a single person. Many of his workers had no trade skills, but he declared them essential and put them to work. As the war progressed and Nazi brutality toward the Jews increased, Madritsch took additional risks to save even more Jews.[5]

In June 1942, the Nazis began "liquidating" the Kraków Ghetto, ruthlessly rounding up Jewish men, women, and children to ship them to newly constructed death camps. A Polish eyewitness recorded the scene:

By the following morning, seven thousand had been assembled. There they were kept throughout the hot summer morning, then driven to the railway station, and sent off to an unknown destination. The round-up was repeated the following day, the 6th of June. The scorching sun was merciless; the heat makes for unbearable thirst, dries out the throats. The crowd was standing and sitting; all waiting, frozen with fright and uncertainty. Armed Germans arrived, shooting at random into the crowd. The deportees were driven out of the square, amid constant screaming of the Germans, who were mercilessly beating, kicking and shooting.

Madritsch managed to save his workers and their families from deportation, eventually moving many of them into living quarters in his factories, but he wanted to save more from the death camps—especially the children. Madritsch had befriended another Austrian, a former bartender from Vienna named Oswald Bosko, who was a sergeant in the police force assisting the SS in the Kraków Ghetto. Even before the "liquidation" of the ghetto began, Bosko had secretly assisted its Jews, smuggling in food and medicine, and warning Jewish leaders of impending Nazi raids. He had also collaborated with Madritsch to help some of his factory workers escape by neglecting to conduct the required workers count as the laborers were marched back and forth to the factories.[6]

As the deportations increased, Madritsch enlisted Bosko to help with a scheme to rescue children from the ghetto. Bosko cut a hole in the barbed wire fencing that blocked a ghetto alleyway, then—under the cover of darkness—he and Jewish coconspirators spirited the children from the ghetto into one of Madritsch's factories. The older children were warned to keep quiet as they escaped, and toddlers were carried out in sacks and cardboard boxes after being drugged to sleep to keep them from crying out. Most would never be reunited with their parents, who were destined for death camps, but many of them would survive the Holocaust. Dozens of children were saved, but two days after the rescue more than eight hundred were either shot by the SS in the ghetto or were shipped away to death camps. When Madritsch was told of the children's fate, he sobbed aloud.[7]

Madritsch knew that the SS would kill him if it caught him helping the Jews, but he did so anyway. A year after the children's rescue, the Nazis learned that Sergeant Bosko had been helping the Jews, and executed him. If tortured before his execution, the heroic sergeant never informed on Madritsch, whose role in the children's escape went undiscovered. Even so, Madritsch lived with the knowledge that his assistance of the Jews could result in his death at any time. One constant threat to Madritsch and the Jews of Kraków was a childhood acquaintance of Madritsch's from Vienna—SS captain Amon Leopold Goeth. Notoriously sadistic and unpredictable, Goeth directed the "liquidation" of the Kraków Ghetto and other Polish ghettos, and commanded a sprawling, infamous slave labor camp located in Płaszów, a suburb of Kraków. The camp housed more than twenty-five thousand forced laborers at its peak, including more than fifteen thousand Jews, and Goeth presided over daily operations like a hovering demon. He personally engaged in bloody beatings, grisly tortures, and savage executions as if suffering and death were his favorite amusements. He patrolled the Płaszów camp on a white horse, and from the second-floor balcony of his home, he would use a Mauser rifle to pick off laborers he deemed to be working too slowly.[8]

The camp was built over Kraków's historic Jewish cemetery, which the Nazis had demolished, using the cemetery's tombstones to pave the street leading to camp headquarters. Trucks arrived regularly from the Jewish ghetto in Kraków and elsewhere, transporting captive Jewish men, women, and children into the camp—where they were routinely lined up and shot, then buried in mass graves. Beginning in 1943, large numbers of the Jewish prisoners were shipped to death camps to be executed by poison gas. At one point, as hundreds of Jewish children were loaded onto trucks bound for a death camp execution, Goeth arranged to have the camp loudspeakers broadcast the German lullaby "Gute Nacht Mutter—"Good Night, Mommy"—while the doomed children's anguished mothers were forced to stand by under guard and watch their children driven away to their doom.[9]

Madritsch had known Goeth in prewar Austria when they were students, and he was aghast at how a seemingly normal person could become so evil. "It was a stain on the honor of Austria that such a man could have been one of her citizens," he later said. He knew that Goeth had been raised as a professing Catholic. In contrast to his own upbringing, however, Goeth's had always seemed to be focused on worldliness rather than faith, and as a boy Goeth always appeared to have been constantly supplied with "whatever he wanted." Even so, Madritsch could not explain Goeth's transformation from a self-indulgent adolescent to a mass murderer. After the war, when Goeth was captured, tried, and executed by a Polish court, Madritsch would recall how the sadistic officer would randomly shoot workers while breakfasting on his house balcony. "He was someone capable of…just sweeping people away," he observed, "as an after-breakfast treat, almost."

At times, in order to rescue more of Płaszów's Jews, Madritsch would try to use his childhood knowledge of Goeth to judge the man's mercurial moods. It was a dangerous gambit, however, and Goeth sometimes appeared suspicious of Madritsch's motives and actions. When the Nazis finally closed the Kraków Ghetto, Madritsch moved his factories and workers westward to the cities of Bochnia and Tarnów, where Jewish ghettos still existed. There he added more laborers from both ghettos, and he also managed to rescue a group of Jews who were hiding in the abandoned Kraków Ghetto, adding them to his workforce. Goeth was also the SS commandant at the Bochnia and Tarnów ghettos, and on the eve of the "liquidation" of one of them he invited Madritsch and Raimund Titsch to his home. They accepted "with mixed feelings," wondering apprehensively what Goeth was planning. Goeth welcomed them cordially to his quarters, then announced that they were his houseguests for the night and abruptly departed—leaving them under the "care" of two SS officers. Madritsch realized that Goeth was probably leading a raid to liquidate the Tarnów Ghetto, and intended to keep him away lest he somehow save his workers and their families.[10]

"Julius Madritsch was a kind man."

Not until dawn did Madritsch and Titsch manage to leave Goeth's guards and home. They immediately drove to the Tarnów Ghetto, where they found the ghetto's Jews being assembled for deportation. Some of them, including some of Madritsch's laborers, were being sent to slave labor on a construction site at a nearby oil refinery. In order to save his workers, Madritsch hastily managed to obtain the contract for the construction project—but he did not stop with just his workers. As his trucks left the construction site to pick up building supplies, he arranged to have them packed with as many Jewish families as possible—who escaped along the way. He also managed to hide workers at his Kraków factories after their work shifts ended instead of sending them back to their barracks at the Płaszów labor camp, then engineered their escape under the cover of darkness.[11]

Goeth realized that Madritsch's workforce was shrinking in numbers, but he did not know how it was happening. To keep them from escaping while going back and forth to work, Goeth imposed a ban on prisoners working outside the Płaszów camp. In response, Madritsch then used his connections with SS officials to move his factories inside the sprawling camp, so he could protect his workers—and he also tried to help other prisoners when possible. At one point, Madritsch and Titsch arranged to have enough fresh bread smuggled into the factories that the workers could secretly carry leftovers to others in the camp. On another occasion, Goeth ordered Madritsch to turn over elderly workers to the SS for execution, stating that they were too old for factory work. Madritsch talked Goeth into backing down, arguing that his oldest workers were the most experienced, and therefore the most valuable. It was a typical Madritsch ploy: Save all you can for as long as you can. "Julius Madritsch was a kind man who was concerned about the welfare of his workers," one of his surviving laborers later recounted.[12]

Eventually, however, as Nazi Germany's military began to crumble under the advance of the Allied armies, there was little need for German army uniforms, and Madritsch was ordered to close his factories. He knew what the order meant: His workers would be executed. He did everything he could to delay the closures, but finally ran out of excuses. He enabled any who could escape to do so, and he managed to transfer one hundred of his workers to a surviving armaments factory operated by Austrian businessman Oskar Schindler, who was a longtime friend of Madritsch's. There they were added to "Schindler's List" of protected workers, and most thus survived the Holocaust. The others—who numbered in the thousands—disappeared into the horrors of the Holocaust and never returned. The day that he had dreaded for long finally arrived, and Julius Madritsch found himself staring at an empty factory floor. There, alone, he could only grieve for the Jews he had tried so desperately to save.[13]

CHAPTER II

HANS CHRISTEN MAMEN

A Norwegian guide leads a group of refugees from Norway into neutral Sweden.
(CREDIT: SOUTHERN COMMUNICATIONS)

"*My*'resistance' was to help as many persecuted Jews as possible."

THE NAZIS WERE coming! The frightening news swept through Norway like a bolt of electricity. It was Tuesday, April 9, 1940, and twenty-year-old Hans Mamen was relaxing at his family's farm outside the Norwegian capital of Oslo. Tall, husky, with an unruly shock of black hair, Mamen was a theology student at a nearby Lutheran seminary—or at least he had been until Hitler's legions had invaded Poland the year before. Taking advantage of the non-aggression pact that had secretly allowed the Soviet Union to claim eastern Poland, Soviet dictator Joseph Stalin had bullied the governments of Latvia, Lithuania, and Estonia into allowing Soviet military forces into their nations—and then, on November 30, 1939, had launched a surprise invasion of neighboring Finland. Although enormously outnumbered by Soviet forces, Finland's tough, courageous army inflicted shocking losses on the invading Russians, and held off Stalin's hordes for three months until forced to capitulate.[1]

Young Hans Mamen was deeply moved by accounts of the suffering in the bloody winter war between the Finns and the Soviets, and he wanted to do *something* to help the Finns. His sacrificial attitude was typical of the young Christian, who had been raised in a devout Lutheran home as one of eight children. At age thirteen he felt a call to the ministry, and when he entered the Norwegian School of Theology five years later, it was the fulfillment of his heart's calling to serve the Lord as a pastor. Midway through his studies, however, he felt that his calling required him to help the beleaguered Finns, so he left school to serve as an ambulance driver with the Norwegian Red Cross in Finland. He was shocked by the brutal reality of warfare, but faithfully did his duty, not only driving Red Cross ambulances, but also holding down wounded soldiers while army surgeons operated on them. After Finland was overwhelmed and agreed to cede territory to the Soviet Union, Mamen came back home—thankful to return to the peaceful family farm. He reenrolled in the seminary, and proposed to childhood sweetheart Ruth Hegelsen. Then, three days after he had returned from Finland, German forces invaded Norway.[2]

The invasion of Norway was part of Hitler's grand scheme to conquer Europe. When Britain and France declared war on Nazi Germany in response to its invasion of Poland in September 1939, Hitler already had a plan in place to defeat the Allied nations. After the Allied declaration of war, the huge but sluggish French army was mustered for action, and Britain sent a force of troops to France. However, the leaders of both nations only halfheartedly prepared for warfare, hoping that Hitler would back down. Instead the Führer intended to strike British and French forces with a surprise attack into France through neutral Belgium. Poor weather repeatedly delayed the German offensive, however, leaving Hitler seething in frustration while the British newspapers dubbed the inaction the "phony war."[3]

While waiting impatiently for spring weather to launch his attack, Hitler shifted his focus to the Scandinavian countries of Sweden, Norway, and Denmark. All three were officially neutral in the new war, and he believed that Sweden would remain so—it held to a centuries-long tradition of neutrality and was a longtime trading partner with Germany. He was concerned, however, that the Allies might somehow block vital supplies of Swedish iron ore that was shipped through Norway. The solution, Hitler decided, was to conquer Norway before invading France, which would secure Germany's iron ore supply and also enable Germany to better attack Britain from captured seaports in Norway. For strategic reasons, he believed, conquering Norway would also require the invasion of neighboring Denmark.[4]

German forces attacked both countries on April 9, 1940. In Norway, German troops made a surprise landing at Oslo's airport and quickly captured the nation's capital, while the German navy overpowered key Norwegian seaports. Unprepared for the invasion, Norwegian defenses were quickly overwhelmed, and Norway's King Haakon VII and his family fled by air to London, where the king established a government-in-exile. Supporting British warships inflicted serious losses on the German navy off the coast of Norway, but nothing seemed able to turn back the well-executed German offensive. Less than twelve hours after the invasion began, a Nazi band was leading German infantry through the streets of Oslo, and two months later all of Norway was occupied by German troops. The victorious Nazis quickly established a collaborationist government, headed initially by a former Norwegian official turned Nazi, Vidkun Quisling, and immediately brought in thousands of SS troops.[5]

The persecution of Norway's one thousand Jews began almost immediately. Some managed to flee the country before Norway surrendered, but more than seven hundred were arrested and shipped to Germany, where almost all were eventually murdered. Others went into hiding, hoping to find a way to escape. Meanwhile Hans Mamen decided to join the Norwegian resistance, which was committed to carrying on the war against the Nazi occupation forces. Soon after the invasion, a secret resistance safe house was set up in the forest near the Mamen family farm, and was initially used by a British special operations team that was sent to help train Norway's resistance fighters. Although most Christians believed that they had biblical grounds for self-defense, especially when opposing the evils of Nazism, Mamen struggled at first with the ethics of joining the resistance. Then he learned what the Nazis were doing to Norway's Jews, and as a Christian, he felt called to help protect them. "*My* 'resistance,'" he later explained, "was to help as many persecuted Jews as possible."[6]

He did not have to wait long to begin. A professor at the Lutheran seminary privately asked if Mamen could help find a hideaway for a Jewish family who had come to him for help. Mamen promptly agreed, and took the Jews to his family farm. But where could they go to be safe? And what about all the other Jews in hiding? Mamen had an inspiration: He would establish a network—an underground railroad—to ferry Jews to the Swedish border and freedom. Remarkably, it came together quickly. Joined by students from the seminary and other friends and contacts, Mamen helped establish a secret organization to assist Norway's Jewish community in its time of danger. Some would hide escaping Jews. Others would provide food and supplies. A select few would become guides or "pilots" to lead Jewish refugees to neutral Sweden. Mamen was active at every level of the organization, but he excelled as a guide.[7]

Relying on his prewar training in a Norwegian boys' scouting organization and his experiences as an ambulance driver in Finland, Mamen repeatedly led groups of escaping Jews through the snow-covered Norwegian forests to the safety of the Swedish border. "I usually took only three people with me at any one time," he later recalled, "because any more became unwieldy and increased the chances of being captured." The escape route he plotted to the Swedish border intentionally meandered through sparsely populated countryside, marked by dense forests and connected by few roads. The isolated country was challenging to cross, but also discouraged heavy German patrolling. Even so, Mamen was careful not to travel after a fresh snowfall, which would have enabled German frontier patrols to follow his footprints. He also arranged for a Swedish lumberjack who lived just across the border to keep a lantern lit at night, so he and his fleeing Jews would know when they had reached the safety of Sweden.[8]

Narrow escapes were common, even before reaching the border country. Once, Mamen was escorting a Jewish couple, Lewis and Edith Adler, who were traveling with their grown son on a bus through Oslo on the first leg of their journey to Sweden. At one point the bus stopped and a Norwegian policeman came aboard to check identification papers as required by the Nazis. The Germans had taken over Norway's national police force, and its ranks were infested with Nazi collaborators. The policeman moved officiously from person to person, examining each identification card. Mamen had been unable to procure forged papers for the Adlers, and their cards bore a large red letter *J* for *Jew*. When the policeman came to Edith Adler, she suppressed her panic and rummaged through her purse, mumbling that she could not find her ID card. He would return when she found it, the policeman told her, and moved on, checking other passengers. When he came to Lewis Adler and his son, each held up his ID card with the red letter *J* covered by his thumb. The policeman glanced at the cards and moved to the next passenger. Eventually he finished his check and came back to Mrs. Adler. Her thumb was too small to hide the *J* on her card, so she just handed it to the policeman, ready to be arrested. The officer studied the card for a moment. Then he handed it back to her and allowed the bus to go on its way. The Adlers made it to Sweden and freedom. Mamen, whose daily life was routinely filled with prayer, later said that he had no doubt *why* the policeman let them pass.[9]

"That child is putting all our lives at risk!"

Many of the Jews rescued by Mamen were children. They had a unique hold on his heart—and each presented a unique challenge: How could he keep a small child quiet on the long, demanding ordeal that was required to reach the Swedish border? "Silence was all-important," he recalled, "because we never knew when and where a patrol would appear." Sometimes small children were given sedatives to put them to sleep, but sometimes no sleeping aids were available, and toddlers did not understand the importance of keeping quiet. Once, when a group of refugees led by Mamen and a Swedish guide had to row a boat across a small lake to the Swedish border, a child in the group began to cry. Nothing could silence him, and the group grew increasingly fearful that a Nazi border patrol would hear the cries. One of the male refugees panicked. "That child is putting all our lives at risk," he frantically whispered. "Kill it!" Mamen's Swedish guide immediately stopped rowing, turned, and confronted the man. "If you stoop that low, I will take you back," he sternly warned. Silent except for the whimpering child, the group finished rowing across the lake and made it safely to the border.[10]

On one escape mission Mamen guided a mother and her three-year-old son, a tousled-haired little boy named Ivar whom Mamen came to view as representative of all the Jewish children whose lives were threatened by the evils of Nazism. After leading the mother and child across Norway to the snow-blanketed forests near the border, Mamen put the little boy on his shoulders as they made the long, demanding hike to Sweden. "I still remember his strong grip in my hair," Mamen later recounted, "and how he bent down and looked at me with his dark eyes. A son of Abraham and a good Norwegian boy he was. This little boy and all of his race were to be killed...?!"[11]

Mamen led the boy and his mother cautiously through the forest. It was nearing dawn, the snow was deep, and he knew that in the daylight their footprints could put Nazi troops on their trail. They moved as quickly as possible, Mamen with the boy on his shoulders and the mother following in his tracks. They listened carefully for any noise that might signal that a Nazi patrol was nearby. Near the border the forest became dense, shutting out the soft starlight and frightening little Ivar, who began to cry aloud. In the crisp winter air any sound could be heard from far away. The boy's mother tried to comfort him, but the child could not be quietened. They could not stop for long for fear of being discovered, and the boy's mother was unable to carry him far. Every cry from the child echoed through the forest like a homing beacon for the Nazi patrols. Mamen knew what would happen if they were captured by German troops. He tried letting the little boy ride on his back in his big knapsack, but even that failed to stop the child's loud sobs. Mamen was desperate—what else could he possibly do? Then he received a flash of inspiration: "You mustn't awaken the birds," he whispered to the boy.[12]

Instantly the child stopped crying. On they trudged through the snow, steadily approaching the border. The child cried no more—not even a whimper. Silently the three continued their escape until they were safely across the border. At last free in Sweden, with the light of sunrise brightening the snow-covered landscape, they began to speak aloud again—all three of them. As the child began to chatter, Mamen realized that it was time for all birds to be awake and singing—they had made it just in time. It had been a nerve-racking escape, hurrying through the dark woods with a crying little boy. And Mamen knew that it had likely been hardest of all for the child—tiny Ivar. "But," he later reminded himself, "he had been saved from the gas chamber."[13]

In December 1942, it was Mamen's turn to flee. Norwegian police working for the Nazis appeared at the door of the family farm, demanding to see Hans Christen Mamen. Someone had talked: The Nazis knew his secret. Mamen's mother acted puzzled and cooperative—her son was attending classes at the Lutheran seminary in Oslo, she explained. When they had satisfied themselves that Mamen was not home, the police left, heading in the direction of Oslo. Hurriedly Mamen's mother telephoned the seminary and sent a coded message to her son: "Pack your suitcase." Mamen was handed the note in middle of a class; immediately he left school and fled to the home of a trusted friend. There he sent word to his fiancée that they needed to flee to Sweden.

Ruth's parents were frightened and tried to persuade her not to go, but she insisted, packed a small bag, and joined Mamen for the escape.[14]

Now he was leading his own getaway. First he and Ruth took a train from Oslo in the direction of Sweden, but got off in the Norwegian city of Mysen well short of the border. Next they boarded an old truck, which Mamen had arranged through his contacts, and hid in the rear under a tarpaulin as the vehicle bumped along toward Sweden. They got out at a safe house located a two-hour hike from the Swedish border, but the house proved to be anything but safe—suspicious Nazi agents were searching the neighborhood for would-be escapees. The forest was nearby, but fresh snow covered the ground, and they feared that the Nazis would follow any tracks they spotted leading toward the woods. At any moment they might hear a knock on the door: What should they do? Then the truck driver, a member of the Norwegian resistance, proposed a daring escape plan. He was a licensed woodcutter, so it would not be unusual for him to drive his old truck to a remote part of the forest near the Swedish border. There a single Norwegian Nazi guarded the border checkpoint on the forest road—and according to the trucker, the man did not like to leave his hut at night. If the guard *did* try to stop them, the resistance fighter said, then he would just "shoot his way through."[15]

Mamen and Ruth agreed with the plan. "Back under the tarpaulin we went," he later recalled. "We held each other close." The driver drove the truck casually through the woods, as if searching for a likely site to cut timber. As darkness fell he approached the border. Ahead, at the Norwegian end of the snow-covered road, lay the border checkpoint—with no one in sight. His gun ready, the truck driver quietly rolled the truck and its hidden human cargo over the border into Sweden. "Finally, we passed the border without hindrance," Mamen later reported. Far away from the

Norwegian border, deep in neutral Sweden, the driver halted the vehicle. "We got down from the truck," Mamen recalled later, "and we went down on our knees to thank God for bringing us to safety."[16]

In Sweden, Mamen continued working with the Norwegian resistance, helping Allied agents slip into Norway to help resistance forces conduct operations. At war's end, when Nazi Germany was defeated and Norway was liberated, Hans and Ruth Mamen returned home. By then they were married and had the first of what would be five children. Mamen completed his seminary studies and began a long and fruitful ministry as a Lutheran pastor. More than sixty years after leading persecuted Jews through the borderland forests to freedom, he was invited to speak at Oslo's new Holocaust Center. There he was introduced to a tall, bearded Norwegian who greeted him with unusual affection for a stranger. His name, he told Mamen, was Ivar Bermann—the Jewish toddler who decades earlier had quieted down in the dark, snow-covered forest so he would not awaken the birds.[17]

CHAPTER 12

GILLELEJE LUTHERAN CHURCH

Safely in Sweden, Jewish refugees pose in the boat they used to escape from Denmark. (CREDIT: DANISH MUSEUM OF RESISTANCE)

"We shall...plainly acknowledge our obligation to obey God more than man."

THE DANISH VILLAGE of Gilleleje was an unlikely-looking site for a life-and-death drama. At the time Nazi forces invaded Denmark and Norway in 1940, Gilleleje was a tiny, four-hundred-year-old fishing village located about thirty-five miles north of Copenhagen in Denmark's North Zealand region. In appearance, it looked a storybook Scandinavian village, marked by a flotilla of small boats, a sprawling cluster of modest houses, and a red-roofed Lutheran church. Its pastoral image, however, belied its importance: the seaside hamlet was a lifeline for Danish Jews desperate to escape the Nazis. Ten miles across the Øresund Strait from little Gilleleje lay neutral Sweden, making the village a critical jumping-off point for Jews seeking safety and freedom.[1]

While the Norwegians briefly but courageously fought the Nazi invasion of their country, Denmark's leaders quickly capitulated. Taken by surprise when German troops swarmed over their borders and dropped from the sky, the Danish military surrendered within four hours. Denmark's seventy-year-old King Christian X trembled as he officially surrendered his nation to a German general, commenting, "You Germans have done the incredible again! One must admit that it is magnificent work!" Intending to make Denmark a model of Nazi occupation rule, Hitler initially allowed the Danish people more freedom than other occupied peoples and spared the country the mass murder that he had inflicted on the Poles. Nazi restraint continued in occupied Denmark until the autumn of 1943. Then the Nazi noose tightened on the small nation.[2]

Many Danes were humiliated and infuriated that their

government had surrendered to the Nazi invaders without a fight, and some were determined to oppose Nazi rule. Slowly a Danish resistance movement gathered strength under the German occupation. By 1943, Allied advances in the Soviet Union, North Africa, and Italy had put Hitler's forces on the defensive, causing German occupation troops in Denmark to worry that the Allies might attempt to strike Germany through Denmark. Sensing the jitters rising within the enemy ranks, the Danish resistance increased operations, sabotaging war production at Nazi-run factories, circulating illegal anti-Nazi pamphlets, and organizing labor strikes among Danish workers in war production plants. In reaction Adolf Hitler declared a state of emergency in Denmark, ordering the nation to be placed under dictatorial powers and ruled "with a hard hand."[3]

Hitler's first priority: Deal with Denmark's "Jewish question"—round up all Danish Jews and ship them to concentration camps. Following the 1940 Nazi invasion, Denmark's Jews had escaped the deadly measures inflicted on the Jewish populations of other nations occupied by German forces—mainly because Hitler wanted to hide his developing plans for the Holocaust from the numerous international news journalists operating in Denmark. By 1943, however, masking Nazi brutality from the world was no longer a priority for the Führer, and he issued orders to round up and ship Denmark's 7,800 Jews to concentration camps. A pragmatic, sympathetic Nazi official in Copenhagen, Georg F. Duckwitz, secretly warned Danish officials of the impending assault on the nation's Jews—and Denmark's population rose up in unified opposition. To Hitler's surprise, the cooperative attitude of the Danish people and their government was transformed into stubborn defiance by the order to give up their Jews.[4]

Almost overnight, Denmark changed from a model of compliance with Nazi rule to a model of national opposition to the Holocaust—becoming an example of unified support for the Jewish people that was unequaled by any other nation in World War II. Danish Jews were also Danish citizens, Denmark's government leaders proclaimed to Nazi occupation commanders, and they would *not* turn them over to the Germans. The government publicly encouraged the Danish people to protect their Jewish neighbors, and the Danes courageously did so. Led by the Danish resistance, Danish citizens throughout the nation took Jewish families into their homes, hid them in schools, churches, hotels, and hospitals, and actively engaged in a nationwide movement to ferry them to safety in neighboring Sweden.[5]

For three weeks in October 1943, while the Nazis mobilized their assault on Denmark's Jews, the Danish resistance hastily recruited the captains and crews of Denmark's countless fishing boats to ferry Jewish refugees across the narrow waterways to nearby Sweden. The departure points were soon filled with hundreds of Danish Jews, lining up with suitcases in hand to board boats small and large for the short voyage to Sweden. Danish universities were closed so students could aid fleeing Jews. Danish police officers looked the other way as caravans of automobiles transported Jewish families to seaside fishing villages. Many came on packed trains. Some arrived hidden in hospital ambulances. At one point, as suspicious Nazi authorities began to set up checkpoints, a fake funeral procession was cobbled together to move carloads of Jewish refugees to a coastal departure point. Meanwhile, led by the Bishop of Copenhagen, the Evangelical Lutheran Church of Denmark issued a public letter to every Lutheran congregation in the nation, noting the Christian belief that God had chosen to become incarnate as Jesus Christ—a Jew—and urging church members to assist Denmark's Jewish community. "We shall fight for the right of our Jewish brothers and sisters to keep the freedom that we ourselves value more highly than life," the letter declared. And in an obvious reference to the book of Acts, chapter five, verse twenty-nine, the letter reminded Denmark's Lutherans of their first priority as Christians: "We shall, if occasion should arise, plainly acknowledge our obligation to obey God more than man."[6]

—

The pastor of Gilleleje's Lutheran church, the Reverend Kjeldgaard Jensen, read the letter aloud to his assembled congregation on Sunday morning, October 3, 1943. He then preached a sermon urging church members to do whatever was necessary to help their country's persecuted Jews. Jensen and his wife, Gudheld, had three small children. They knew the risks involved in helping Jews in Nazi-occupied Denmark—and they acted anyway. Under Jensen's leadership, church members joined in an organized outreach to the Jewish refugees pouring into the seaside village, working with members of the Danish resistance to help Jewish families escape to Sweden. Church members sheltered the arriving Jews in their homes, shops, garages, and attics. Many provided food and drink, helped with the children and elderly, or contributed money to pay local fishermen for fuel and possible loss of their boats as they secretly ferried boatloads of Danish Jews across the Øresund Strait to Sweden in the dark of night.[7]

Boat after boat left and returned, then repeated the round-trip voyage, ferrying more Jewish families to safety with each trip. Organized and encouraged by the Danish resistance, fishermen at numerous other ports opposite the Swedish coast also transported scores of escaping Jews to freedom. Although short—usually ten miles or less—the nighttime voyages were dangerous. Some boats were swamped and sank, drowning some of the refugees. Other craft were forced to turn back by bad weather or the appearance of German patrol boats. Some resistance members involved in rescue attempts were arrested and imprisoned; others died in concentration camps. Several were lured into a trap by Gestapo agents and were shot dead on the spot. Despite the risks and losses, the makeshift fishing boat evacuation continued night after night, and thousands of Danish Jews made it to Sweden.[8]

The large number of Jewish refugees descending on tiny Gilleleje soon threatened to overwhelm the village's hiding places. Then, on the night of October 5, 1943, the problem severely worsened—a train from Copenhagen rolled into the village bearing approximately three hundred more Jewish refugees and a handful of resistance organizers. It was a stormy night and the Jews needed shelter. Pastor Jensen's church members and other villagers scrambled to provide housing, putting scores of them in the church, and hustling others into shops, warehouses, fish markets, and any other place that could hide them. The next morning Pastor Jensen, church lay leaders, and other villagers met with resistance leaders in the local butcher shop, trying to figure out how to move so many refugees to Sweden. By their count more than five hundred Jewish escapees were trying to hide in Gilleleje. Despite efforts to conceal them, many were walking the streets, carrying their luggage, presenting easy targets if the Gestapo arrived. Trying to transport so many people aboard the village's fishing boats would take too much time—there had to be a better way.[9]

Then someone mentioned that a large schooner, the *Flyvbjerg*, had sought shelter from the previous night's storm in Gilleleje's harbor. What if they could lease the ship and transport most or all of the refugees with a single voyage? To hire the schooner and its crew, Pastor Jensen and the others calculated that they could raise fifty thousand Danish kroner. The *Flyvbjerg*'s captain agreed to the deal, and they began alerting the refugees, passing the word that they would be escorted to the ship at the proper time. Many refugees were too anxious to wait, however. Soon Gilleleje's dockside was lined with hundreds of people dressed in traveling clothes, carrying suitcases, pulling trunks, and even pushing baby carriages.[10]

The evacuation's organizers tried to keep order among the long line of nervous refugees as they slowly boarded the ship, but those in the rear became increasingly restless. At one point a local fisherman began yelling at stragglers to stay in line. Hearing a commotion in the rear, the refugees at the front of the line mistakenly concluded that the Nazis had arrived, and panicked. "The Gestapo! The Gestapo!" some yelled. Hearing the alarm, the *Flyvbjerg*'s captain also panicked, and ordered the crew to cast off lines and get under way. Although only half-filled with passengers, the ship quickly steamed away, leaving scores of frantic refugees stranded ashore. The organizers calmed the crowd, and placed as many people as possible on local fishing vessels, but by dark more than a hundred refugees were still trapped in Gilleleje. Where could so many people hide in the little village? Pastor Jensen volunteered his church's facilities. About eighty people were hidden in the church attic, and about twenty more took shelter in the darkened parish hall. Pastor Jensen addressed the group in the parish hall, then climbed the steps to the church attic and spoke to the refugees huddled there. They were welcome in the church, he explained, and he would do everything possible to care for them until boats could be commandeered to take them over to Sweden.[11]

"Get out! The Germans are coming!"

Jensen and his church members brought the refugees food and drink, set up makeshift restrooms, and tried to make the frightened families comfortable, but everyone understood the danger. If the refugees could make it through the night, Jensen and other leaders could disperse the group to farms and houses outside the village until a way could be found to get them to Sweden. Shortly after midnight, however, someone frantically pounded on the church's door, shouting, "Get out! The Germans are coming!" Before anyone inside could react, the building was illuminated by the headlights of a circle of trucks—it was a Nazi raid. Apparently alerted by a Nazi sympathizer, a large force of Gestapo agents and German troops had surrounded the church, led by the region's

Gestapo commander, a German officer named Hans Juhl. Nazi troops beat on the door, but the church members inside refused to open it.[12]

Pastor Jensen rushed to the church from his house, intent on opening a small panel behind the altar so the people inside could escape out the back. He was stopped by German troops, however, who demanded keys to the church. He tried to stall for time, explaining that the church sexton kept the keys at his home. Juhl loudly announced that if the Jews inside did not surrender, he would burn down the church with everyone in it. Left with no other option, those inside the church opened the doors, and the Jewish men, women, and children inside were herded into trucks to begin the journey to a Nazi concentration camp. One young boy, sent to hide in the church belfry, was the sole survivor of the raid, and was taken in by a village family. The Gestapo made threats, but did not arrest Jensen or other church members that night. Later, after surveying his empty church, Jensen penned a sad notation in his parish record book: "It was a terrible day for the town of Gilleleje. May God protect His ancient and stubborn people and keep them from harm."[13]

The next day, instead of cowering after the raid, church leaders, resistance members, and other villagers met again, discussing how to rescue Jewish refugees who were hiding with villagers and on farms outside Gilleleje. Pastor Jensen was not present; he had collapsed from the strain of the ordeal. Other church leaders took his place, however, and the group developed a plan: They would lease another large schooner—one was available nearby—and this time they would anchor it far out at sea and ferry the refugees to it by small boat. And instead of lining up at Gilleleje's dock, the escapees would hide on the brushy shoreline outside the village. This time their plan worked. The schooner made numerous trips during the following nights, always eluding searching patrol boats, and within a few days almost all the remaining Jews hiding in the Gilleleje area were safely in Sweden. A Jewish woman who made it to freedom with her family later recalled their escape:

> Each of the four passengers and the organizer were hidden under a bush by the shore.... We lay a whole day, waiting for darkness. At seven o'clock in the evening, a strange sight revealed itself. From the bushes along the beach, human forms crawled on their stomachs. We discovered these were other passengers of whose presence we were unaware. After a while we reached the fishing boat and were herded into the hold, like herrings in a barrel.... Would we ever be saved? At seven o'clock in the morning, land was sighted. But *what* land? The boat approached the coast. We hoped that liberty was at hand. We were *really* in Swedish waters! People threw their arms around one another and cried for joy.[14]

The Gilleleje evacuation was duplicated at other sites along the Danish coast. Like Pastor Jensen and the members of the Gilleleje Lutheran Church, countless Danes put their lives at risk to save their Jewish countrymen. Their courageous, united stand produced an extraordinary result. Of the 7,800 Jews living in Denmark in 1943, approximately 95 percent escaped the Holocaust—a statistic unmatched by any other Nazi-occupied nation. In 1953, the State of Israel established Yad Vashem, the Jewish nation's memorial to the victims of the Holocaust, and a decade later created the honor of Righteous Among the Nations to officially recognize "non-Jews who risked their lives to save Jews during the Holocaust." When Yad Vashem officials attempted to bestow the Righteous honor upon veterans of the Danish resistance, such as those who had aided the Jewish refugees at Gilleleje, the Danes requested that the Danish resistance "be commemorated as one group." As for Pastor Kjeldgaard Jensen and the members of the Gilleleje Lutheran Church, they had the additional blessing of knowing that they had faithfully followed the biblical call to "obey God more than man."[15]

CHAPTER 13
JOSEPH PEETERS

Comblain-au-Pont's sleepy appearance belies its role as a refuge for Belgium's perse-cuted Jews, who sought Father Joseph Peeter's help at the village church.

(CREDIT: SOUTHERN COMMUNICATIONS)

"Until the last moment, he smiled."

FOR ONCE, FATHER Joseph Peeters found little to smile about. The Germans were invading his country—again. Peeters was the local priest at the tiny Catholic church in the village of Comblain-au-Pont, which was located in Belgium's hilly, forested Ardennes region. At age forty-three, he was a beloved figure in the village: a tall man with close-cropped salt-and-pepper hair who was respected for his inspiring pulpit homilies, but who was clearly not a typical priest. To visit his parishioners, he roared through the countryside on a motorcycle he had named Fury, wore overalls as often as a cassock, and was an accomplished woodworker who could often be found making or repairing church furniture. He was also an enthusiastic hunter and gun collector who joyed in prowling the forests of the Ardennes. In other ways, he was the ultimate pastor. He was revered for his servant's heart: No chore necessary to aid his congregation was beneath his dignity, including emptying bedpans for disabled parishioners. Affable and witty, he was a former youth minister and enjoyed a special rapport with the village children. Despite a serious limp caused by a childhood affliction, he often led them in games on the village soccer field, then would gather them around him for Bible stories. During the First World War, he had served in combat with the Belgian army and was said to be utterly fearless—yet he was best known for his hopeful, optimistic faith and his habitual smile. Some called it "an unwavering smile."[1]

There were few smiles to be found in Belgium on May 10, 1940. On that date, Adolf Hitler unleashed the Nazi blitzkrieg, or "lightning war," against French and British forces with a surprise attack through Belgium, Luxembourg, and Holland. All

three nations were officially neutral, but Hitler ignored that distinction and struck them with a powerful surprise attack similar
to what he had unleashed on Poland, Denmark, and Norway. The
attack came on a gorgeous spring day—the weather that Hitler
had been chafing for since his invasion of Poland the previous
fall. The once-muddy roads of winter, now hardened by warm
weather, easily supported overwhelming columns of panzer tanks,
which led German ground forces unchecked through the Belgian
and Dutch countryside, supported overhead by waves of *Stuka* dive
bombers. His main target was the combined French and British
armies, which were deployed on a defensive line along the eastern border of France, where they had been positioned following
the invasion of Poland and the outbreak of war. There the Allied
troops had languished in boredom, waiting for a German offensive
and still devoted to the outmoded trench-style military tactics of
the First World War, which left them vulnerable and unprepared
for Hitler's blitzkrieg juggernaut.[2]

The fearsome German blitzkrieg struck with a one-two punch,
striking first through Holland and central Belgium. Allied forces
reacted with a mighty counterattack that raced forward—right
into a German trap. The Allied commanders responded just
as Hitler had hoped, and once he had drawn them into a huge
pocket, he unleashed his second punch: another giant force of
tanks and troops that advanced unexpectedly through Belgium's
rugged Ardennes region. Led again by the German air force—the
Luftwaffe—and speedy divisions of German panzers, this powerful German second strike knifed across Belgium, tiny Luxembourg, and northern France to hit the Allied rear, entrapping the
combined French and British armies near the English Channel
port of Dunkirk. En route the German army captured so many
French prisoners that it could not imprison them all—most were
ordered to discard their weapons and were sent trudging toward
Paris, unguarded, defeated, and dejected. From Paris, French

premier Paul Reynaud excitedly telephoned London and spoke to Winston Churchill, Britain's new prime minister. "We have been defeated!" he exclaimed. "We are beaten!"[3]

On June 14, 1940, a little more than a month after Hitler launched his grand offensive, victorious German troops were parading beneath the Arc de Triomphe in Paris, and soon afterward, France agreed to an armistice. By then the other invaded nations had already given up. Luxembourg surrendered after one day; Holland after four. Belgium, which had suffered brutally from a German invasion in the First World War, held out longer—for almost three weeks—until King Leopold III surrendered on May 28, 1940. Meanwhile, in an extraordinary rescue that became known as the Miracle of Dunkirk, more than three hundred thousand British troops were rescued from the French port of Dunkirk by the British navy, aided by hundreds of English civilian vessels. Hitler immediately placed occupation troops in all the conquered countries, including Belgium, where Nazi totalitarian rule was gradually implemented.[4]

Jews in Belgium were forced to quit posts in government, and could no longer serve as judges, lawyers, government workers, journalists, or educators. Despite protests by Belgian officials, Jewish-owned shops and businesses had to display signs identifying their Jewish connections. Yellow Stars of David were issued to all Jews—an act that had to be enforced nationwide by German troops when Belgian officials refused to hand them out. Many Belgian authorities also refused to provide lists of Jewish citizens, but Nazi officials demanded that the nation's Jews identify themselves, and arrested any that failed to do so. Eventually Nazi leaders in Belgium ordered the nation's sixty-five thousand Jews to be relocated in four major cities; then, in 1942, they ordered all Jews rounded up and shipped to concentration camps. Almost half of Belgium's Jews were killed in the Holocaust, which, shockingly, actually gave Belgian Jews one of the highest survival rates in Europe. The survivors included more than four thousand Jewish children—"the hidden children," they were called—who were secretly taken in by Belgian citizens. Belgium was predominantly Catholic, and many of the Belgians who risked their lives to protect Jews were priests, nuns, and Catholic laypersons. Although Belgium's Catholic cardinal would be criticized for doing too little to help the nation's Jews, the Bishop of Liège—Monsignor Louis-Joseph Kerkhofs—secretly advised priests and nuns of his diocese that protecting the Jews was their Christian obligation.[5]

Pastor Peeters's church was in the monsignor's diocese. He met with Kerkhofs soon after the German invasion, readily agreed to comply with his appeal, and took up the cause with his typical zeal. Soon a fleeing Jewish couple appeared at his church seeking help. The ever-smiling priest welcomed them and took them in. Others arrived, and he helped them too. Soon Jewish refugees were knocking on Peeters's rectory door almost daily. He usually arranged for them to be housed in the countryside with members of his church, who risked imprisonment or worse for aiding the Jews. Aided by other priests, he established a secret network of safe houses. "They saved our lives," a Jewish survivor later observed, "knowing if they got caught they would get the death penalty." On Fury—his beloved motorcycle—Peeters raced around the countryside, his priestly garments flapping in the breeze, and regularly checked on his Jewish escapees. In the summer he loaded vegetables from his rectory garden into a small motorcycle trailer and hauled them to the safe houses. As the number of Jewish refugees in the network increased, he supplied them with forged identity papers and counterfeits of the food coupons the Nazis required to buy food, both of which he obtained from the Belgian Resistance.[6]

After seeing the evils of Nazi rule firsthand, Father Peeters apparently had no qualms about joining the Resistance. He was a natural leader, a combat veteran as well as a pastor, and "the smiling priest" soon emerged as a regional Resistance commander as well as Comblain-au-Pont's protector of the Jews. To counter Nazi propaganda, he set up a hidden radio receiver in the church, which enabled him to gather news from the British BBC radio network and report it in a clandestine newspaper that was distributed throughout the Ardennes region. He hid British airmen whose aircraft had been shot down on bombing raids over Germany, concealed weapons for the Resistance, delivered forged documents to Jews and others, and directed Resistance attempts to block rail shipments of Nazi war materials through the Ardennes. "You had to have seen him at work in the long, secret fight against the Occupation to understand what was great and exceptional about him," a friend and fellow Resistance member later recalled. "He was always cheerful as he went about his duties. Thanks to our good priest, we did important work. He was the soul of the Resistance."[7]

Always he tried to help the Jews. Not only did he provide them food, shelter, and protection against the Nazis, but he continuously used the power of the pulpit to denounce their persecution. His boldness as a preacher was reminiscent of an Old Testament prophet. "He showed his patriotic faith," recounted an observer. "*His* party was the oppressed and those who resisted. His reputation made him the very picture of a man who was bold and fearless." Through it all, Papa Peeters, as he became known, continued to encourage his fellow believers to keep the joy of their salvation even in the darkest days of the Nazi occupation. "He was so encouraging," one later explained. "We would talk with Father Peeters and we would regain our joy. It was more than just receiving encouragement from a priest—he taught us to trust in the Providence of God."[8]

"A sentence of death and five years of hard labor—which should I do first?"

In August 1942, a fellow priest who belonged to the Resistance came to Peeters's rectory, desperately seeking help to escape from pursuing Gestapo agents. He asked Peeters to accompany him to a hotel in a nearby town, where he was scheduled to meet a Resistance guide who would escort him to Switzerland and safety. Peeters agreed, and took the nervous clergyman to the meeting. It was a trap: Gestapo agents were waiting, and arrested both priests. During interrogation Peeters braved shouts, threats, and beatings without compromising his hidden Jews or the Resistance—and infuriated his Gestapo interrogator by calmly replying to every demand with a smile. Finally the Gestapo gave up and charged him with assisting Jews and the Belgian Resistance. A panel of Nazi judges imposed a death sentence as well as five years of hard labor. Afterward, his fellow prisoners were dismayed to learn his fate, but he cheered them with a joke. "Hmmm," he said. "A sentence of death and five years of hard labor—which should I do first?"[9]

He was transferred to the Belgian city of Liège, where he was confined for months on death row at the Citadel of Liège, a seventeenth-century fortification that the Germans used as a prison. It was a grim existence, marked almost daily by the execution of a prisoner. Most were killed by firing squad, and the sound of gunfire reverberated through the prison's ancient halls day after day. In the gloom and oppression of prison, Pastor Peeters believed he had received a new call from Christ—to minister to those awaiting execution. Worship services were forbidden, but Peeters managed to conduct them secretly—and was never caught. Not only did he minister to the prisoners' spiritual needs, but he also kept up their morale by playing chess and cards, and even organizing arm wrestling matches. When the day dreaded by every prisoner finally arrived, and another victim was summoned to execution, Peeters prayed with the doomed man if possible, and prayed for him if not. "His quiet courage, his serenity, his steadfast faith—all gave us great hope," recalled a former prisoner. Often, when his fellow prisoners seemed overwhelmed by despair and hopelessness,

Peeters would lead them in a song he had taught the children of his village. It was called "Smile!"

When everything seems against us,
that's the very best time
to entertain a smile.
For all things are allowed
by God for our good,
and even this is somehow Divine.
So smile![10]

On Tuesday, August 31, 1943, it was Father Peeters's turn. He was given notice the night before his execution. After an initial look of surprise, he resumed his cheerful demeanor, and moved from prisoner to prisoner, talking, praying, encouraging, bidding good-bye. He penned an entry in his diary: "All things work together for the good of those who love God. Neither prison, nor tribulations, nor death can separate me from the love of Christ." In the early morning he held a final worship service. Then it was time to go. As he was led through the prison hallways to the execution site, he sang the hymn the Magnificat, praising aloud, "My soul magnifies the Lord and my spirit rejoices in God my Savior." Later in private, a German prison guard who had grown to respect the cheerful priest shared the details of Peeters's execution with some of the prisoners. With his hands bound behind him, the pastor was tied to a stake and blindfolded. Then a red cloth heart—a target—was placed on his chest. In Latin he began to loudly recite, "Into your hands, O Lord, I commend my spirit. You have redeemed us, Lord, God of truth"—until a volley of gunfire silenced him. The guard concluded with a final observation: "Until the last moment, he smiled."[11]

CHAPTER 14
MADELEINE ROUFFART

With crematorium chimneys looming ominously ahead, newly arrived Jewish families at Auschwitz are marched unknowingly from their railroad cars to execution in gas chambers. (CREDIT: YAD VASHEM)

"Whoever saves a life, it is considered as if he saved an entire world."

ELEVEN-YEAR-OLD SIMON GRONOWSKI dangled from the moving train, held only by his mother's hands. Then she let go. Young Simon and his mother had been on a train to certain death at the Auschwitz concentration camp when a chance for escape suddenly occurred—and Chana Gronowski quickly seized the opportunity to save her son.

Chana, her husband Léon, young Simon, and his eighteen-year-old sister Ita, were Jewish, and were living in a suburb of Brussels when Nazi forces conquered Belgium in 1940. Decades earlier Léon and Chana Gronowski had immigrated to Belgium from Poland. For years Léon had shoveled coal in a Belgian coal mine, enduring the backbreaking work until he could save enough money to move to Brussels and open a leather goods shop. Over the years, with hard work and disciplined frugality, their business had prospered and the family of four had enjoyed a happy, comfortable life—until the Nazis came.[1]

Léon and Chana Gronowski knew what had happened to the Jews in Germany, and Belgium's Jewish community was awash in rumors about unspeakable horrors unleashed against Poland's Jews, so they had tried to flee to France when the Nazis invaded Belgium. Their attempted escape was blocked when Nazi aircraft bombed and strafed the roads, even though they were packed with fleeing civilians. Then they learned that Nazi forces had also invaded France, so they reversed course and worked their way back to their home and leather shop in Brussels. To their surprise the German occupation of Belgium did not seem so threatening at first. Nazi propaganda repeatedly claimed that the invasion was intended merely to prevent Belgium from being overrun by British and French armies, and even with food shortages and the presence of German uniforms on the streets, life seemed bearable. German soldiers proved to be their best customers at the leather goods shop. They were polite, paid without haggling, and seemed grateful when the Gronowskis conversed with them in German.[2]

Slowly, however, conditions worsened. The Nazis somehow identified the Gronowskis as Jewish, and ordered Léon to post a sign on the front of his shop that read "Jewish-Owned Business." Soon afterward the family was ordered to obtain yellow cloth Stars of David, which each of them had to wear on their clothing over their hearts. Then, in late 1941, Léon Gronowski received a letter from the Nazi occupation government demanding a written inventory of the items in his leather goods shop and a list of financial assets. Within months Nazi authorities had confiscated the little shop that provided the family's income. To avoid losing his house too, Gronowski rented it to the brother of his next-door neighbors, Remacle and Madeleine Rouffart, and covertly moved the family into a tiny attic apartment in another neighborhood. The Rouffarts, who were Catholic, were willing to risk their lives to help the Gronowskis. Together the couples secretly planned the moving arrangements in an attempt to prevent the Nazis from stealing the Gronowskis' home and belongings.[3]

Madeleine Rouffart was the store manager at the Gronowskis' leather goods shop, and the two families were longtime friends. The Rouffarts' daughter Maggy and Ita Gronowski were high school classmates and best friends. Likewise the Rouffarts' son Raymond was eleven-year-old Simon's best friend, and both boys belonged to the same troop of Belgium's version of the Cub Scouts. Madeleine Rouffart was more than just a key employee to the Gronowski family: She was a devoted friend and was like a second mother to young Simon. With the assistance of her husband Remacle, she managed the Gronowskis' secret underground life, setting up the plan to protect their home, arranging for their hideaway apartment through another Catholic family, bringing them groceries, and providing regular updates on Nazi activity in Brussels. The Gronowskis rarely left their apartment for fear of being discovered. Young Simon, a dark-headed, stocky little boy who loved the outdoors, made the best of life in hiding. He discovered a crack in the wall that allowed him to view the street below without being seen. It became his favorite spot, and he sat there much of the day, beginning in the early morning when he could watch other children walking to school.[4]

The plan worked for more than six months. Then a collaborator in the Gronowskis' new neighborhood realized the family was Jewish, and reported them to Nazi authorities. One Sunday morning in March 1943, Chana Gronowski had just sat down to have breakfast with Simon and Ita when they heard a rush of footsteps coming up the stairs to their apartment. Léon Gronowski was not home at the moment; he had risked going to a nearby hospital to get examined for some troubling health issues that had developed while he was in hiding. Suddenly Gestapo agents burst into the Gronowski apartment. Her face paled in fear, but Chana Gronowski remained calm. The agents confiscated the family's identification papers and demanded to know Mr. Gronowski's whereabouts. Thinking quickly, Chana Gronowski replied that she was a widow. The Nazi agents arrested Chana, Ita, and Simon and brusquely herded them out of the attic and off to a Nazi jail. Within minutes of the family's arrest, someone notified Madeleine Rouffart. She immediately dispatched her husband and a friend to the hospital, where they located Léon Gronowski and hustled him away to a safe house that Madeleine Rouffart had set up with some friends.[5]

Simon, his sister, and his mother were imprisoned in an enclosed four-story masonry army barracks about thirty miles north of Brussels at the city of Mechlin. There they joined thousands of other captive Jews who thought they were being housed in a labor camp. Instead it was a transit camp—a station on the way to a Nazi death camp. A detachment of thuggish-looking SS soldiers searched all incoming prisoners, confiscating everything of value—jewelry, watches, fur coats, money, food coupons, keys, and even family photographs. It was a shocking environment—especially for an eleven-year-old boy. "It was a reign of terror," recalled Simon, decades later. "It was a constant uproar—the sounds of people being beaten, the yelling of the SS guards and the cries of victims." Back in Brussels, Madeleine Rouffart persistently lobbied Belgian officials, arguing for the Gronowskis' release. When her efforts failed, she repeatedly made her way to Mechlin, exchanging letters and bringing the family food parcels and writing materials for as long as her visits were allowed.[6]

On April 19, 1944, more than sixteen hundred Jewish prisoners at Mechlin were forcibly assembled and herded onto a waiting train, which stood, hissing steam, just outside the camp. They ranged in age from a ninety-year-old grandfather to a five-week-old baby. Their final destination lay more than seven hundred miles away— the notorious Auschwitz death camp in Poland. Recalled Simon, "It was one vast assembly of innocent people, unaware that they had been condemned to mass execution very soon." Despite Madeleine Rouffart's desperate efforts to get her friends released, among those selected to be gassed to death at Auschwitz were Chana and Simon Gronowski. As an eighteen-year-old born in Belgium, Simon's sister Ita was set aside to be shipped to the camp later with other native-born Belgian Jews. As SS guards moved Simon toward the train alongside his mother, he craned for a final look at the older sister he adored, who always called him *mon petit Simon chéri*—"my dear little Simon." For a brief moment he saw her, standing far away in the distance, weeping.[7]

Simon and his mother were packed with other prisoners into a wooden boxcar, which was ventilated by a single, small, wired-over window. Nazi guards shut the car door and locked it. It was night-time before the train was fully loaded on its way toward Germany and—seven hundred miles away—Auschwitz. "It was stifling," Simon later remembered. "There was no food, no drink [and] no seats, so we either sat or lay down on the floor. I was in the rear right corner of the car with my mother. It was very dark." At about nine thirty p.m., the train suddenly slowed and then lurched to a stop. Simon and his mother had no way of knowing it, but they were traveling on transport number 20, which would become famous as the "Twentieth Convoy"—the only Nazi train during the Holocaust to be ambushed by members of the Resistance while en route to a death camp. And the attack was under way.[8]

The assault force consisted of only three people: Robert Maistriau, Jean Franklemon, and Youra Livchitz. The three were friends, all in their twenties, and were members of the Belgian Resistance— and Livchitz was Jewish. They despised the Nazis and their brutality toward the Jews, and had developed a simple but bold plan to stop a death camp train and try to free as many prisoners as possible. They were armed with a single small-caliber handgun, a makeshift emergency lantern, wire cutters—and an enormous amount of courage. They had picked a spot on the railway near the Belgian town of Boortmeerbeek, which lay less than ten miles southeast of Mechlin, and there, on the railroad tracks, they placed a lantern covered with red paper to simulate an emergency stop signal. And then the train appeared. "We were lying in the thicket," Robert Maistriau later recounted. "Thumping hearts. The grinding of brakes. It was unreal. The train rode through a signal; that I could see from my position. We looked at each other. Suddenly, the realization. It stopped. It stopped!"[9]

The three scrambled from their hiding places and ran toward the train. Livchitz began wildly firing his revolver in the direction of the Nazi guards at the rear of the train, trying to simulate an attack by a large force. Meanwhile Maistriau and Franklemon ran from one boxcar to another with their wire cutters, cutting the wires that held the car doors shut, sliding open the doors, and shouting, "*Sortez! Sortez!*"—"Get out! Get out!" To Maistriau's surprise, when he pulled open the door of one boxcar, a matronly-looking woman peered at him in the darkness and said calmly, "What do you expect us to do now?" Exasperated, Maistriau paused for a moment, pointed to the south, and replied, "Madame, Brussels is that way. . . . Sort it out for yourselves. I've done all I can." Then he ran on to the next car.[10]

From every boxcar that the three Resistance fighters managed to open, prisoners spilled out and tried to run away in the darkness. Atop the rear of the train, German troops opened fire, dropping escapees who were slow to run or who stood waiting for family members to jump down from their car. In a few minutes, the train began to move forward again, but the train engineer—a Belgian railway worker named Albert Dumon—realized what was happening and intentionally kept the train's speed slow as long as he could. When the train began rolling forward again, Maistriau, Franklemon, and Livchitz ran to nearby bushes where they had hidden three bicycles and hurriedly pedaled away. Livchitz would later be caught and executed by the Nazis, but Maistriau and Franklemon would survive the war. More than 230 Jewish prisoners escaped from the Twentieth Convoy, and more than a hundred evaded recapture.[11]

———

The Resistance fighters did not reach the boxcar where Simon and his mother were imprisoned, but men in the car realized other prisoners were escaping and managed to pry open the boxcar door. By then the train was moving, but some inside jumped out anyway. Realizing this might be her only chance to save her son, Simon's mother gave him a hundred-franc note and told him to hide it in his sock. She then worked her way through the crowded car to the door with Simon in tow. Then, holding Simon by his shoulders, she lowered him toward the ground, which was racing past beneath his feet. "The air was crisp and cool and the noise was deafening," Simon later recalled. "I saw the trees go by and the train was getting faster." His mother kept a firm grasp on him and waited for the right moment, but the train picked up speed. Simon yelled that she could let go, but the train was moving too fast. "It's too fast," she yelled back—in what would prove to be the last words Simon would ever hear from his mother. Then the train suddenly slowed for a moment. "Now I can jump!" Simon yelled up to his mother—and she let go.[12]

Simon landed on the ground unhurt, and stood up. He looked back for his mother, waiting for her to jump too. But the train was going faster now, and no one else jumped from his car, which was quickly receding into the darkness. Then the German guards began shooting from the moving train and Simon saw some of the other jumpers fall, hit by gunfire. "I wanted to go back to my mother," he recounted later, "but the Germans were coming down the track toward me. I didn't decide what to do, it was a reflex. I tumbled down a small slope and just started running for the trees." He ran until he was out of breath and was sure that no one was following him. When he stopped he was deep in the woods in the middle of the night. Instead of being frightened, he found the surroundings comforting—he had spent many nights camping in the Belgian forests as a scout.[13]

He kept walking, with no plan except to get far away from the German guards who were shooting people at the railroad. If he could just get back to Brussels and Madame Rouffart—his second mother—surely she could somehow reunite him with his father. So he kept walking. The dense woods gave him a sense of security, but even as a scout he had never been left alone to find his way through the forest at night, and he was now very conscious of being a little boy. To keep up his morale, he hummed a song that his sister Ita loved to play on the family piano—Glenn Miller's "In the Mood." He walked all night, sometimes slogging through muddy bogs. Finally, at daybreak, he came to the edge of the woods. Ahead he could see a small house. Working up his courage—and thinking of a cover story—he knocked on the front door. A middle-aged woman opened the door and was surprised to find a little boy in muddy, torn clothes. Simon blurted out his cover story: He had been playing with friends and had gotten lost—could she please help him get home to Brussels?[14]

The woman walked him to another house, and when the door opened he found himself looking up at a man in uniform—a policeman. For the first time since his family had been arrested, he shivered in fear. But the policeman—Officer Jan Aerts—was secretly a member of the Belgian Resistance. He knew about the train ambush—the bodies of three dead Jews from the train had been brought to the local train station—and he realized that young Simon had somehow escaped. Aerts's wife fed the boy breakfast, gave him a bath, and washed and mended his clothing. Then Officer Aerts escorted him to a remote train depot, bought him a ticket to Brussels, and put him on a departing train. Somehow the eleven-year-old managed to ride the train all the way to Brussels without anyone asking to see his identification papers.[15]

"Madame Rouffart cared about me very much."

Back in Brussels he managed to find his way through the city to his old neighborhood, where he knocked on another door—at the home of Madame Rouffart. He was exhausted, haggard-looking, dressed in stitched-up clothing, waiting for his second mother to open her door. When Madeleine Rouffart saw him—the lost little neighbor boy she so adored—she was both shocked and overjoyed.

"Madame Rouffart cared about me very much," Simon would always remember. She immediately put him under her care, and made plans to place him back in hiding. As soon as possible, she took him to the safe house she had arranged for his father—and the two were joyfully reunited. It was thought too risky for both to be in hiding together, however, so Madame Rouffart set up another safe house with friends from church and Simon went there to live. He remained there, safely hidden, until Belgium was liberated at war's end.[16]

Much later he learned that his mother had been gassed to death at Auschwitz immediately upon arrival. His sister Ita was eventually transported to the death camp too, and was also murdered in the gas chamber. His father survived in hiding until Belgium was liberated by Allied forces in September 1944, but soon afterward died of a heart attack. Of the four members of the Gronowski family, Simon alone survived the Holocaust. Madame Rouffart arranged to have him live with an aunt and uncle, and little Simon Gronowski—who had survived so much horror—grew up to become an accomplished Belgian attorney, father, and grandfather. Never would he forget his second mother, Madeleine Rouffart, who had risked so much to help his family and save his life. Although she had been unable to protect the rest of the family from destruction, she had the solace of knowing that little Simon had survived. One child saved among so many lost. And yet to have helped save a single life was an extraordinary accomplishment, as noted in the Jewish Talmud: "And whoever saves a life, it is considered as if he saved an entire world."[17]

CHAPTER 15

BASTIAAN JAN ADER

The ruins of Rotterdam's four-hundred-year-old St. Lawrence Church tower above the heart of the shattered city, which was flattened by German saturation bombing in the 1940 invasion.

(CREDIT: NATIONAL ARCHIVES)

"It's not about me."

Fourteen-year-old Hansie Dobschiner heard the noise and ran to the window. Her family's apartment overlooked one of the many canals on the south side of Amsterdam, and on this Friday morning—May 10, 1940—she could hear a loud humlike roar growing steadily louder overhead. Yanking back the curtains and peering out her window, she could see the neighbors milling around in the street below, some in their pajamas, all looking skyward. Looking up, she was shocked at what she saw. Dense formations of German aircraft with huge black-and-white crosses on their wings were passing over the city. As a member of a Dutch Jewish family, Hansie was especially alarmed to see the sky filled with Nazi warplanes. Then, beneath the aircraft heading in the direction of the Amsterdam airport, white blossoms began appearing—hundreds of them. German paratroopers were landing in Holland.[1]

To Adolf Hitler, the 1940 surprise invasion of Holland, Belgium, Luxembourg, and France was officially known as Case Yellow—and it unfolded with a speed and success that far exceeded the Nazi dictator's most optimistic predictions. Even before the German blitzkrieg rolled across Belgium, Luxembourg, and northern France toward the English Channel, German forces crossed the long Dutch-German border from the east, led by columns of panzer tanks. They were preceded by heavy bombing and by legions of German airborne troops, who were dropped by parachute to seize key bridges, airports, and other strategically important targets. Greater numbers of airborne forces quickly followed when the airports were captured, brought in by convoys of transport aircraft. Soon greenish-gray German army uniforms seemed to be everywhere in Holland.[2]

Dutch forces fought back bravely, inflicting serious losses on the invaders in some places, but they were outnumbered and taken by surprise by the German paratroop assault. "White dots suddenly appeared like puffs of cotton," a Dutch army officer reported. "First, there were twenty of them, then fifty, then over a hundred of them! And still they came!" Surprised by the Dutch resistance, Hitler ordered the terror bombing of Rotterdam, even as the city's defenders were negotiating a surrender. Massed formations of German bombers carpet-bombed the city, killing more than eight hundred Dutch civilians in less than fifteen minutes, and leaving almost eighty thousand others homeless. After only five days of fighting, Holland surrendered. British operatives managed to spirit Holland's Queen Wilhelmina to safety in Britain, where she established a government-in-exile like those of other defeated European nations.[3]

Hitler planned to do more than just conquer Holland. He considered the Dutch ethnically kindred to the Germans—part of what he believed was a Nordic master race—and he intended to make Holland part of Greater Germany just as he had done to Austria. Therefore he wanted Holland's Jewish population erased as quickly as possible. Within months of the Nazi occupation, Dutch Jews were stripped of their jobs in government and at universities and schools. Jewish physicians and attorneys were ordered to give up their practices, Jewish businesses and assets were seized by the Nazis, and the hateful yellow star became a fixture of Jewish attire. To Hitler's surprise, however, most Dutch loathed the thought of being part of a Nazi master race, and protested Nazi persecution of the nation's Jews. Dutch shipyard workers, metalworkers, and streetcar employees went on strike in support of the Jews, and the rapidly growing Dutch resistance began setting up safe houses for Jews who wanted to escape. Hitler responded with typical ruthlessness: strike leaders were arrested, the deadly hunt for members of the resistance was launched, and in a single day, more than four hundred young male Jews were stopped in the streets of Holland by SS soldiers, who beat them up and hauled them away, never to return. Then, in the summer of 1942, the SS began to systematically round up all of Holland's Jews for deportation to death camps. Of the nation's 140,000 Jews, more than 110,000 would perish in Nazi hands.[4]

———

In the spring of 1943, as the deportations increased, Hansie Dobschiner was a freckle-faced, dark-eyed Jewish seventeen-year-old who worked as an aide in a day nursery at a Jewish hospital in Amsterdam. Her dream was to become a nurse. She was bright, imaginative, sensitive, and kind-natured—and was terrified of the Nazis. Her two older brothers had perished in the SS roundup of young Jewish men, and her parents—devout Orthodox Jews—had taken in two Jewish orphans whose parents had been deported. Hansie shared her room with the two children, with her bed separated from theirs by a partition. Late one night in April 1942, she was awakened by a commotion downstairs—the sound of boots scuffing on the steps and voices shouting in German. Instantly she knew SS troops were raiding the apartment. Frozen with fear and still weak from a recent bout of scarlet fever, she lay unmoving in her bed behind the partition. She heard the SS soldiers enter her room—speaking in German—and someone took the two orphans from their bed. But no one looked behind the partition. The commotion moved outside, then she heard her mother's voice, yelling that she had forgotten to turn off the electricity and the gas. Seconds later her mother suddenly appeared over her bed, whispered for her to be quiet, and the two exchanged a frantic, heartbreaking good-bye. Then Hansie was alone.[5]

For hours she silently lay in the darkness until she was certain no one else was in the house. Without turning on any lights, she quickly dressed and packed a suitcase. She was afraid to remain at home—looting sometimes followed Nazi raids on Jewish homes—but Jews were under a nighttime curfew and she was fearful of being arrested on the street. All night she sat in the darkness, waiting tensely for six a.m., when the curfew would end. When the time came she walked out of the apartment, wondering as she left if she would ever see her family there again. She reached the Jewish hospital without incident, where her colleagues gave her a knowing look when she stated simply, "They came last night...the whole family." Later that morning a line of German army trucks rolled to a stop across the street from the hospital, at a theater that had been converted into a processing center for captive Jews. As lines of Jewish families were herded out of the theater and into trucks, Hansie watched the distressing scene from a hospital window, hidden by a curtain. There—for a quick moment—she saw her parents file from the theater and climb into a truck. As she boarded the covered vehicle, her mother covertly glanced at the hospital—and Hansie had to suppress an instant urge to run to her parents, but she was afraid to even wave. She would never see them again.[6]

A friend at the hospital took Hansie into her home, but two months later the Nazis raided there too, and Hansie found herself with scores of other arrested Jews under armed guard at a train station, awaiting deportation to a concentration camp. All around her were frightened children who had been separated from their parents. Suddenly she felt completely calm and confident. Her family had lived in Berlin when she was young, and she spoke excellent German with a Berliner's accent. With the children swarming beside her, she turned to nearby rifle-toting SS soldiers and said confidently, "Can I do anything to help?" One of the soldiers looked at her aide's uniform and, mistaking her for a nurse, told her to take care of the children. She kept them close until they were reunited with their parents, then she was moved at gunpoint to a crowded cattle car with other captives. As she helped a family with a small baby climb aboard, she noticed the baby had a facial rash—probably just a heat rash, she thought—but it looked just like scarlet fever and instantly a plan came to her mind. "Hurry! Hurry!" she yelled to the nearest SS troops. "Infectious disease!" When the soldiers ran over, she boldly told them to stay back—and to immediately remove the family from the car. Obediently one of the soldiers ordered the family off the train and back into the station terminal, where a savvy Dutch doctor arranged for Hansie and the family to be taken to the Jewish hospital. Thus they all escaped.[7]

But not for long. To protect her, hospital officials promoted Hansie to nurse, even though she lacked training, but the ploy failed—another raid swept away all short-term hospital employees, including Hansie. Back at the Amsterdam railway station she was loaded onto another overcrowded cattle car, still in her nurse's uniform, but some in the car begged her to get out when they learned she had worked in an infectious disease ward. When she climbed down from the car, an SS soldier hurried over to her with a leveled rifle. "It's no use," she boldly told him in perfect German. "They won't have me on the train because I worked in the isolation unit for infectious diseases. I think I had better go back to the hospital." Dutifully the soldier called to a departing guard and said, "Drop this nurse at the hospital, will you?" Again she escaped the death camp train.[8]

A month later Hansie was treating a patient at home when the SS again raided the Jewish hospital, and this time they emptied the building, sending everyone there to a death camp. Again Hansie was left alone. Feeling isolated and unworthy to live when so many others were dying, the seventeen-year-old considered surrendering to the Nazis to share the fate of her family. Before she could act, however, she was approached by a Dutch Christian, who offered her escape to a safe house. She was instructed to stand outside a house in an Amsterdam neighborhood, pretend to sneeze, and then take a handkerchief from her pocket with her right hand.

She did as instructed, and a tall, lanky, blond Dutchman took her inside. He was friendly and reassuring, but she still feared a trap—until he cut the yellow star from her dress. She could call him Domie, he said—which was a shortened form of the Dutch *dominee*, or "pastor."[9]

His name was Bastiaan Jan Ader, and he was a thirty-four-year-old pastor in the Dutch Reformed Church. His church was located in the village of Nieuw-Beerta, which was located in the rural farmland of northeastern Holland not far from the German border. There he and his wife Johanna had converted their home—the church manse—into a safe house for Jewish refugees such as Hansie. He had a keen mind, a heart for the Lord, and a matchless amount of energy. He had been accepted into a Dutch Reformed seminary at age seventeen, had become a gifted organist as well as a minister, and had come to the Nieuw-Beerta church as its pastor five years earlier in 1938. There he and his wife had ministered to the tiny congregation: Bastiaan preached, taught, and counseled; Johanna led the church women's group and raised the couple's two children. Before he accepted the pastorate, Ader had spent six months bicycling around biblical sites in the Holy Land. There he had been befriended by numerous Jewish families, and had grown to love the Jewish people. When Nazi forces invaded Holland, he considered it his calling as a follower of Christ to help the persecuted Dutch Jews, as directed by Scriptures such as Hebrews 13:2–3:

> Be not forgetful to entertain strangers: for thereby some have entertained angels unawares. Remember them that are in bonds, as bound with them; and them which suffer adversity.[10]

He had sheltered refugees from the Polish invasion, and immediately took up the cause of protecting Dutch Jews after Nazi forces occupied Holland. The first Jew the Aders hid in their home was one of Johanna Ader's personal friends. Soon more came. Eventually eighteen were hidden in the Ader home, which prompted Bastiaan to develop a network of safe houses in northeastern Holland. A regional network was not enough—he wanted a national network of safe houses. He joined the Dutch resistance, quickly rising in leadership, and with his typical energy he and others managed to establish safe houses throughout Holland. He also helped downed British bomber pilots escape back to Britain, assembled food coupons for fugitive Jews, and once even broke into a government office after hours to filch documents so false identity cards could be made for the Jews in his safe-house network. Worried that the Nazis were preparing to deport the residents of a Jewish old-age center in Amsterdam, he devised a plan to secretly move as many as possible to safe houses, which rescued dozens of elderly Jews from death camps.[11]

"He died to secure my life in this world."

The Gestapo suspected Ader of aiding Jews, and raided his home, ransacking every room, but failed to find any hidden Jews or evidence of resistance work. His tension-riddled lifestyle kept him constantly on the move throughout Holland, traveling from one region to another under cover to maintain his network of safe houses. Trying to stay ahead of Nazi collaborators and searches, Ader developed an ingenious method of moving the Jews from his home to other safe houses. Brazenly, he moved them in pairs on a late-night train from Germany that was usually crowded with German troops returning from furlough. Nazi officials assumed no one with anything to hide would be brazen enough to travel with a trainload of German troops, so they seldom checked identification cards. Thus, under the noses of German soldiers, most of the Jews from Ader's home made it to other safe houses, including Hansie Dobschiner, who turned eighteen while in hiding.[12]

While hiding Jews from the threat of death, serious Christians faced a dilemma: Should they share their faith with the Jews in their care? Some believed sharing the Gospel was the ultimate expression of love, and did so. Some believed sharing their faith with a "captive audience" under duress was inappropriate, and thus chose to witness by lifestyle rather than words. Others, particularly those from the Reform tradition such as Pastor Ader, trusted God's providence and timing. While staying in Ader's home, Hansie browsed through Domie's library one day and discovered a children's Bible, which she read in her attic hideaway. As a devout Jew she was familiar with the Old Testament stories, which she had learned from the Hebrew Bible, but knew nothing about Jesus. Why did she not know about this famous Jewish prophet, she wondered. From the children's Bible, she moved to the New Testament, reading the four Gospels, and began to understand why Domie and Johanna Ader were willing to risk their lives to help those in danger—it was because of their faith in Jesus as Christ or Messiah. "As the weeks and months passed," she later recounted, "His life became part of mine. I enjoyed the company of my Bible and my new-found prophet and hero." On her own while in hiding, Hansie pondered New Testament passages such as John 3:16 and messianic prophecies in the Hebrew Bible such as Isaiah 53:5. Steadfastly embracing her Jewish heritage and identity, she later explained, she eventually came to profess faith in *Yeshua Ha Mashiach*—Jesus Christ—as the Jewish messiah and her personal Savior.[13]

Always she would remain grateful to Bastiaan Ader and his wife for providing her with safety and shelter. In the summer of 1944, Pastor Ader was caught by the Nazis. He was arrested by the Gestapo in the city of Haarlem while escorting a Jewish girl to a safe house. For six months he was imprisoned, beaten, and tortured, but he refused to reveal the names of any of his associates or the locations of his safe houses. On November 22, 1944, six months before the end of the war, Pastor Bastiaan Ader and five other prisoners were taken to a remote wooded spot in the country and executed by the Gestapo. They were shot to death one at a time, and Ader reportedly asked if he could be shot last so that he could minister to those awaiting execution. His wish was granted. Earlier, in prison, suspecting that his death was near, he wrote a poem that later reached Johanna:

> *I yearn for freedom and cry for justice.*
> *Yet, I know ... it's not about me.*
> *I have fought the good fight ...*
> *And now I sail away to a distant bright shore.*

After the war, resistance veterans concluded that Bastiaan Ader had saved the lives of almost three hundred Dutch Jews. Hansie Dobschiner was among them. She would live to become a nurse, a wife and mother, and the organizer of a charity that supported the nation of Israel. Of Pastor Ader she said, "He died to secure my life in this world. Christ died to secure it in the next."[14]

CHAPTER 16

THE TEN BOOM FAMILY

Casper ten Boom and his wife, Cornelia, pose in the center of a family photograph surrounded by their four children. Left to right: Nollie, Corrie, Willem, and Betsie.
(CREDIT: YAD VASHEM)

"It would be an honor, for me, to give my life for God's ancient people."

SURROUNDED BY DOZENS of girls in uniform, Corrie ten Boom stood at attention and saluted the flag as tears streamed down her face. It was the summer of 1940, and the forty-eight-year-old Dutch woman was the founder and leader of the Nederlandse Meisjesclubs (Netherlands Girls Clubs), a Christian version of the Girl Scouts. Through Ten Boom's organization, thousands of Dutch girls in Holland and its colonies had grown in their faith and developed a heart for the Lord and others, but after conquering Holland the Nazis had outlawed all such organizations. Now, at a final assembly, Ten Boom and her girls ceremoniously lowered the club flag, folded it, and prepared it for storage until a better day. "Girls, we mustn't cry," she told the numerous teary-eyed faces looking toward her. "We had great fun in the clubs, but it wasn't just for a good time that we have come together. We have learned the important facts of what makes us strong, even in times of disaster. The Lord Jesus gives us security even in the insecurity of wartime."[1]

Corrie ten Boom's deep faith and her hope in Jesus Christ was typical—of her and her family. For generations the Ten Boom family had operated a watch and clock shop in the Dutch city of Haarlem, which was located twenty miles west of Amsterdam. The patriarch of the family and its highly regarded watchmaking business was eighty-one-year-old Casper ten Boom, who was assisted by Corrie and her oldest sister, Betsie. Corrie's sister Nollie was a teacher, and her brother Willem was a pastor in the Dutch Reformed Church, to which all of the family belonged. Her mother, who had died early, had also been devout.

A single woman who wore her dark blond hair in a bun, Corrie was a skilled watchmaker, but her greatest calling was serving the vulnerable and disadvantaged. Motivated by Jesus's admonition that "Inasmuch as ye have done it unto one of the least of these my brethren, ye have done it unto me," she led the Netherlands Girls Clubs, tended to foster children, and taught Bible classes for learning-disabled children in Sunday school. Her father—who was her spiritual mentor—was especially supportive of her ministry to special-needs children. "Corrie," he once told her, "what you do among these people is of little importance in the eyes of men, but I'm sure in God's eyes it is the most valuable work of all."[2]

From childhood Corrie and her siblings had been taught the biblical doctrine that the Jews were God's chosen people—the elect—and her father believed that Nazi Germany would eventually suffer God's punishment for abusing them. "I pity the Germans," he said. "They have touched the apple of God's eye." In May 1942, a Jewish woman appeared at the Ten Boom home with suitcase in hand. The Nazis had seized her husband, she explained, and she had been told that the Ten Boom family had hearts for the Jews—could they help her? They promptly took her in, and the next night two more Jewish escapees appeared at the Ten Boom door. The family decided it was their biblical obligation to help protect "the apple of God's eye" from persecution. The Ten Boom home was too close to the neighborhood police station to be a long-term hideaway, so they decided to use it as a halfway house, from which they would transfer refugees to safe houses through Pastor Willem, who had contacts with the Dutch resistance.[3]

Soon the entire family was assisting the resistance, and Corrie emerged as a key operative, directing an eighty-person network that operated safe houses for Jewish families, procured the ration cards required to buy food, and provided medicine for anyone who was ill. The flow of customers in and out of the family watch shop provided an effective cover for the arrival and departure of refugees. Although they aided anyone seeking safety from the Nazis, the family's main calling was helping the Jews. On the third floor of the Ten Boom home—in Corrie's bedroom—a resistance member who was skilled at constructing hideaways built a tiny secret room behind a false brick wall, and camouflaged it with stained paneling and an aged bookcase. It was about two and a half feet deep, and was accessed by a cleverly designed sliding panel. The family called it "the hiding place." If the Gestapo suddenly raided the Ten Boom home, Jews and resistance members who might be sheltered there could scramble into the hiding place. For almost two years, the Ten Booms successfully conducted their clandestine operation, helping rescue more than eight hundred Jewish men, women, and children.[4]

Then, on February 28, 1944, Gestapo agents raided the Ten Boom home. Tipped off by a Dutch informant, they stormed into the watch shop and spread out through the family's living quarters. At the time four Jews and two resistance members were staying in the Ten Boom home. With only seconds to spare, Corrie helped them scramble into the hiding place behind her bedroom. The raiders ransacked the house, but failed to discover the hiding place and its frightened occupants. They set up a trap, however, and took more than thirty people into custody, including friends attending a prayer service at the Ten Boom home. After a rough interrogation, the prisoners were marched to the nearby Haarlem police station, then transported to Gestapo headquarters in The Hague. Most were eventually released—but not Corrie, Betsie, and their father. The Gestapo commander took a long look at Casper ten Boom, who at eighty-four wore a long white beard. "I'd like to send you home, old fellow," the officer said. "I'll take your word that you won't cause any more trouble." The aging Ten Boom patriarch stood erect, looked the Nazi in the eye, and gently replied, "If I go home today, tomorrow I will open my door again to any man in need who knocks."[5]

Soon afterwards, Casper ten Boom became ill and died in prison. Upon learning of his death, Corrie and Betsie found peace in the promises of Scripture that their dear father was in heaven and not in a concentration camp. They could remember the words he had spoken long before his arrest: "It would be an honor, for me, to give my life for God's ancient people." Corrie and Betsie were initially imprisoned in a penitentiary the Nazis had commandeered in the Dutch city of Scheveningen, then they were transferred to Vught, a Nazi transit camp located in southern Holland. Although Vught was a temporary camp for Jews, resistance members, and others awaiting deportation to labor or death camps, it too was operated by the SS, and conditions there were brutal. Prisoners were routinely starved and still forced to work at hard labor. Countless inmates died of illness, and any infraction of camp rules could result in hanging. At one point seventy-four women were crammed into a tiny cell as punishment, causing at least twelve to suffocate. A crematorium was kept busy disposing of prisoners bodies. Soon, however, conditions for the Ten Boom sisters worsened drastically: they were deported to Ravensbrück concentration camp, a notorious Nazi prison located about fifty miles north of Berlin. There more than 120,000 people from more than forty nations were imprisoned, including more than twenty thousand Jews. Over the course of six years, an estimated thirty thousand died—most of whom were women and children.[6]

"In the darkness God's truth shines most clear."

At Ravensbrück the Ten Boom sisters and other prisoners were forced to work as slave laborers, producing products for the Nazi war effort. Corrie and Betsy were housed in a filthy, overcrowded, and flea-infested barracks beside the room where prisoners were punished. "From there," Corrie later recalled, "all day long and often into the night, came the sounds of hell itself. They were not the sounds of anger, or any human emotion, but of a cruelty altogether detached: blows landing in regular rhythm, screams keeping pace." Soon after their imprisonment, Corrie and Betsie managed to obtain a small-sized Bible and took turns hiding it in a sack they wore under their prison uniforms. It became their daily saving grace. "Life in Ravensbrück took place on two separate levels, mutually impossible," Corrie later wrote. "One, the observable external life, grew every day more horrible. The other, the life we lived with God, grew daily better, truth upon truth, glory upon glory."[7]

With their precious contraband Bible—illuminated by the single dim lightbulb in their barracks—the sisters held secret nighttime Bible studies and worship services for the other prisoners. As they shared the Word of God in Dutch and German, the Scripture would race through the crowded barracks in a multitude of languages. "They were services like no others, these times in Barracks 28," Corrie recollected years later. "They were little previews of heaven, these evenings beneath the light bulb.... And I would know again that in the darkness God's truth shines most clear." To Corrie her sister Betsie set an example of hope and truth in the sovereignty of God that modeled Christ's love. As they prayed and talked together, they optimistically discussed what they would do when the war ended. Betsie's vision was to build a center where they could minister to concentration camp victims—one with soothing green walls and beautiful flowers.[8]

Betsie sickened, and in December 1944 she died. Shortly before her death, she encouraged Corrie to persevere, even in Ravensbrück. "There is no pit so deep," she said, "that He is not deeper still." Two days after Betsie's death, Corrie was summoned to Ravensbrück's headquarters and told that her sentence was completed and she would be released. Two weeks later she was on a train back to Holland and the house above the watch shop. Later she would learn that her release from Ravensbrück had been the result of a clerical error, and that a week after she left, all the women of her age had been sent to the gas chamber. After the war she followed the vision that she and Betsie had received in Ravensbrück, and established rehabilitation centers for victims of Nazi brutality. One center was set up in a former concentration camp in Germany. In keeping with Betsie's dream, she requested that the buildings be painted pastel green and all windows adorned with flower boxes.[9]

In the decades that followed, Corrie ten Boom felt called to share what God had shown her in prison, and she became a popular international speaker. Her message was a simple one: "Jesus can turn loss into glory." She authored numerous books, including a best-selling account of her wartime experiences—*The Hiding Place*—which became a widely popular motion picture that helped expose the reality of the Holocaust to a new generation. She died in 1983, on her ninety-first birthday. Her story exposed countless people to the barbarity of the Jewish Holocaust, and also brought a message of personal forgiveness. In *The Hiding Place*, Corrie revealed that while speaking at a postwar church service in Munich, Germany, she was approached by a man from the audience whom she recognized as a brutal SS guard from Ravensbrück. He explained that he had recently come to accept Jesus Christ as Lord and Savior. "To think," he said, "that as you say, He has washed my sins away!" He then extended his hand and asked for Corrie's forgiveness too. Anger and the desire for revenge welled within her: This monster had inflicted so much pain on so many— including her beloved sister Betsie. "I tried to smile," she wrote, "I struggled to raise my hand. I could not." Then she silently prayed, "Jesus, I cannot forgive him. Give me your forgiveness." Immediately she felt an overwhelming peace and love that enabled her to take the former Nazi's hand and forgive him. "And so," she wrote, "I discovered that it is not on our forgiveness any more than on our goodness that the world's healing hinges, but on His. When He tells us to love our enemies, He gives, along with the command, the love itself."[10]

CHAPTER 17
JEAN HENRI WEIDNER

Jean Weidner, an experienced skier, poses in the rugged mountainous terrain through which he led so many Jewish refugees to freedom in Switzerland.

(CREDIT: YAD VASHEM)

"I did what I think everyone should have done."

ADOLF HITLER WAS jubilant. Wearing a German army uniform bedecked with his First World War Iron Cross medal, he sat opposite a line of defeated French generals in a railway car near Compiègne, France. It was the same car in which German commanders had been forced to surrender to the Allies in the First World War. France had preserved it as a museum and national historic site. Now, on June 21, 1940, Hitler required French officials to surrender on the same spot and in the same rail car where Germany had been disgraced twenty-two years earlier. "I observed his face," wrote an observer of Hitler. "It was grave, solemn, yet brimming with revenge. There was also in it, as in his springy step, a note of the triumphant conqueror, the defier of the world. There was something else—a sort of scornful, inner joy."[1]

In the recent German blitzkrieg invasion of Holland, Belgium, Luxembourg, and France, Hitler's forces had defeated the Allied armies in a mere six weeks. The Maginot Line—the supposedly impregnable French defense fortification that stretched along the French-German border—had fallen easily to German paratroopers and flamethrowers, after having been rendered useless by the flanking German juggernaut attack through Belgium and Holland. British forces had been driven back to Great Britain, and the highly lauded French army had been thoroughly defeated. "Civilians and French troops, their faces distorted with terror, lay huddled in ditches, alongside hedges, and in every hollow beside the road," German general Erwin Rommel reported. "The French troops were completely overcome by surprise at our sudden appearance, laid down their arms and marched off to the east beside our columns."[2]

After the French commanders penned their names to the surrender document, Hitler had the railway car in which they had been humiliated hauled off to Berlin as a souvenir. Then, touristlike, he took a breakneck three-hour tour of Paris, the defeated French capital—a city he had dreamed of visiting as a disgruntled young artist. Now he came as a triumphant conqueror. He toured the Palais Garnier—the Parisian opera house—was driven down the Champs-Élysées, posed for a photograph at the Trocadero with the Eiffel Tower behind him, circled the Arc de Triomphe, and at Les Invalides stood solemnly above the ornate tomb of French emperor Napoléon Bonaparte. There, at the graveside of another dictator who had conquered much of Europe, Hitler proclaimed, "This is the finest moment of my life."[3]

In contrast, Hitler's conquest of France would produce the worst moments of life for countless French citizens—and would bring an end to life to more than seventy-five thousand French Jews. He ordered defeated France divided into two regions. Occupied France—which included the nation's northern half and its Atlantic coastline—would be occupied by German troops; Vichy France, the remainder of the country, would be ruled by a puppet government from the city of Vichy. Eventually Hitler would order the entire country placed under Nazi rule. Hitler's demands also required France to turn in all anti-Nazi refugees who had fled Greater Germany—mainly Jewish escapees. Soon after German forces were deployed to occupied France, the familiar Nazi pattern of persecution descended upon French Jews. It was executed slowly—France was a large country and Nazi resources were stretched by the demands of war—but it increased in severity, and eventually mass deportations to death camps began. Tens of thousands of French Jews fled to Vichy France, only to discover that there too they were targeted by the Nazis.[4]

Almost two weeks before the surrender, twenty-seven-year-old
Jean Henri Weidner stood in the heart of Paris and watched a
flood of panicky Parisians surging through the streets, desperately attempting to escape the advancing German army. "Everyone spoke with a kind of devastated astonishment," a refugee later
recalled. "They...headed out of Paris on foot, past the city gates,
dragging their bags behind them in the dust, then into the suburbs,
all the time thinking, 'This can't be happening! I must be dream-
ing!'" Days earlier many of these same people had been seated
at sidewalk cafés, leisurely sipping coffee or wine, and express-
ing their confidence that the invincible French army would repel
German forces while the enemy was still far from Paris. Then
the French army collapsed and columns of German tanks rum-
bled toward the city, prompting the French government to go
on the radio and order Paris's two million residents to evacuate.
Soon German troops were parading shoulder to shoulder beneath
the Arc de Triomphe, and the Nazi swastika was flying atop the
Eiffel Tower. Eventually, as France was sectioned into occupied
France and Vichy France, most Parisian refugees returned home,
and—like other Frenchmen—learned to make do with life under
German occupation. But they were not Jews.[5]

After France succumbed to Nazi rule, Jean Weidner happened upon a roundup of French Jews by SS troops, and watched
in horror as a black-uniformed SS officer heartlessly murdered a
Jewish infant because the child would not stop crying. Nearby
other SS officers laughed and joked at the incident. The shocking experience solidified Weidner's determination to do *something*
to rescue Jews from Nazi evil. Weidner was a devout Christian, a
Seventh-Day Adventist, and the son and grandson of pastors. He
was not a Christian in name only: As with other serious believers,
his relationship with Jesus Christ was central to his daily existence.
And he believed fervently that every Christian was obligated to
oppose evil and help the helpless.[6]

His family was Dutch, but he had grown up in Collonges-sous-Salève, a small town at the foot of the French Prealps on the Swiss border, where his father was a professor of Greek and Latin at France's Adventist University. The only boy among four children, he learned his way around the rugged, mountainous terrain and trails around the Salève, a four-thousand-foot-high French peak that towered over the nearby city of Geneva, Switzerland. From his parents he also learned the meaning of commitment to Christ and an appreciation for the Jewish people. "My mother and father taught us that Moses got the instruction from God that tells us to love our neighbor as we love ourselves," he later explained. "And we also knew from the Bible that Jesus Christ, who was Himself a Jew, had said that the greatest commandment was 'to love God and to love your neighbor as yourself.' "[7]

While the family was temporarily living in Switzerland during Weidner's childhood, the Swiss government required students to attend public school on Saturday, which is observed as the Sabbath by Seventh-Day Adventists. Swiss authorities refused to grant the family a reprieve, and told Weidner's father he would be sentenced to a day a week in jail if his children did not attend school on Saturdays. Instead of abandoning his convictions, Weidner's father surrendered himself for jail every Saturday until the family moved across the border to France. "As a little boy," Weidner later recounted, "that impressed me, the idea that if you believe in something that is right, you have to be able to accept the consequences of it." Likewise, Weidner held a conviction that he was biblically and morally obligated to help Europe's oppressed Jews.[8]

Tall, blond, and blue-eyed, Weidner had a soft-spoken, humble demeanor, but it concealed a bold, fierce determination. Before the war he had established a thriving textile manufacturing plant in Paris; after the German occupation, he forgot about making profits and turned to saving lives. He relocated the business to a new site in Vichy France and used it as a cover to ferry fleeing

Jews out of the country. "It was very dangerous to help Jews and it was not easy because it was so difficult to travel from one place to another," he later explained. "We had to find safe places along the way where people could sleep for one night or two and also ways to feed them. Then there were other problems: Where could we get false papers? Where could we find money to pay for papers and food? Where would we find people to help us? Could we trust the people we found?" Despite the challenges, Weidner's escape network became so efficient that the Nazis posted a five-million-franc reward for his capture.[9]

One escape route moved Jews from France into neutral Spain; the other moved them via a chain of safe houses through the Prealps into Switzerland. Weidner not only directed operations, but also led many Jews to safety himself. "In setting up an escape route," he later explained, "I tried to avoid the roads to find a passage from one side of the mountain to the other side, down the cliff. There, with the help of friends, we could watch during the night and then reach the border. We could avoid the guards, cut the barbed wire, and go into Switzerland." He survived numerous narrow escapes. Once, while hiking toward a rendezvous with Jewish refugees, he was discovered by a patrol of German troops who pursued him with search dogs. With the hounds baying only yards behind him, he dodged German gunfire as he raced through the terrain he knew so well from his childhood. When the pursuing troops appeared to have cornered him, he disappeared down a deep mountain crevasse, climbing down a vertical cliff to safety.[10]

A strong, nationwide resistance movement arose in France after the German occupation, and soon Weidner's network was also rescuing downed Allied aircraft crewmen. Many of the Jews moving through the network were from Holland, so Weidner's escape route became known as "Dutch-Paris." Twice Weidner was captured but escaped. He was arrested and beaten by the collaborationist Vichy police, but was released for lack of evidence. Once he jumped from a moving train to escape capture. On another occasion he swam across the Rhine river in the dark of night under machine-gun fire. At one point he was taken into custody by members of the infamous Milice française, a pro-Nazi French militia, who brutally tortured him. Praying desperately for strength, he held out without revealing the name of anyone in his network. Finally Milice officials gave up and ordered him turned over to the Gestapo. Weidner believed he would be executed within hours. However, a sympathetic Milice officer who had discovered a Bible in Weidner's coat pocket felt moved to look the other way, allowing Weidner to climb out a prison window. He dropped three stories to the street below, somehow landed unhurt, and escaped.[11]

"If I have one hero, it is God."
Eventually Weidner's network involved more than three hundred operatives. Over the course of the German occupation, his Dutch-Paris network saved the lives of more than one thousand Jews and rescued more than one hundred Allied airmen. In February 1944, however, disaster struck. A network operative was arrested by Gestapo agents, who discovered a notebook in her possession that contained the names of several hundred people secretly working in Dutch-Paris. She had violated a life-and-death rule: All of Weidner's agents had agreed never to write down another agent's name. Her disobedient carelessness produced deadly consequences. More than 150 members of Dutch-Paris were arrested and sent to concentration camps, where more than forty died. Among them was Weidner's sister Gabrielle, who was seized at a church service by Gestapo agents and later perished at Ravensbrück. Weidner, who was slated to be shot if caught, narrowly escaped capture.[12]

It was not such near-death moments that Weidner would remember in his old age: What haunted him most was the irrational hatred for God's special people, the Jews, that he observed so often in the Nazis. "What I particularly remember was their voices," he recounted decades later. "They sounded inhuman, hard. They didn't speak like human beings, or act like human beings. They were a brutal force without brains, without thinking." After the war Weidner was celebrated as a hero by the French, English, Belgian, and Dutch governments, but he never considered himself heroic. In Nazism he had seen firsthand the destructive power of unchecked sin in humanity, and it left him humbled. It was his salvation through Jesus Christ, he believed, that had spared him from such a slide into a heart of darkness. "During the war I did what I think everyone should have done," he later stated. "I am nothing exceptional. If I have one hero, it is God." At war's end he determinedly pursued one last mission: He tracked down the young woman whose disobedience had cost the lives of his sister and so many others—and forgave her.[13]

CHAPTER 18
ANDRÉ TROCMÉ

Led by Pastor André Trocmé, the Huguenot Christians of Le Chambon-sur-Lignon made their village into a hiding place for scores of Jewish refugees.

(CREDIT: SOUTHERN COMMUNICATIONS)

"Do the will of God, and not of men."

PASTOR ANDRÉ TROCMÉ stood in the pulpit of his church and looked down at the uplifted faces of his congregation. Tall, blond, and bespectacled, the forty-one-year-old minister was a Protestant Huguenot and pastor of the Reformed Church of France congregation in the village of Le Chambon-sur-Lignon, centered in a cluster of villages in the remote, mountainous region of the Plateau Vivarais-Lignon—which lay in what was designated as Vichy France. On this Sunday morning in August 1942, Pastor Trocmé felt called to deliver a sermon that he knew would threaten his life, the lives of his wife Magda and their four children, and the lives of his entire congregation. Yet his faith in Jesus Christ compelled him to preach it. Just weeks earlier French policemen under orders from Nazi officials had rounded up more than thirteen thousand Jews in Paris—including six thousand children—and now Vichy police were arresting thousands of Jews in the unoccupied zone. Reports claimed they were being shipped to internment camps such as Beaune-la-Rolande, Drancy, and Pithiviers, where they would await deportation to concentration camps in Poland and elsewhere—from which few people ever returned.[1]

Already Trocmé had taken actions that had made him a target of Vichy officials and their Nazi rulers. Anxious to please Nazi authorities, the puppet Vichy government had ordered all schools in Vichy France to observe a daily salute to the Vichy flag, and to display a large photograph of Marshal Philippe Pétain, the First World War French military hero who led the puppet government under the Nazis. Trocmé had established a Christian school in Le Chambon, and as its head he refused to make its students swear allegiance to anything or anyone connected to the evils of Nazism.

When faced with totalitarian rule, Trocmé believed, Christians were obligated to react with nonviolent resistance. Trocmé was mindful of the biblical admonition to submit to governing authority—unless human law violates God's law. Whenever man-made laws attempted to usurp the higher law of God, Trocmé believed, Christians were compelled to follow God's law regardless of the cost. "Do the will of God," he urged his congregation, "and not of men."[2]

So as France was slowly cloaked in the darkness of Nazi rule, Pastor Trocmé urged his congregation that morning to resist the growing godlessness with the love of Christ—even at risk to themselves. "Tremendous pressure will be put on us to submit passively to a totalitarian ideology," he said. "If they do not succeed in subjugating our souls, at least they will want to subjugate our bodies. The duty of Christians is to use the weapons of the Spirit.... Loving, forgiving, and doing good to our adversaries is our duty. Yet we must do this without giving up, and without being cowardly." Trocmé knew that such a response would not be easy, but he believed that God would provide the grace to face adversity. "We shall resist whenever our adversaries demand of us obedience contrary to the orders of the Gospel," he said. "We shall do so without fear, but also without pride and without hate." As Christians, Pastor Trocmé told his flock, the Huguenots of Le Chambon had an obligation to resist evil by housing and protecting Europe's persecuted Jews—along with any other refugees who came their way. One Sunday morning soon afterward, Trocmé stood in the pulpit and announced, "Three Old Testaments have arrived today." Everyone understood his code: three Jewish refugees had come to Le Chambon seeking help. Immediately an aging farmer rose and spoke: "I'll take them," he said.[3]

The village of Le Chambon had a long heritage of helping the oppressed. As the Protestant Reformation spread through western

Europe in the sixteenth century, it was embraced by many in Germany, Holland, England, and elsewhere, but was ruthlessly opposed by the monarchies of Spain, Portugal, and France, which resisted the Reformation doctrine that every person—whether a prince or a pauper—is of equal value in the eyes of God. With the blessing of France's King Charles IX, more than ten thousand Huguenots were slaughtered throughout France on a single day in 1572, in what became infamous as the Saint Bartholomew's Day Massacre. Many Huguenots fled to the remote, mountainous area around Le Chambon-sur-Lignon. The region thus became a Protestant haven, whose inhabitants developed a tradition of providing sanctuary for others: Catholic clergy fleeing the antireligious violence of the French Revolution, displaced people from the First World War, refugees from the Spanish Civil War in the 1930s, and early political opponents of Nazi Germany. It was a legacy that Trocmé loved. Soon after accepting the Le Chambon pastorate in 1934, he wrote that "the old Huguenot spirit is still alive. The humblest peasant home has its Bible and the father reads it every day. These people... do not stand on the moving soil of opinion but on the rock of the Word of God."[4]

Now they would welcome fleeing Jews. Not only did the Huguenots of Le Chambon open their homes, but so did others in surrounding villages and farms. It was a quiet resistance—the people had learned to keep silent about their guests—but they were determined to help, motivated by their faith. It was "a conspiracy of goodness," some called it—and it was inspired by Pastor André Trocmé. The Huguenots led simple lives and had few possessions—many wore wooden shoes—but they opened their homes and shared all that they possessed. "The peasants and villagers of the area took in the Jews who came," observed Pierre Sauvage, then a Jewish child refugee who would grow up to make an acclaimed documentary about the remarkable event. "And the Jews kept coming. And the people of Le Chambon kept taking them in—individuals, couples, families, the children, the elderly—people of all ages. . . . Doctors, merchants, intellectuals, homemakers—from Paris, Vienna, Warsaw, Prague."[5]

News of the exodus to Le Chambon reached Vichy leaders, who dispatched a high-ranking official to Le Chambon, where he confronted Pastor Trocmé and demanded to know where the Jews were hiding. "We do not know what a Jew is," Trocmé calmly replied. "We know only people." Soon afterward Vichy police raided the town, but Le Chambon's Jewish refugees were well hidden, and the Vichy trucks drove away largely empty. However, Trocmé and his congregation knew that the police would someday return. Six months later they did. By then the war had dramatically widened. On December 7, 1941, Japanese military forces launched a surprise attack on the US Navy's Pacific Fleet at Pearl Harbor in Hawaii, killing more than 2,300 American military personnel and prompting the US Congress to declare war on Imperial Japan. Honoring Nazi Germany's mutual defense treaty with Italy and Japan, Hitler then declared war on the United States. When he learned that the United States was joining Great Britain in the war against Nazi Germany, British prime minister Winston Churchill later recalled, he "went to bed and slept the sleep of the saved and thankful."[6]

"I have never seen a farewell like this, never!"

In November 1942, Allied American and British forces landed in French North Africa, defeated Vichy French defenders, and launched the long campaign that would drive German and Italian forces from North Africa. In response to the Allied landings, Hitler ordered Vichy France occupied by German forces, which increased the danger to little Le Chambon and its swelling population of Jewish refugees. Two hotels in the town were commandeered by the German military for the recuperation of wounded and weary German troops, so German uniforms routinely appeared on the streets of Le Chambon. Pastor Trocmé's

Protestants went about their daily lives as usual, giving little evidence that they were secretly hiding Jews. Some hid Jewish children in plain sight, dressing them in the clothing distinctive to the region and equipping them with false identification cards. So many Jews were hiding in and around Le Chambon by early 1943 that the village became a center for the production of high-quality forged ID cards. More raids occurred, but they usually failed to discover hidden Jews. "We were always afraid of being caught by the Germans," a Jewish survivor later remembered. "We were always on the alert."[7]

Pastor Trocmé and his wife kept dozens of Jewish refugees in their home, shuttling them off to a network of safe houses they had established, and sometimes into Switzerland. Trocmé made the rounds of the safe houses, just as he had always checked on the members of his congregation, sometimes on a bicycle and at times hiking through heavy snow. It was his duty as a Christian and a pastor, he believed. "These people came here for help and shelter," he explained at one point. "I am their shepherd. A shepherd does not forsake his flock." In February 1943, Vichy police arrived at Le Chambon, cordoned off all roads leading from the little town, and disconnected the telephone to Trocmé's home. Two police officers—a major and a lieutenant—knocked on the Trocmés' door. Magda Trocmé greeted them, explained that her husband was at church youth group meeting, and invited them to wait in his study. When he arrived the police officers informed him that he was under arrest, and told him to pack a suitcase.[8]

He was allowed to say good-bye to Magda, who had just finished cooking dinner. The two spoke, then—mindful of the Scripture "If thine enemy be hungry, give him bread to eat"—they turned to the two police officers and invited them to dinner. The officers looked shocked. They hesitated, then agreed, and the policemen and their prisoner sat down to eat. Before they finished, news of the beloved pastor's arrest had spread through the village, and members of the congregation began appearing at the house one by one, bearing hard-to-find gifts for Trocmé's imprisonment. Someone brought a can of sardines. Another brought a pair of socks. Someone left chocolates. Another person brought a candle. When Magda Trocmé commented that they had no matches to light candles, the police lieutenant contritely contributed a pack— and the police major began crying. "I have never seen a farewell like this," he said, "never!" Dinner finished, Trocmé embraced his wife and children and said good-bye, not knowing if they would ever see each other again. The police officers then escorted the pastor out the front door toward a waiting police car down the street. To their surprise the snowy street was lined on both sides by members of Trocmé's congregation. No one did anything threatening, or even spoke harshly. Instead, as the pastor passed between the rows of Christians, they spontaneously began singing the sixteenth-century Martin Luther hymn "A Mighty Fortress Is Our God."

> *Did we in our own strength confide,*
> *our striving would be losing,*
> *were not the right man on our side,*
> *the man of God's own choosing.*
> *Dost ask who that may be?*
> *Christ Jesus, it is he;*
> *Lord Sabaoth, his name,*
> *from age to age the same,*
> *and he must win the battle.*[9]

———

Pastor Trocmé survived. He and his associate pastor, Edouard Theis, were imprisoned at a transit concentration camp. After more than a month, they were offered their freedom if they would sign an oath of allegiance to the Vichy government. Both refused, even though they knew most of the camp inmates were being shipped to Nazi death camps. "What is this?" the camp commandant demanded. "This oath has nothing in it contrary to your conscience!" Trocmé politely disagreed, pointing out that the Vichy government was turning thousands of Jews over to the Nazis to suffer unknown horrors. "When we get home," he admitted, "we will certainly continue to disobey orders from the government. How could we sign this now?" Without explanation the commandant released them. Trocmé returned to Le Chambon, but only temporarily. Warned of an impending assassination by Nazi agents, he went into hiding, moving from location to location, continuing meanwhile to do what he could to help the French Resistance. Meanwhile Magda Trocmé kept the safe houses operational, while more Jews continued to arrive in Le Chambon to be cared for by the villagers.[10]

On D-Day, June 6, 1944, Allied forces successfully landed in France, then battled their way through Normandy, liberated Paris, and began their drive toward Germany. In early September 1944, Le Chambon was liberated by Allied troops. Pastor Trocmé was reunited with his family, and peace came to Le Chambon. It was later estimated that more than three thousand Jews and two thousand others had been saved from death camps by Trocmé and the Huguenots of the Le Chambon area. "Nobody asked who was Jewish and who was not," a Jewish survivor of Le Chambon recalled. "Nobody asked where you were from. Nobody asked who your father was or if you could pay. They just accepted each of us, taking us in with warmth." In the decades to come Pastor Trocmé and his wife Magda engaged in a fruitful ministry, serving, speaking, writing—and sharing the biblical admonition that the Huguenots of Le Chambon had so faithfully illustrated with their lives: "Do the will of God, and not of men."[11]

CHAPTER 19
LOIS GUNDEN

Whisked away from a teaching job in Indiana, young Lois Gunden found herself in Vichy France keeping Jewish children out of harm's way.

"God, make me strong. Help me not to cringe."

IN 1941 TWENTY-SIX-YEAR-OLD Lois Gunden was happily immersed in her life as a French language instructor at Indiana's Goshen College when a church official contacted her with a startling proposal: How would she feel about going to France and helping operate a convalescent home for refugee children? A devout Mennonite, Gunden was a 1936 graduate of Goshen College—a Mennonite school—and had returned there two years earlier after earning a master's degree in French studies at Peabody College. A native of the Illinois farmland, the dark-haired, dark-eyed young woman was a demure Christian who to some might have appeared far too youthful and sheltered to be dispatched to a nation recently conquered by the Nazi war machine. Gunden's winsome ways and meek personality were misleading, however: she was also a bright, competent, and resourceful young woman who was bold in her faith. She had mastered the French language, and after prayerfully considering the offer, she was convinced that helping refugee children was her call from God "for such a time as this." [1]

The job was in a town called Canet-en-Roussillon, which was located on the Mediterranean Sea just north of the Spanish border in Vichy France—the portion of France not occupied by German forces at the time. Although President Franklin D. Roosevelt was encouraging a buildup of the US armed forces for possible warfare, most Americans were still reluctant to enter the war in 1941, and an isolationist movement remained strong in America. With the fall of France and other European nations in 1940, Great Britain had been left to oppose Nazi Germany alone, and in 1941 the United States was still officially neutral—and Vichy France remained accessible to American travelers. Soon, accompanied by an older Mennonite woman, young Lois Gunden was sailing across the Atlantic aboard a passenger ship, which took her to neutral Portugal. There, as she sipped bouillon at dockside, she saw her first sign of war: circling above the harbor was a German observation aircraft bearing the broken-cross Nazi swastika on its wings. From Portugal, Gunden traveled through Spain and into Vichy France, arriving finally at Canet-en-Roussillon and Villa Saint-Christophe—an aging seaside villa that the Mennonite Central Committee had rented for a children's home.[2]

The demands of her post befell her immediately: dozens of children arrived at the home even as she did—child refugees fleeing fascist Spain's dictatorship, homeless French Gypsies, and scores of Jewish children from displaced families. Most were officially interned at a French transit camp called Rivesaltes, which was located about twelve miles away on a former French military post. Refugees were placed there until Vichy French officials could decide what to do with them, and officials at the overcrowded camp gladly allowed the Mennonite social workers to move orphans and sickly children from the camp to Villa Saint-Christophe. Upon recovering, the children were supposed to be returned to the camp. Gunden visited Rivesaltes soon after assuming her job, and was confronted with shocking, squalid conditions—and a babel of languages caused by a recent influx of Jews from countries conquered by the Nazis. "Unforgettable memories...," she penned in her diary. "Sight of bunks with people sitting hunchbacked on them...dirty and bare kitchens...eagerness with which the children drank milk."[3]

When she and the other workers brought children from Rivesaltes to the convalescent home, they immediately faced the challenge of doctoring and washing long-neglected, grimy little bodies and battling legions of lice. "Each new [child] from the camp is immediately combed with a fine comb," she noted in her diary. "If a boy has [lice], off goes his hair. If it is a girl, her hair is cut quite short." The small Jewish boys seemed especially shy about stripping for baths, Gunden thought at first—then she realized that their parents had taught them to hide their circumcision for fear of being persecuted as Jews. Suddenly the plight of Europe's Jews was no longer merely a vague newspaper account or impersonal statistics: it was real, shocking, and personal—and it made the rumors of distant horrors in faraway camps immediately believable. For Gunden's American colleague, it was all too much: She collapsed with a nervous breakdown and had to be sent home. Not Gunden. She believed God had called her to help every Jewish child placed in her care. "God, make me strong," she wrote. "Help me not to cringe."[4]

At age twenty-six, Gunden soon found herself in charge of most operations at the children's home. When the Vichy government implemented its Nazi-inspired roundup of Jews in the summer of 1942, the number of Jewish families forcibly interned at Rivesaltes increased—and so did the number of sick and orphaned Jewish children brought to the Mennonite children's home. Gunden's mentor at the home was an experienced, savvy Irish Quaker social worker named Mary Elmes who visited the home regularly for a support agency and advised Gunden on the realities of life in Vichy France. As Vichy police rounded up Jews by the thousands in the summer of 1942, Elmes confided in Gunden: She had learned the intended fate of Jewish prisoners in France's transit camps, and it was not good. Gunden wrote in her diary, "Mary informed me about the return of Polish and German Jews to Poland—where death by starvation awaits them." In fact, the full horror of the Holocaust was still largely unknown: The mass slaughter of Europe's Jews by poison gas was already under way at death camps such as Auschwitz.[5]

Gunden knew she was powerless to save the thousands of Jews being herded aboard train cars at Rivesaltes for shipment to distant concentration camps, but would it not be worth the risk if she could save even a few children? After praying about it, she was convinced that God had called her to save as many Jewish children as possible. Now when she removed orphaned and sick children from Rivesaltes to the convalescent home, she had no intention of returning them to the camp. Instead she planned to keep them at the home until the threat of deportation ceased, or a relative could be found who would hide them. One by one, in twos and threes, she brought more Jewish children from Rivesaltes to the villa—until almost seventy were housed there. She wanted them to experience as much childhood joy and learning as possible, so she arranged for them to romp on the nearby beach almost every sunny day, to learn the responsibility of household chores, to help prepare meals—and to experience loving attention every day. It was a determined attempt to provide a sense of normalcy in an abnormal time. "May I show the kindness and gentleness to the children that they do not get from others," she wrote.[6]

"Finally his sobs died down."

Not only would she rescue ill and orphaned children, she decided, but she would also take in any Jewish children whose parents made the heart-wrenching decision to give them up to save them from death in a faraway concentration camp. "When I got back, [I] found a little boy crying," she wrote in one entry. "Miss Elmes had brought us 3 Jewish boys in an attempt to save them when their parents leave. Had quite some time quieting the poor little fellow; but finally his sobs died down." In some cases, when she reunited formerly sick children with their parents at the camp, she tried to persuade the parents to let her keep them—if the family was about to be deported. Witnessing parents struggling with the decision to give up their children to save them was excruciating for Gunden. "Began to feel faint [while returning from the camp]," she wrote once. "When we arrived...everything went black before my eyes, and a kind lady and a gentleman helped me from the tram."[7]

Twelve-year-old Ginette Drucker was one Jewish child whose mother tearfully turned her over to Gunden on the eve of deportation to Auschwitz, where the child's father had already perished. "At the time I was certainly scared," Drucker recalled as an adult, "but Lois Gunden was kind and passionately determined to take me and these other Jewish children out of Rivesaltes to protect them from harm." After being removed from the transit camp, many of the children Gunden rescued were apparently forgotten by Vichy officials, who had no problem meeting the quota of deported Jews demanded by the Nazis. One day, however, two Vichy policemen appeared at the convalescent home and asked for three Jewish children—the Landesmanns. The children were under arrest, they told Gunden, and they were there to take them away for deportation. Frantically, Gunden prayed a silent prayer. The children were playing on the beach at that moment, so she told the policemen that they were not available and asked them to come back at noon. Several hours later the police returned, but Gunden again asked them to come back later because she had not finished packing the children's clothes. Again the policemen agreed, but now Gunden was out of excuses. Inexplicably, however, the policemen never returned. Hurriedly Gunden managed to put the children into hiding with relatives. Later, when she thought about how the children "were finally snatched from the fate hanging over them," she wrote, "I felt as if God must have prevented anyone from coming after them."[8]

In most cases, when a child's parents were deported from Rivesaltes, they were never heard from again. "Some of the children...have been without news from their parents for some time," Gunden noted in her diary, "and are therefore fearful of what that might mean. I have been telling them that they may have news any day, but I will not be able to keep telling them the same thing forever." Eventually, under Gunden's guidance, more than seventy children were housed in the villa. "[I] woke with the noise of happy children outside the window," she wrote at one point, "children singing, playing games and running on the beach." October 31, 1942, was the first anniversary of Gunden's arrival at the convalescent home. She marked the occasion with an entry in her diary: "My year's experience in relief work over here has taught me more than ever that one has to live only a day at a time and that God's faithfulness toward those who put their trust in Him can be counted upon."[9]

By then Nazi Germany was at war with the United States, and soon afterward German troops occupied Vichy France. Gunden and other Americans under Nazi occupation were considered enemies. Soon afterward, at the wedding of an American colleague in Lyon, Gunden and the other Americans present were detained by German troops and became prisoners of war. She was not allowed to return to the convalescent home at Canet-en-Roussillon. She later learned that when German troops arrived in the area, the staff had managed to move the home's children and place them in different locations. From Lyon she was sent by rail to Baden-Baden, Germany, where she was interned under guard at a hotel with American diplomats, journalists, and other relief workers. After more than a year, the Americans were shipped from Baden-Baden through France and into Portugal, where they were released in exchange for German diplomats. "We thought when we arrived in Lisbon that we all had stood internment very well," one of the American detainees later recalled, "and we were proud of ourselves. Later, someone told me he had never seen such a bunch of zombies! I guess our condition may have been less healthy than we thought." As for Lois Gunden—after what she had witnessed at the Rivesaltes transit camp, she had few problems enduring internment in a German hotel.[10]

Back home in Indiana, Gunden returned to her teaching post at Goshen College. Ahead of her awaited marriage, family, teaching, speaking, and writing—all of which allowed her to share her faith in Jesus Christ. She never learned how many of the Jewish children she had tried to rescue actually escaped death. She did, however, have the comfort of knowing that she had tried hard to fulfill what she considered to be a God-given calling, and that for a while at least in the lives of some Jewish children, she had been allowed to replace persecution and fear with love and laughter. Never would she forget the children of Rivesaltes. Nor would she forget the lessons she had learned during that single year in Vichy France. Decades later she wrote, "Do we find ourselves shrinking from a difficult situation that calls for sacrifice, dedication or surrender? Might we do well to consider whether God may have placed us in that very situation for the purpose of saving His people through us?"[11]

CHAPTER 20
PRINCESS ALICE OF BATTENBERG

*When Germany invaded Greece, Princess Alice of
Battenberg—the future mother-in-law of Britain's
Queen Elizabeth II—defied Nazi threats and pro-
tected a Jewish widow and her children.*
(CREDIT: WIKIMEDIA COMMONS)

"Well, they tell me that you don't hear the shot that kills you. . . ."
NAZI FORCES CONQUERED Greece easily. Hitler unleashed the invasion in April 1941, but he did so reluctantly and with seething frustration. He was coiling his military forces for a massive strike against the Soviet Union, and having to conquer Greece was a distraction. He did so only because his closest ally, Italian dictator Benito Mussolini, had botched a surprise invasion of Greece. To fulfill his own vision for conquest—a new Roman Empire— Mussolini had already conquered Ethiopia and Albania, and had invaded Egypt from the Italian colony of Libya. He had also attempted to join Hitler's 1940 blitzkrieg with his own fumbling invasion of a corner of France. Eager for more territory, he had ordered an Italian invasion of Greece in October 1940—without notifying Hitler in advance. Italian troops had been humiliated, however, by a stubborn Greek defense reinforced by British troops. In April 1941, Hitler felt it was necessary to bail out Mussolini, and ordered simultaneous invasions of Greece and Yugoslavia. German forces overwhelmed Yugoslavia in ten days, and conquered Greece in two weeks. When both countries were occupied by German troops, the familiar pattern of Nazi horrors toward the Jews progressively followed: All Jews were first identified, then persecuted, and finally deported to death camps. Of an estimated seventy-five thousand Jews in Yugoslavia, approximately sixty-six thousand were killed. In Greece 85 percent of the nation's eighty thousand Jews died.[1]

When Nazi forces invaded Greece, there was a princess in Athens. And she was deaf. Officially she was Victoria Alice Elizabeth Julia

Marie, and she was the great-granddaughter of Queen Victoria, who had been Great Britain's longest-ruling monarch. Her son Philip would someday become *Prince* Philip by marrying another British monarch—Queen Elizabeth II. Her mother was Queen Victoria's granddaughter, and her father was a German prince from Battenberg, so Alice was known as Princess Alice of Battenberg. In 1902, at the coronation of Britain's King Edward VII, she resembled a storybook princess, graced by beautiful features, fashionably upswept hair, and an exquisite lace-lined dress—all at age seventeen. There the princess fell in love with a prince— Andrew, youngest son of the king of Greece. "She was absolutely dotty about him," said a member of the British gentry. "Really, deeply in love." The two married, and she moved to Athens to live the life of nobility as Princess Alice of Battenberg. But what appeared to be a fairy-tale existence belied a grim reality: Princess Alice faced a life of adversity.[2]

She had been born deaf and grew up in a life of silence. Her determined and devoted mother had her taught lipreading and sign language, and with a determination of her own, the young princess mastered not only English but also three other languages. She also mastered a sympathy for the downtrodden and oppressed that was rare for nobility, and was born, perhaps, of her hearing affliction. As a Greek princess, she bore five children—Philip being the youngest—and put aside the trappings of nobility to become a volunteer nurse and pursue a simple lifestyle. A revolution overthrew the Greek monarchy in 1917, and again in 1921, and both times she and family were forced to flee the country to save their lives. On the second escape, marked by a race to a waiting British warship, she carried baby Philip to freedom in a scavenged orange crate. The family settled in Paris, living in a house provided by members of the Greek royal family.[3]

Princess Alice had professed faith in Jesus Christ as a teenager, and as a young woman had grown in her faith under the influence of an aunt—Grand Duchess Elizabeth—who had married into the Russian czar's family, and was later murdered by Communist revolutionaries. Eventually, Alice moved from the Anglican Church to the Greek Orthodox Church, abandoned the affluence of royalty for a simple lifestyle, and devoted herself to helping homeless refugees. At age forty-five she suffered a nervous breakdown. Over her protests her prince husband arranged for her to be put away in a Swiss sanatorium—while he absconded to the French Riviera with a mistress. After two years Princess Alice managed to free herself of her sanatorium incarceration, and while she never divorced her husband, their marriage was never restored. By then her four daughters were married, and British relatives were overseeing young Philip in the boarding school life expected of British nobility.[4]

In 1938, as Philip prepared for service in the British navy, Princess Alice returned to Greece, living in Athens in a two-bedroom apartment and working as a volunteer with the poor, devoting herself to "the least of these" in a hands-on manner that was rare for anyone, especially nobility. When Greece was invaded by Italian and, later, German forces, most of the Greek royal family fled to distant exiles, but Princess Alice refused to leave. She was invited to move into a three-story Athens home that had been vacated by a royal relative, and she made it into her wartime headquarters. From there she ventured forth to engage in a variety of selfless causes—working with the Red Cross, lobbying for medicine for the homeless, setting up shelters for wartime orphans, and serving the hungry in a soup kitchen. She had little to eat herself, and when her exiled royal relatives sent her food parcels, she gave them away. When fighting raged near her house, she went into the streets on an errand of mercy, and was chided by a friend. She replied, "Well, they tell me that you don't hear the shot that kills you, and in any case I'm deaf, so why worry about that? I wouldn't know, would I?"[5]

In 1943, as the Nazis began the mass arrest of Jews in Greece, Princess Alice learned about the plight of a Jewish woman named Rachel Cohen—the widow of a member of the Greek parliament—whose hiding place had been betrayed to the Germans. She sent for the woman and her daughter, who made it to her back door in the middle of the night. Later they were joined by a son. As it was in other countries occupied by the Nazis, protecting Jews in Greece could be punishable by death, but Princess Alice took in the family without hesitation. She housed them in the upper floor of her home, passing them off as beneficiaries of one of her charitable causes—war refugees she had taken in.[6]

"It never occurred to her that her action was in any way special."
Already Princess Alice was under watch by Greece's Nazi occupiers. As a member of the British royal family, she could have been imprisoned by the Germans or used in some way as a hostage. Now she was hiding Jews. Some of her German-born relatives were serving in the German armed forces, and Nazi officials apparently thought that Princess Alice, despite her British pedigree, was sympathetic to the German war effort. Instead of hiding behind that cover, however, Princess Alice discarded it at the first opportunity. A German general called on her at her home, obviously intending to curry favor with a supportive member of the British monarchy, but he was undoubtedly surprised when the princess appeared dressed more like a nun than like royalty. He extended his hand, but she ignored it. "Is there anything I can do for you?" he solicitously asked. Princess Alice was unswayed and unintimidated. "You can take your troops out of my country," she evenly replied.[7]

Gestapo agents reportedly kept her movements under surveillance, but—unaware that she was secretly protecting Jews—found little suspicious about her soup kitchen and aid to orphans. Even so, on several occasions a Gestapo agent appeared at her home to interrogate her. He discovered nothing: Princess Alice explained that her deafness made it very difficult to understand the Nazi's questions, conveniently ignoring her ability to read lips and speak fluent German. The Nazis systematically massacred more than seventy thousand Jews in Greece, and Princess Alice risked her own safety to protect Rachel Cohen and her children.[8]

At war's end, with Greece liberated by the Allies, the Cohens were safe and free, and Princess Alice continued her life of charity and self-sacrifice. She had preserved her princess's jewels through the war, and when it ended, she sold them to establish a ministry within her church—the Christian Sisterhood of Martha and Mary—and to build an orphanage in a poor neighborhood of Athens. After another coup in Greece in 1967, Prince Philip— now married to the Queen of England—brought his mother to Buckingham Palace in London, where she continued to live quietly and modestly. Only after she died at age eighty-four, in 1969, did it become public knowledge that she had helped to save the Cohen family. In 1993, at Yad Vashem—Israel's official memorial to the victims of the Holocaust—Prince Philip spoke at a ceremony recognizing Princess Alice as one of the Righteous Among the Nations. Referring to her decision to house the Cohens, he said, "I suspect that it never occurred to her that her action was in any way special. She was a person with deep religious faith and she would have considered it to be a totally human action to help fellow human beings in distress."[9]

CHAPTER 21
DANIIL TYMCHYNA

Father Daniil Tymchyna poses with the boys of his Ukrainian orphanage. Hidden in their ranks were Jewish refugees. (CREDIT: YAD VASHEM)

"Monk Daniil instructed us three Jewish children how to be cautious."

DANIIL TYMCHYNA WAS a burly middle-aged man with a bushy black beard and the large, rough hands of a laborer. Despite his intimidating appearance, children loved him—and children were central to his life. In 1941 Tymchyna was a priest and monk in the Ukrainian Eastern Rite Church and oversaw an orphanage for boys in Uniow, a village in the western part of the Ukraine, which was then a sprawling republic of the Soviet Union. Orphanages were desperately needed in the region where Tymchyna ministered: It had been racked by turmoil in the past half century, harshly ruled by Poland, Hungary, Russia, the Soviet Union, and, now, Nazi Germany. Always the children had suffered—and never more than under the Nazis, who were determined to exterminate anyone in the Ukraine they deemed to be an enemy, especially Jews. And that created a lot of homeless children.[1]

On June 22, 1941, Hitler launched a massive surprise invasion of his recent ally, the Soviet Union, less than two years after engineering the nonaggression pact between Germany and the USSR. "My pact was only meant to stall for time," Hitler had confided to his high command. "We will crush the Soviet Union." Hitler's goal was to seize control of the Soviet Union's gigantic store of natural resources for the German war effort, destroy Soviet Communism—the bitter left-wing enemy of Hitler's right-wing fascism—and place the Slavic peoples of eastern Europe and Russia under the German "master race." The Nazi plan was revealed with brutal clarity by Erich Koch, the Nazi official Hitler put in charge of the Ukraine. "We are the Master Race and must govern hard," Koch stated when in command. "We...must remember that the lowliest German worker is racially and biologically a thousand times more valuable than the population here." As he conquered the Soviet Union, Hitler also intended to rid the world of the three million Jews in Soviet-controlled territory. [2]

Hitler code-named his Russian invasion Operation Barbarossa, and it unfolded on a staggering scale: More than one million German troops advanced into the Soviet Union on a two-thousand-mile front that stretched from the Black Sea in the south to the Arctic Circle in the north. Disaster had befallen Napoléon Bonaparte when he attempted to conquer Russia a century earlier, but Hitler was confident he could do it in ten weeks. "Just kick in the door," he told his generals, "and the whole rotten structure will collapse." Initially his rash aggression again seemed successful: Everywhere, Soviet force retreated from the German juggernaut. "The dead bodies [lay] by the side of the road," one Soviet private recalled, "[alongside] burning wheat fields and the rising black smoke that completely blotted out the sky." Reported another, "It was a dismal picture. By the time we reached Minsk, we were leaderless." Collapsed Soviet military resistance was due not just to the German blitzkrieg; Soviet dictator Joseph Stalin was also responsible. Fearful of a military coup, he had wiped out the senior leadership of the Soviet Armed Forces on the eve of World War II, executing more than thirty thousand military officers. As successor to Vladimir Lenin, the ruthless founder of the Soviet Communist state, Stalin would eventually be blamed for the deaths of more than ten million people, most of whom had been his Soviet countrymen.[3]

More than twenty million Soviet civilians would perish in the German invasion and occupation—just as Hitler had deliberately planned. "There is no doubt," recorded a secret Nazi projection, "that...many millions of persons will be starved to death." Countless others—political leaders, Communist Party members, Gypsies, and, especially, all Jews—were also targeted for immediate death on a mass scale. Including areas seized by the Soviet Union as part of the 1939 pact with Hitler, the Jewish population of the Soviet Union numbered more than five million. By the beginning of 1942, German forces had driven Soviet defenders in retreat across the Ukraine, Belorussia, and the Baltic states, pressing toward Leningrad, Stalingrad, and Moscow. The Soviet Union had to be destroyed and its people subjugated, Hitler believed, so he could establish a New Order for Europe—making it a Nazi-governed continent in which all non-German people would exist solely to serve the Nazi empire. As for Europe's Jews, by then Hitler had settled upon what would infamously come to be known as the Final Solution—he would try to kill them all. "The Jews," reported Berlin-based journalist William L. Shirer, "were the *Untermenschen* or sub-humans. To Hitler they had no right to live."[4]

Therefore, for Jews living in the Soviet Union, mass death accompanied the German advance. Hitler's Final Solution was intended to wipe out the Jewish people through a mass killing machine of concentration camps—death camps—that would use poison gas to murder the Jews in almost incomprehensibly large numbers. In the Soviet Union as in Poland, however, Hitler would not wait for the necessary number of death camps to be built: The mass death of Soviet Jews began with the German invasion. Using the savage techniques they had perfected in the Polish holocaust, the Nazi SS Einsatzgruppen, or death squads, unleashed an imaginable slaughter—and in the Soviet Union, Hitler insisted that the German general army—the Wehrmacht—join the mass murder. "Thus," a German officer confided to his diary, "the Army must now assume the onus of the murders and burnings which up to now have been confined to the SS." Some Jewish families escaped into the vast Soviet forests; some joined the Russian partisans fighting the Germans—but most perished.[5]

Embittered by the harsh domination of Soviet Communism and desperate for national independence, many Ukrainians initially welcomed the Germans as liberators, and more than two hundred thousand Ukrainians joined the German army. Scores of Ukrainian police and anti-Semitic civilians collaborated with the Germans in the persecution and mass murder of the Ukraine's Jewish population, which numbered about 1.5 million people. Thousands at a time were rounded up throughout the Ukraine, reportedly for deportation to labor camps or even to faraway Palestine, but instead they were marched to preselected killing sites. There they were routinely forced to strip and surrender all personable valuables—and then they were shot to death and buried in gigantic mass graves.[6]

Outside the Ukrainian capital of Kiev in late September 1941, the city's Jews were assembled and forcibly marched to a broad ravine called Babi Yar, and there, in a two-day slaughter, more than thirty-three thousand Jewish men, women, and children were systematically massacred. The executioners were SS troops, led by an Einsatzgruppe, and assisted by Ukrainian police from Kiev. A Ukrainian truck driver impressed into service by the SS later described the horror of Babi Yar:

The Jews went down into the ravine through two or three narrow paths. When they got closer to the edge of the ravine, members of the *Schutzpolizei* [Police] grabbed them and made them lie down over the corpses of the Jews who had already been shot. It took no time. . . . As soon as a Jew lay down, a [guard] came along with a sub-machine gun and shot him. . . . Walking over the corpses toward a new victim who had already laid down, the machine gunner shot him on the spot. It was an extermination machine that made no distinction between men, women and children.[7]

At another execution site near the Ukrainian city of Dubno, a civilian eyewitness recorded a similar mass murder of Jewish families:

> Without screaming or weeping these people undressed, stood around in family groups, kissed each other, said farewells and waited for a sign from another SS man, who stood near the pit, also with a whip in his hand.... An old woman with snow-white hair was holding a one-year-old child in her arms and singing to it and tickling it. The child was cooing with delight. The parents were looking on with tears in their eyes. The father was holding the hand of a boy about 10 years old and speaking to him softly; the boy was fighting his tears. The father pointed to the sky, stroked his head and seemed to explain something to him.... An SS man sat at the edge of the narrow end of the pit, his feet dangling into the pit. He had a tommy gun on his knees and was smoking a cigarette.... They went down into the pit, lined themselves up against the previous victims and were shot.[8]

When they learned of such horrors, many Ukrainians abandoned the mistaken notion that the Germans were liberators. Throughout the Ukraine, untold numbers of devout Christians defied Nazi rule and attempted to protect their Jewish neighbors—even though they knew that the Nazis could kill them for doing so. Leading the outreach to Jews were Ukrainian Baptists, Seventh-Day Adventists, and priests in the Ukrainian Eastern Rite Church—including Daniil Tymchyna.[9]

In late 1941, Tymchyna learned that he would be receiving three new boys at his orphanage. He was director of the orphanage, which was located on the grounds of an Eastern Rite monastery outside the village of Uniow, and sheltering children was nothing new for him. However, these boys were different. The request to protect them had come directly from the head of the Ukrainian Eastern Rite Church—Metropolitan Andrey Sheptytsky—and the three boys were endangered Jews. The seventy-six-year-old Sheptytsky was a prominent leader in the western region of the Ukraine, where the Eastern Rite Church had many members. Sheptytsky was a lifelong defender of Ukrainian rights, and had continuously resisted the Soviet government's attempts to replace religion in the Ukraine with Communist atheism. He too had initially welcomed the German occupation, hoping that it would be an improvement over Soviet domination of the Ukraine, but the Nazi mass murder of Ukrainian Jews changed his mind. Boldly, he sent an official church protest to SS head Heinrich Himmler, denouncing Nazi actions against the Jews, and he threatened to excommunicate any member of the church who aided the Nazis in persecuting the Jews. He also personally hid Jews in his residence, and placed them in hiding through his monks and priests.[10]

The three Jewish boys Sheptytsky placed in Tymchyna's orphanage were Leon Chameides, Adam Rotfeld, and Oded Amarant. Six-year-old Leon Chameides was a Polish boy whose family had fled from Poland to the Ukraine to escape the 1939 German invasion. When the Germans invaded the Ukraine, they fled again. As they had elsewhere, SS troops and German military police systematically rounded up the Jews in the western area of the Ukraine and massacred them. Their vacated homes were then looted by the police, and afterward anti-Semitic civilian gangs took what was left. Frantic to save their little boy from death and burial in a mass grave, Leon's parents hurriedly left him at a local Eastern Rite church, where the local priest hid him. As the Germans intensified their search for and seizure of Ukrainian Jews, Leon was moved from church to church by priests until he was brought to Metropolitan Sheptytsky, who arranged for him to be secretly taken to Tymchyna's orphanage. The second Jewish boy, Adam Rotfeld, was only three years old. Except for one sister, his entire family had been murdered by the Germans. No one seemed to know anything else about him. Somehow an Eastern Rite priest had rescued the little boy, and had been directed by Sheptytsky to quietly bring him to Tymchyna's boys' home.[11]

The third boy, Oded Amarant, was a six-year-old from Palestine. His parents had emigrated there from Poland almost a decade before. After a visit to family in Poland, Oded's mother had returned to Palestine and had left the boy to return home with his grandparents, who were preparing to leave for Palestine too. On the eve of their departure, however, Hitler invaded Poland, and the family went into hiding, as did so many other Jews. They made their way to the remote village of Uniow, to live with Oded's aunt and uncle, and there they hoped to be safe. The aunt and uncle were young and healthy, so the Germans had forced them to work in an armaments factory instead of deporting them. During the day Oded's grandparents stayed out of sight at home, and Oded's aunt and uncle took him with them to the armaments factory, where he was allowed to stay in a makeshift day care with other Jewish children. One day Oded and his aunt came home to find their house empty: The Nazis had raided the home and carried away Oded's grandparents. Oded would never see them again, but they had left a final message: Hanging from a ceiling light fixture was a pair of Oded's little shoes, apparently tossed there as a last act by his grandparents as they were hustled away by the Nazis. Their message: *Take care of our grandson.*[12]

"A German soldier...shined his flashlight in my direction."

Soon afterward German troops raided the factory where Oded's aunt worked, and seized all Jewish children who were too young to work as slave laborers. She managed to hide Oded under a table covered by a cloth. Knowing he might be there for hours, she told the six-year-old to keep quiet and gave him an empty bottle to use if he needed to urinate. Decades later Oded still vividly remembered the terror of that time under the table. "I sat there trembling with fear," he recalled, "and never stopped peeing. Soon the bottle was full and the floor and my shoes got wet." German troops were methodically moving through the factory, searching for stray Jewish children, and the puddle beside the table was an obvious giveaway. "A German soldier lifted the tablecloth and shined his flashlight in my direction," Oded recounted. "Our eyes met, but he dropped the tablecloth and moved on." Of the dozens of children in the factory day care, only Oded and three others survived the raid.[13]

Afterward Oded's uncle took him to Metropolitan Sheptytsky's residence, where he met with the church leader and asked him if he and his priests would hide a little Jewish boy from the Nazis. "I well remember our entering a large room filled with books," Oded later recollected. "In that room sat an elderly person with a long white beard. On his side stood two priests." The surroundings were strange for a Jewish child, and Oded did not know what to expect from the big white-bearded man. Would he be turned over to the bad Nazis or have to hide under a table again? But Oded soon relaxed. "He talked to my uncle and patted me on the head," he recalled. "After consulting with the other priests, Metropolitan Sheptytsky gave me a Ukrainian name, and asked one of the priests to take care of me." Oded was taken to Daniil Tymchyna's orphanage, where he joined Leon Chameides and Adam Rotfeld. There the monk took a deep interest in the persecuted boys, taught them to call him "Monk Daniil," and personally supervised their care.[14]

The boys could speak Ukrainian, so Tymchyna decided to hide them in the midst of the other orphans—but he had to take precautions to keep their Jewish identities secret. Like Oded, Leon and Adam were called by Ukrainian names while they were in hiding, and the boys were told not to talk about their families or background. When it was bath time at the orphanage, Tymchyna would allow the boys to bathe separately from the other orphans, so their circumcision would not betray their true identities. They joined the other boys at working in the orphanage garden, help- ing tend to livestock, and picking berries and mushrooms in the nearby forest, and also attended school. Slowly their lives acquired a measure of stability and normalcy—but always they were on the alert. "Monk Daniil instructed us three Jewish children how to be cautious," Oded recalled. If German troops were nearby, Tym- chyna would discreetly shepherd the three boys away from the others and hide them in a small room deep in the orphanage until it was safe for them to emerge.[15]

Under his care they survived the Holocaust. In 1944, German forces retreated from the Soviet Union. The turnaround was a shock to Hitler after his armies had been so successful in the initial attack against Soviet forces. By mid-1942, after advancing rapidly on their thousand-mile-long front, German forces had besieged the city of Leningrad, where more than one million Soviet civil- ians died of starvation or froze to death; the Germans then fought their way to the outskirts of the Soviet capital of Moscow, and bat- tled into the vital Soviet industrial city of Stalingrad in the south. With the capture of Stalingrad, Hitler intended to seize Soviet oil fields to fuel the Nazi war machine, then send his legions south- ward into the Middle East to eventually link with German forces in Egypt—but Stalingrad instead became the killing field where Hitler's Soviet invasion began to reverse course.[16]

Aided by tanks and aircraft sent from the United States and Britain, along with phenomenal weapons production by the enforced labor of the Soviet people, Stalin had reorganized the Soviet armed forces—which then inflicted massive casualties on the German invaders. So did the deadly Russian winter weather, which Hitler's forces were unprepared to endure. Empowered by a mighty offensive, the Soviet Red Army drove back Hitler's freezing and battle-weary forces at Stalingrad in November 1942, capturing two entire German armies along with their joint commander and twenty-two generals. More than one million Soviet troops were lost at Stalingrad, but so were more than eight hundred thousand Germans—and Hitler could not replace those losses. In the summer of 1943, German forces in the Soviet Union tried to regain the initiative at the Battle of Kursk—the largest tank battle in history—but there too they were turned back by the Soviets. The war against the Soviet Union, which Hitler had thought could be won in a few months, instead proved to be a slaughterhouse for the German army, which was forced into a long, bloody retreat from the Soviet Union.[17]

By the autumn of 1944, German forces had been driven from the Ukraine, and the village of Uniow was no longer under German occupation. Soon Soviet troops arrived in the region, and the three Jewish boys in Daniil Tymchyna's care no longer had to live in hiding. The priest arranged for all the boys to be transported into Poland, where they were placed in the care of a rabbi. Leon Chameides and Adam Rotfeld were eventually placed with surviving relatives in Poland, and Oded Amarant was finally reunited with his parents in Palestine, from which would soon emerge the Jewish state of Israel. Leon Chameides grew up to become the minister of foreign affairs for the independent nation of Poland. Adam Rotfeld was brought to the United States after the war, and there became a respected pediatric oncologist. Oded Amarant became an accomplished textile engineer in Israel. Their rescuer, Daniil Tymchyna, faced a darker future after the war. In most areas of eastern Europe that were "liberated" by Soviet forces, Soviet dictator Joseph Stalin replaced the fascist oppression of Nazi rule with the Communist oppression of Soviet rule. Ukrainian hopes of independence were again crushed, and the Ukraine returned to Soviet control. To suppress Ukrainian nationalism—and to reinforce the official atheism of Soviet Communism—Stalin ordered the arrest of all leaders in the Ukrainian Eastern Rite Church. By then the aging leader of the church, Metropolitan Andrey Sheptytsky, had died, but Daniil Tymchyna was arrested for his faith and was deported to a Soviet gulag prison camp as a slave laborer. He would not be released for ten years.[18]

CHAPTER 22

IOSIF AND ANNA NAZARUK

Baptist pastor Iosif Nazaruk, seated left, and his wife, Anna, seated far right, with five of their seven children. (CREDIT: YAD VASHEM)

"This is the wish of the Lord."

HINKA MINAKER RAN for her life. She was frantic, lost, stumbling
and running through the woods—and a Nazi death squad was
chasing her. She had no idea where she was running, but she had
to escape what she had just seen. It was October 14, 1942, and she
and four thousand other Jews from her hometown of Kobryn, in
the Soviet republic of Belorussia, had been marched through the
city streets and into the wooded countryside on the outskirts of
town. For more than a year, Jewish families from Kobryn had been
forced to live in two sealed-off ghettos in the city, where they were
weakened by starvation and illness. "There was great hunger," a
survivor later recalled. "The Jews looked like skeletons, thin with
big eyes. A lot died from hunger and infection." In July 1942, one
of Kobryn's ghettos had been emptied and all its residents shipped
by rail to a remote railroad spur at a place called Bronna Gora,
where the German *Ordnungspolizei* (Order Police) had excavated
a giant burial pit. The Order Police were German military police
considered too old for combat, but who proved themselves more
than fit to execute tens of thousands of Belorussian Jews. Assisted
by collaborationist Ukrainian police, they used machine guns to
slaughter more than fifty thousand Jews at Bronna Gora, thousands of them from Kobryn.[1]

On October 14, the Nazis came for Hinka Minaker's ghetto,
but the Jews there knew what was coming and fought back. At least
five hundred escaped. The rest, including Hinka, were marched to
the forest outside the city, where a sprawling burial pit awaited
them. There German and Ukrainian military police ordered those
at the head of the line to undress, then forced them into the pit,
where they were killed by machine-gun, rifle, and pistol fire. "I

walked in the third row, exhausted," one of the few survivors later wrote. "What kind of thoughts went through the minds of [other] Kobrin Jews at this time? Did they understand that they were to be slaughtered like cattle in a very short time? One could not think. The pain, the shock, the fear paralyzed us completely.... [When the Nazis opened fire] you could see Jews, barefoot, hungry and thirsty, trying to escape. But the Ukrainian police were sent to catch those Jews. Young Jewish girls threw themselves into wells instead of falling into their hands." Such was the fear that drove Hinka Minaker to frantically race through the forest away from the piled-up bodies behind her.[2]

Adolf Hitler was determined to find a way to kill the Jews more efficiently and in larger numbers—and Soviet Belorussia was his testing ground. In December 1941, Hitler had convened a meeting of leading Nazi officials in the private quarters of the Reich Chancellery—the German White House—where he discussed the fate he intended for the Jews of Europe. By then he realized that the Soviet Union would not be defeated easily. The Japanese had attacked American forces in the Pacific, and Hitler had declared war on the United States. Germany was now engaged in a world war of unprecedented scale—and Hitler irrationally blamed it on the Jews and not himself. Earlier he had vowed that if a world war blocked his goals of conquest, he would oversee "the extermination of the Jewish race in Europe." At the Reich Chancellery meeting, he announced his intention to fulfill that vow. "With respect of the Jewish Question," Nazi propaganda minister Joseph Goebbels wrote afterward, "the Führer has decided to make a clean sweep.... The world war is here, and the annihilation of the Jews must be the necessary consequence." A little more than a month later, at what would infamously become known as the Wannsee Conference, Nazi leaders met at a plush Berlin villa and developed a plan to achieve Hitler's goal of wiping out Europe's Jews. They called it the Final Solution.[3]

Already great numbers of Jews from Nazi Germany and the countries it had invaded were being systematically killed by death squads with firearms—tens of thousands at a time. But the Final Solution proposed mass murder on a previously unimaginable scale—one that required sadistically efficient killing centers or death camps. The Nazis had built scores of labor camps and several death camps—but over the course of the next two years, many more would be built, bearing names that would become synonymous with unimaginable horror. Labor and transit camps were constructed throughout the Nazi-occupied nations, while the death camps were concentrated in Poland, which had the largest Jewish population in Europe. Over the next two and a half years, gigantic numbers of European Jews and others declared to be enemies of the Nazi state would be imprisoned, worked to death, executed, or killed by illness in notorious labor and transit camps such as Dachau, Buchenwald, Gross-Rosen, Mauthausen-Gusen, Theresienstadt, and Ravensbrück. Meanwhile, at infamous Nazi killing centers and death camps such as Chełmno, Bełżec, Majdanek, Sobibór, Treblinka, and Auschwitz, newly designed gas chambers would kill Jewish men, women, and children on a scale of slaughter previously unknown in history. The numbers were staggering: 35,000 at Theresienstadt, 89,000 at Majdanek, 152,000 at Chełmno, 170,000 at Sobibór, 430,000 at Bełżec, 900,000 at Treblinka, and more than a million at Auschwitz.[4]

The Soviet republic of Belorussia proved to be Hitler's practice field for his Final Solution. When Nazi troops invaded Belorussia in 1941, the same program of mass murder that the Nazis had pursued in Poland, the Ukraine, and the Baltic states was unleashed on the Jews of Belorussia. First Belorussian leaders were killed—attorneys, teachers, engineers, government officials. More than three thousand were shot to death in the city of Minsk in a single day. More than four thousand were killed in Pinsk, an estimated five thousand in Brest-Litovsk, and more than nine thousand in Slonim. In short order, with the famed German efficiency, more than two hundred Jewish ghettos were established throughout Belorussia. There healthy adults were forced to work as slave laborers twelve hours a day on starvation rations; children, the ill, and the elderly were fed nothing. Within months tens of thousands were dead—six thousand in the Pruzhany Ghetto alone. Then the Nazis began to "liquidate" the ghettos, killing their Jewish inhabitants in mass shootings: more than thirty thousand at the Minsk Ghetto, another thirty thousand at Białystok, twenty-five thousand at Bobruysk, twenty-two thousand at Slonim, twenty thousand at Mahilyow, eighteen thousand in Mozyr. In Rakov, more than nine hundred Jews were forced into a synagogue, and then it was burned down with all inside. In some locations the Jewish population ceased to exist.[5]

Despite such a massive harvest of death, Hitler demanded larger numbers, quicker results. In Belorussia, Hitler's handpicked Nazi governor, Wilhelm Kube, pushed for a more efficient killing system, and an SS Einsatzgruppe commander named Arthur Nebe, a former Berlin police commissioner, began experimenting with mobile gas chambers—large, vanlike trucks that were rigged to use carbon monoxide to kill Jewish captives locked inside. Earlier, in a policy called *Sonderbehandlung*, or "special treatment," Hitler had ordered the execution of more than seventy thousand German civilians deemed to be "unworthy of life" by Nazi standards. Carbon monoxide gassing had been used to euthanize the mentally ill, people with epilepsy, the blind, the deaf, the "feeble-minded," children and adults with physical deformities—anyone deemed likely to negatively affect the future of the Nazi master race. It worked on a smaller scale, and the experiment in Belorussia proved that it could be equally deadly in larger operations: Over a three-day period twenty-seven thousand Jews were gassed to death in Belorussia. Gas chambers using carbon monoxide gas were constructed at Chełmno and Bełżec. After deadly experiments at Auschwitz, a highly poisonous pesticide called Zyklon B became the standard killing agent at Nazi death camps, most of which were located in German-occupied Poland. In Belorussia the combination of gassing and shooting killed more than eight hundred thousand Jews—including those at the Kobryn massacre that Hinka Minaker desperately tried to escape.[6]

When the Nazis opened fire and people began to scream and fall, Minaker dashed panic-stricken into the forest. Her Nazi pursuers were only seconds behind her—close enough for her to hear their shouts. How long could she keep ahead? Then she burst out of the woods in front of a rustic farmhouse—and in its open door stood a man hurriedly motioning to her to come inside. "Come in and go down to the basement," he whispered urgently, pointing to an opening in the floor as he rushed past her into the farmhouse yard. As she scrambled for the basement door, she caught a glance through the window of men in uniforms running past the house. Her rescuer was pointing them down a lane, away from the house. The Nazis ran on in a vain pursuit, and did not return. Hinka Minaker had escaped the Kobryn massacre.[7]

Later the man who had saved her brought her up from the basement into the farmhouse parlor. He introduced himself as Iosif Nazaruk—a Baptist pastor. His wife, Anna, stood beside him, weeping with fear. Nazaruk gently tried to comfort her. "This is the wish of the Lord," he said. "Once she is in our house," he continued, referring to Hinka, "we cannot throw her out. And may the Lord help us." The Nazaruks had no intention of making Hinka leave, even though some Kobryn residents turned in Jews for a bounty. Instead they hid her, knowing the Nazis would kill them and their seven children if they were found harboring a Jew.

As they prepared a place for her to hide inside the house, and gave her food, they learned that Minaker was married, and that her husband had been taken to a Nazi slave labor camp. She had been living in the Kobryn Ghetto with her mother, but the two had become separated when Minaker was rounded up with most of the Jews in the ghetto and forced to make the march into the country.[8]

"I stayed there a whole year and got well again."

Belorussia had few Baptists, but the Reverend Nazaruk pastored a tiny congregation in the rural countryside outside Kobryn. Protecting a persecuted Jew was his obligation as a follower of Christ, he believed, and his wife, Anna, willingly shared the risks. As Hinka Minaker settled into a routine at the Nazaruk farmhouse, the pastor made careful inquiries about her husband and mother through the members of his congregation. He learned that her mother was among the few survivors still in the Kobryn Ghetto—all of whom were likely facing execution by the Nazis. Somehow Pastor Nazaruk managed to free the mother from the ghetto and arrange for her to be secretly brought to the Nazaruks' home. There she went into hiding with her daughter. Then the pastor used his congregational contacts to arrange for the release of Minaker's husband Shimon from the Nazi labor camp, and also hid him at their farm, along with another Jewish couple.[9]

With five Jewish fugitives and seven children, the Nazaruks did not have enough room to keep everyone in their farmhouse. Perhaps because of illness she had contracted in the Kobryn Ghetto or the trauma she had suffered escaping from the massacre, Hinka suffered from chronically poor health. Therefore the Nazaruks hid her in their home, and concealed the others in a nearby barn and a potato cellar. Although they had little food themselves, the pastor and his wife managed to feed their seven children and all their Jewish refugees throughout the winter of 1942–43. "He fed us," Hinka later recalled. "He had seven children, and he himself would grind the wheat and bake the bread. He was a pastor.... I stayed there a whole year and got well again." For the Nazaruks and the Jews they hid, the threat of discovery and death was constant, but through his church members, Nazaruk managed to remain aware of possible Nazi raids.[10]

Not only did the Jews of Europe resist the Nazis by going into hiding, but in some cases they managed to arm themselves and fought back—especially in Belorussia, Poland, and elsewhere in eastern Europe. At Sobibór in 1943, Jewish prisoners overpowered and killed about a dozen SS and Ukrainian guards, cut telephone and electric wires, set the camp on fire, and broke out. About six hundred were involved in what became known as the Sobibór Uprising, and approximately three hundred escaped, although only about fifty survived the war. In the Belorussian city of Raduń, about 175 miles north of Kobryn, Jewish men who were ordered to dig their own graves by SS troops suddenly turned on their guards, hitting them with their shovels, and managed to escape. Elsewhere in Belorussia other Jews escaped the killing fields, fled into the territory's dense forests, and formed groups of resisters called partisans who fought the German occupation troops. "We did not go to our deaths quietly and submissively," sixteen-year-old Yitzhak Arad would later explain. "We battled as best we could—often with our bare hands." Communist partisan bands, which included former Russian soldiers, received weapons and supplies sent by air by the Russian army, and managed to win control of large regions of Belorussia. Although thousands of fighters joined the Belorussian partisans, many Belorussians were anti-Semitic, and Jewish fighters were not always welcomed, especially by the Communist partisans.[11]

In late 1943, after Pastor Nazaruk's Jewish refugees had successfully hidden from the Nazis for more than a year, a large force of Communist partisans appeared at the Nazaruk farm. Hinka Minaker was too ill to go outside, but the other Jews came out of hiding and greeted them as allies. Instead of responding in kind, however, the Communists seized Hinka's husband and mother and the two other Jews, and took them away to work as forced laborers building partisan defenses. None survived. Hinka alone remained alive and in hiding at the Nazaruk farm. A year later, in the summer of 1944, the Soviet Red Army drove out Nazi forces and "liberated" Belorussia. At war's end, Pastor Nazaruk and his wife Anna resumed their ministry under the repressive policies that governed the officially atheistic Soviet state. Hinka Minaker eventually remarried, and she and her husband managed to emigrate to the newly established nation of Israel. Even with a new home and a new life, she never forgot the courageous Baptist pastor and his wife who had risked everything to save her as she ran for her life through the forest.[12]

CHAPTER 23
ANTON SCHMID

German officers indulge in a wartime celebration. Yards away from such a gathering, Sergeant Anton Schmid made plans to rescue imperiled Jews. (CREDIT: SOUTHERN COMMUNICATIONS)

"All I did was save people."

ON THE EVE of his execution, Toni Schmid sat in his prison cell
and wrote his wife and daughter a final good-bye. "I am inform-
ing you, my dearest," he wrote, "that I must depart from this
world, I am sentenced to death. Please remain strong and trust
in our dear God, who decides the destiny of each of us." It was
April 13, 1942, and Anton "Toni" Schmid was a German soldier
condemned to death for rescuing Jews. Six years earlier, when
Nazi Germany took over his native Austria, Schmid had been a
thirty-eight-year-old shopkeeper selling radios in Vienna. A year
later, when Germany invaded Poland, he was drafted into the
German army and was forced to leave his wife and daughter. He
was among those Austrians who had no love for Adolf Hitler or
Nazi Germany, but his age and aptitude earned him the rank of
sergeant in the German army. Eventually he was placed in charge
of a *Versprengtenstelle* post—a rear-echelon collection center where
stragglers and other troops separated from their units worked until
reassigned. The dark-haired, mustached Schmid was responsible, forthright, and considerate—traits that endeared him to the
soldiers serving under him, and that reflected his personal faith:
Schmid was a deeply committed Christian.[1]

His upright character and compassionate heart were immediately assaulted in 1941, when he was posted to Vilnius, the capital
of Lithuania. The Baltic states of Lithuania, Latvia, and Estonia
had been occupied by Soviet forces following the German-Soviet
nonaggression pact of 1939, but were quickly conquered in the
German invasion of the Soviet Union two years later. More than
three hundred thousand Jews lived in the three small nations, and
more than 90 percent perished in the Holocaust. They were killed

in the same style of mass murder inflicted on the other Jews of the Soviet Union by German forces, led by the SS Einsatzgruppen and aided at times by anti-Semitic Baltic police and militias. Vilnius, where Schmid's unit was posted, was such an important center of Jewish cultural life in eastern Europe that it was known as the Jerusalem of Lithuania, and a full quarter of its population was Jewish.[2]

Over the course of several months, beginning in the late summer of 1941, the Germans murdered more than forty thousand Jewish men, women, and children in a wooded region outside Vilnius known as the Ponary forest. A firsthand account of the slaughter was recorded by Kazimierz Sakowicz, a Lithuanian writer who lived in a cottage in the Ponary woods, and who safeguarded his report by burying it in sealed lemonade bottles. An excerpt:

> In a group of 200, a middle-aged emaciated Jewish woman in a navy blue dress with white dots walks arm in arm with a man.... Many children aged twelve to fifteen years old [are brought in] and old people who are carried.... They shoot in groups, from behind, in the back, or with grenades or machine guns when it's raining or late.... After a moment, [I hear] a volley, later a few individual shots, then everything quiets down.... One [Jew] escaped in his underwear.... He was hunted down and shot.... With trembling hands I write the words.

Although he had nothing to do with the Ponary Massacre, Sergeant Schmid happened to see SS troops executing Jewish children, and the sight horrified him. He became convinced that it was his obligation as a Christian to somehow help the Jews—but what could he do?[3]

One night soon afterward, as he walked along a darkened street in Vilnius, puffing on a cigarette, a desperate young Jewish woman who was half-mad with fear suddenly appeared out of the shadows and irrationally asked Schmid—who was wearing a German uniform—to hide her from the SS death squads. He could have turned her over to Nazi authorities, or simply ignored her, but instead he hid her in his small apartment overnight, then took her to a Catholic priest he knew, who agreed to issue her a certificate identifying her as a member of his congregation. Using her new identity, Schmid presented the Jewish woman as a civilian employee from his military unit whose documents had been seized by the retreating Soviets. In a single day he walked her through the German bureaucracy, enabling her to obtain an official identity card, rent an apartment—and stay alive. At about the same time, he met a young Jewish man who was also hiding from the death squads. Schmid had just received the military identity papers of a German soldier whose death had gone unreported. He found a German army uniform for the Jewish refugee, gave him the dead soldier's papers, and put him to work in his office as a military aide. Soon other Jews found their way to the meek but courageous German sergeant who had a heart for the oppressed. Almost overnight—in the words of a Jewish leader—Sergeant Schmid became "a secret one-man relief organization" for the Jews.[4]

"To us in the ghetto the frail, quiet man in the [sergeant's] uniform was a sort of saint."

Through his emerging Jewish contacts, Schmid broadened his activities to assist increasing numbers of Lithuanian Jews. At his military post, he oversaw workshops in Vilnius that employed convalescing German soldiers, Russian prisoners of war, and Jews who had been spared immediate execution because their skills were deemed essential to the German war effort. Although he was officially allowed only fifteen slots for Jews, Schmid issued enough documents to bring in dozens of Jewish workers, sparing them from the Ponary forest death squads. Vilnius's surviving Jews had been crammed into an overcrowded ghetto as they awaited their fate, and Schmid began slipping into the ghetto at night, handing out food, medicine, and even milk-filled baby bottles that he had kept warm in his pockets. He warned Jews in the ghetto of pending Nazi raids, and when his Jewish workers were caught in roundups and placed in Vilnius's notorious Lukiškės Prison, he boldly went there and obtained their release. "He did all these things without ever waiting for anyone to thank him," a Jewish survivor later recalled. "He did it out of the goodness of his heart. To us in the ghetto the frail, quiet man in the [sergeant's] uniform was a sort of saint."[5]

Schmid's duties occasionally gave him access to German army vehicles, and he began hiding escaping Jews in the covered rear of trucks bound for German-occupied areas of the Soviet Union, where he hoped the Jews would fare better than in Lithuania. In response to the mass murder of Jews in Ponary forest by the Nazis and their Lithuanian collaborators, a Jewish resistance movement arose in the Vilnius Ghetto. Some of its leaders made contact with Schmid, who secretly advised them of pending German operations, helped transport Jewish resistance fighters out of Vilnius, and even supplied stolen German weapons to the movement. He allowed resistance members to meet in his apartment, at one point hosting a meeting while German officers were partying in the apartment above his. Once Jewish resistance leaders shared with him their dream of a newly re-created nation of Israel—and said that surely Israel would give him a medal for all he had done to rescue the Jews of Lithuania. In response Schmid solemnly replied, "I will wear it with the greatest possible pride."[6]

By April 1943, Schmid had enabled almost three hundred Jews to escape capture or murder by the Nazis in Lithuania. Gestapo agents had grown suspicious of him, however, and began to follow him. That month, as he prepared to move five Jewish men from Vilnius, the Gestapo raided his apartment. Schmid was visiting the

Jewish ghetto at the time, and escaped capture. As he was returning home, some of the soldiers who served under him stopped him
and warned him that Gestapo agents were waiting for him. He
fled, and managed to escape capture for several weeks, but was
finally caught, quickly tried by a Nazi court, and sentenced to
death. "I won't be able to write you anymore," he wrote to his
wife, Stefi, and their daughter hours before his execution. "But be
sure that we will meet in a better world with our Lord."[7]

On April 13, 1942, Sergeant Anton Schmid was shot to death
by a Nazi firing squad. "All I did was save people...," he wrote his
wife in a final letter. "Now I close my last lines, the last I can write
to you, and send you my love. I kiss you both, and another kiss to
you, Stefi, you are everything to me in this world and the next,
where I will soon be in God's hand. Many kisses, love forever
from your Toni." The prison chaplain administered Communion
to Schmid moments before his death, and his last words were the
Lord's Prayer. Then he was executed—alongside the five Jewish
men he had tried to save. Years later one of the many Jews who
had escaped through Schmid's "secret one-man relief organization" was asked how he felt about the devout German sergeant
whose faith in Christ had propelled him to risk his life helping the
Jews. "Schmid became one of us," he said, "a family member."[8]

CHAPTER 24
ALDO BRUNACCI

While visiting Germany, Italian dictator Benito Mussolini shares a laugh with the German Führer.

(CREDIT: NATIONAL ARCHIVES)

"There are times when heroism is required."

ATTIRED IN THEIR brown, hooded robes, they looked like the many other Catholic monks moving about the sprawling monastery in Assisi, Italy. But they were neither Catholic nor monks. The monastic clothing was camouflage: the "monks" were actually Jews attempting to evade capture and murder by the Nazis. They were the Viterbi family—father, mother, and two daughters—and they had fled to Assisi after German troops invaded their distant hometown. As the war engulfed Italy in the autumn of 1943, hundreds of displaced Italians fled to Assisi, located in the hill country of central Italy about 120 miles north of Rome. It was the home of twelfth-century cleric Saint Francis of Assisi, and the Catholic order named for him. Amid Assisi's sprawling Basilica of San Francesco d'Assisi and numerous other monasteries, churches, convents, and shrines, Italian war refugees sought shelter—and among them were scores of Jews fleeing from the Nazis.[1]

When Benito Mussolini—Italy's bombastic fascist dictator—came to power in 1922, Italy's Jews were initially spared the severe persecution suffered by German Jews under Hitler. Italy's Jewish community was well integrated into all sectors of Italian society, and anti-Semitism in Italy was infrequent compared to what existed on the eve of World War II in Germany, Poland, and the Baltic states. Reluctant to provoke the political opposition of the Italian people, Mussolini hesitated in persecuting the nation's Jews—until he led Italy into the Axis treaty with Nazi Germany. Even then, persecution of the Jews was resisted by the general public and even Italian government officials in many places. The threat to the Jewish population increased, however, in the summer of 1943, as the war shifted direction in Italy. Following up on their victory in North Africa, American and British forces invaded Sicily and defeated its Italian and German defenders. Weary of the war and Mussolini, antifascist Italian leaders aided by British intelligence operatives managed to overthrow and imprison Mussolini. They then formed a new government, joined the Allies, and declared war on Nazi Germany. Meanwhile Allied forces landed in Italy, prompting Hitler to rush German troops into the country, which became engulfed in ferocious fighting.[2]

As German forces battled advancing Allied troops, the SS turned on Italy's population of approximately forty-five thousand Jews, targeting them for deportation to Nazi death camps. In October 1943, the Nazis attempted to deport all the Jews in Rome—estimated at about twelve thousand—and in a two-day raid managed to round up some twelve hundred Jewish men, women, and children. Raids in other Italian cities captured more than five thousand others. As the Holocaust unfolded, the Vatican, which was located in Nazi-occupied Rome, officially said little about persecution of the Jews. The Vatican was officially neutral in the war, but Pope Pius XII's official silence would later earn him severe criticism. However, while appearing diplomatically timid to some, the pope was reported to have privately encouraged Catholic priests and nuns throughout Italy to actively shelter Jews in churches, monasteries, convents, and parish houses. Even more Jews were protected by Catholic laypersons, who took their Jewish neighbors into their homes at the risk of their own lives. In so doing, courageous Catholics managed to save more than 80 percent of Italy's Jewish population from the Holocaust. "Through this," observed Jewish historian and Holocaust survivor Mordecai Paldiel, "they epitomized the best and most elevated form of religious faith and human fidelity."[3]

In the fall of 1943 Father Aldo Brunacci was a tall, dark-haired, bespectacled, thirty-year-old Catholic clergyman serving as the chief aide or secretary to the Bishop of Assisi, Giuseppe Nicolini.

One day the bishop called Brunacci into his office and held up a letter. "He said he had received the letter from Rome," Brunacci later recalled, "and he read what it said—that the Holy Father wanted us to see to it in our diocese that something would be done to ensure the safety of the Jews." The operation would be top secret—even their fellow clergy would be on a need-to-know basis only, the bishop emphasized—and he wanted Brunacci to take charge of the undertaking. Brunacci agreed, and immediately went to work building a regional underground network designed to protect every Jewish refugee in the Assisi area. Prior to the war, Assisi had had no Jewish residents; now scores were arriving, hoping to find safety in a historic site famous as a national center of Christianity.[4]

Among them were the Viterbi family, who arrived in Assisi after a harrowing escape from their faraway home via trains and roads clogged with German troops. They had been on vacation when German forces invaded Italy, and their hometown had been occupied by enemy troops. "That was when the real persecution began," recalled Grazia Viterbi, then seventeen years old. "The hunt for the Jews was on." Grazia's father, Emilio Viterbi, feared for the family's safety if they returned home, so he decided to lead them to Assisi. He was a university professor who was familiar with Saint Francis of Assisi, and hoped his family might somehow receive better treatment in the venerated city of Saint Francis's birth than elsewhere. They traveled by train, then by foot—only to learn as they neared their destination that the German army had established a military hospital in Assisi. Adding to the fear provoked by that discovery was a white-knuckle interlude when a German officer apparently mistook the family for pro-German Italian refugees, and insisted on giving them a ride in a vehicle loaded with wounded German soldiers.[5]

In Assisi the family checked into a hotel, but Emilio Viterbi knew that public lodging was likely to be routinely searched by

Nazi police. As he pondered what to do next, he was visited by Father Brunacci, who had somehow learned of the Viterbis' arrival and identity. Soon the Viterbi family was secreted away in a nearby monastery, where they were temporarily disguised as monks until Father Brunacci could arrange lodging for them in a safe house. Brunacci was gifted with exceptional organizational skills, and, using church contacts and resources, soon established an efficient underground network that provided Jewish refugees with shelter, food, and forged identity papers. The Viterbi family became the Vitellis, and their cover story was that they had fled their hometown in southern Italy—a town selected because it was occupied by Allied forces and thus the Germans could not contact it to check identities.[6]

Assisted by another priest, Father Rufino Nicacci, Aldo Brunacci routinely checked on the network's Jewish families, traveling by bicycle—a form of transportation he had often used for priestly duties. At times he bunked overnight with Jewish refugees, many of whom were housed by local Christian families. "Our first concern," he later recalled, "was to get them safely lodged in the various monasteries and convents or with reliable families who would 'forget' to comply with the police regulations to denounce any strangers in their homes." On his bicycle Brunacci also delivered forged identity papers to Jews in hiding, sometimes sparing himself uphill pedaling by holding on to the rear bumpers of German army trucks—even as he traveled with forged papers hidden in his bicycle handlebar.[7]

"They understood that they had been welcomed in a bond of love as brothers and sisters."
To obtain false identity cards, Brunacci turned to a Catholic layman he knew, Luigi Brizi, who operated a souvenir shop in Assisi that was equipped with a small printing press. Together Brunacci and Brizi managed to produce authentic-looking forgeries of the

identity papers required by the occupying German army. All that was missing was the official government seals, which another forger expertly produced. Brizi's son routinely borrowed Brunacci's bicycle to travel to the distant seal-maker. The townspeople of Assisi kept quiet about Father Brunacci's Jewish rescue network, even when pressed by German officials about suspicious activities.[8]

There were close calls aplenty. One of the convents under Brunacci's care was designated as the site of secret kosher meals during Jewish observances, which Brunacci carefully arranged for Assisi's hidden Jews. He liked to joke that Assisi boasted the only Catholic convent with a kosher kitchen. The ingredients were assembled discreetly, and the nuns learned how to prepare the Jewish dishes to perfection—all within yards of passing German troops. "When the guests sat down to take their first meal," Brunacci later recounted, "they understood that they had been welcomed in a bond of love as brothers and sisters." On another occasion Brunacci was visiting a local convent when a German officer and an Italian fascist policeman appeared at the convent entrance and demanded they be allowed to conduct a search. When Brunacci objected, the policeman pulled his service revolver and aimed it at the priest's face. After a tense moment, the German officer intervened, ended the standoff, and led the policeman away. [9]

Once an elderly Jewish woman who lived secretly in one of Brunacci's many safe houses died of natural causes. Jewish funeral rites were conducted in private prior to burial, and the woman was buried in a church cemetery with little ceremony. As the pallbearers carried her casket down an Assisi street, however, they encountered a passing body of German troops. Assuming that he was encountering a Catholic funeral procession, the German officer respectfully ordered his troops to halt and stand at attention for the passing of the deceased—not realizing he had ordered his soldiers to salute a Jewish funeral party.[10]

After almost six months of clandestine activity, however, Nazi officials became suspicious of Father Brunacci's actions. On May 15, 1944, Brunacci was walking home when he was stopped by two German policemen near his house. He was under arrest, Brunacci was told, on suspicion of assisting Jews. He asked if he could go to his study long enough to retrieve his breviary—his ministerial book containing church liturgies. The policemen agreed, but accompanied him home. As they reached the front door, Brunacci suddenly remembered that the entire Viterbi family was in his study—waiting for a scheduled meeting with him about housing for a relative. Suppressing his panic, he paused at the door and asked the policemen if they would please wait outside just long enough for him to get his book. To his surprise they agreed. He stepped into his study, where he found the Viterbis waiting for him as planned. He whispered to them not to move, picked up his breviary, and rejoined his police escort. He was imprisoned for three weeks until Vatican officials arranged for his release with the promise that he would be taken to the Vatican in Rome and not be allowed to return to Assisi.[11]

Allied forces, meanwhile, were slugging their way up the Italian peninsula, driving back the German army. Boosted by thirty-six thousand troops landed on the nearby Italian coast at Anzio, Allied forces captured Rome in June 1944, defeating and driving out the city's German occupiers. Eleven more months of bloody fighting lay ahead until German forces were driven up the Italian peninsula and finally forced to surrender, but one region of Italy after another was liberated by the Allies. As for Benito Mussolini—he had been rescued from imprisonment by German commandos dispatched by Hitler, who had then arranged for the Italian to rule a small puppet state protected by German forces in northern Italy. When the German army in Italy finally capitulated in April 1945, Italian resistance fighters captured and executed Mussolini and his mistress and hung their bodies from a lamppost in Milan.[12]

When Rome was liberated by the Allies, Father Brunacci was

free to return to Assisi. There he resumed his ministry. At war's end, he assisted in relief efforts for the several thousand war refugees who had fled to Assisi—including many Jews. Why, he was once asked, did he and others in Assisi risk their lives to save Jewish people they did not even know? "Because we had to," he replied. "It's what the Gospel asks a Christian to do." Only later—decades later—did Father Brunacci learn that the underground network he had established at the request of Bishop Nicolini had rescued more than three hundred persecuted Jews—and that not one had been deported or killed by the Nazis. Never did he express regret for endangering himself as he labored to help his new Jewish friends in wartime Assisi. "There are times in everyone's life in which it is easy to confuse prudence with a calm life," he observed, "[and] there are times when heroism is required."[13]

CHAPTER 25

JANE HAINING

*Jane Haining was a schoolteacher from Scot-
land who taught in a predominantly Jewish
school in Hungary. When the Nazis came for
her students, she went first.*

(CREDIT: YAD VASHEM)

"How much more will they need me in the days of darkness?"

WHEN SHE HEARD the wail of approaching sirens, Jane Haining knew what it meant: the Nazis were coming. The date was April 4, 1944, and Haining was a Scottish schoolteacher in Budapest, Hungary, presiding over a boarding school composed mainly of Jewish children. Teaching and caring for her Jewish students was Jane Haining's life work. It was a call that she had accepted as a Christian more than twelve years earlier. In 1932, she had been a thirty-four-year-old single woman working as a secretary in a textile factory in Scotland. She was a member of the Church of Scotland, holding to Reformed or Presbyterian doctrine, and one night she attended a life-changing church missions program. There she learned about a church ministry in Hungary that included a school for Jewish orphans. Turning to a friend sitting beside her, she stated confidently, "I have found my life-work."[1]

An attractive young woman with dark hair, a light complexion, and sparkling blue eyes behind her round spectacles, Haining had a delicate appearance that belied a strong Scottish personality and a bold faith in Jesus Christ. She had grown up in a large farming family among the rugged, rocky blue ridges of southwestern Scotland, had lost her mother when she was only five, and had acquired an independent spirit and a zeal for learning. A bright student in her village grammar school, she was awarded a scholarship to a highly regarded Scottish academy, and then attended college in Glasgow and Edinburgh. She had become a Christian as a girl, had taught Sunday school while still a teenager, and was elated at the opportunity to become headmaster of the girls' elementary program at the Scottish school in Budapest. There she thrived. She already spoke German, quickly learned to speak fluent Hungarian, and—despite a no-nonsense style in the classroom—soon became a beloved figure to her Jewish students, many of whom were orphans. "She was a very sympathetic person," a former student later recalled. "So kind. So good. Everyone loved her very much."[2]

She returned the affection. Perhaps because she had lost her mother at an early age, she had a tender heart for children and especially for orphans. "We have one new little six-year-old, an orphan without a mother or a father," she wrote in a letter home. "She is such a pathetic wee soul to look at, and I fear, poor lamb, has not been in too good surroundings.... She certainly does look as though she needs heaps and heaps of love." About another child she wrote, "We have one nice little mite who is an orphan and is coming to school for the first time. She seems to be a lonely little wee soul and needs lots of love. We shall see what we can do to make life happier for her.... What a ghastly feeling it must be to know that no one wants you." As the evil stain of Nazism spread through Europe and war erupted, the Scottish boarding school in Budapest became a sanctuary for its Jewish students. "Anti-Semitism presented itself in many places and forms in those times," recalled a former student decades later, "but in the Scottish school I never sensed it either from the teachers or another student, either directly or indirectly. The Scotch was a warm nest. In the upper classes, I gained morality and that lasts a lifetime."[3]

Children who found themselves in need of a "warm nest" soared in numbers as World War II enveloped Hungary—especially in the nation's Jewish community. An independent nation on the eve of the war, Hungary was headed by a regent, Miklós Horthy, who had been commander in chief of the Austro-Hungarian Navy in the First World War. He tried to steer Hungary on a course between fascism and communism, but under pressure from Hitler he reluctantly aligned the nation with Nazi Germany and sent the Hungarian army to fight alongside the Germans in the 1941 invasion of the Soviet Union. By late 1943, however, Hitler's military forces had suffered reversals almost everywhere: The German army was being driven out of the Soviet Union toward Poland and Germany, had suffered defeat in North Africa and Sicily, and was in retreat in Italy. The Hungarian army, meanwhile, had suffered more than a hundred thousand casualties fighting the Soviets on the Eastern Front, and Regent Horthy did not want Hungary to go down with Nazi Germany, so he attempted to negotiate an armistice with the Allies. In response Hitler ordered German troops to invade Hungary in March of 1944, imprisoned Horthy, installed a fascist puppet government, and kept the Hungarian army in the fight against the Allies.[4]

Hitler also demanded that Hungary's eight hundred thousand Jews be deported for annihilation as part of the Nazi Final Solution. Already Hungarian Jews were under persecution, and more than forty thousand Jewish men had been sent to the Eastern Front as slave laborers, most never to return. Until the German invasion, however, Horthy and other Hungarian leaders had managed to keep most of Hungary's Jews from being deported and killed in the Holocaust. Eventually, however, with the help of a savage Hungarian equivalent of the Nazi Party called the Arrow Cross Party, the SS and the Gestapo deported more than half a million Hungarian Jews to death camps, where most of them were murdered. Holocaust organizer Adolf Eichmann, now an SS lieutenant colonel, arrived in Budapest the day the German army invaded, and with a contingent of six hundred troops took command of the Jewish deportations. Within ten days of his arrival, Hungarian Jews were forbidden to travel, use telephones, do any work besides common labor, or withdraw money from their bank accounts—and they were all ordered to wear a yellow cloth Star of David on their clothing. Soon thousands of Jews were being assembled in Budapest and herded into railway boxcars for deportation to Auschwitz and other death camps.[5]

As she sewed the yellow stars on her students' clothing, Jane

Haining wept. Upon learning that the German army had invaded Hungary, officials in the Church of Scotland ordered Haining and the other Scots who worked at the Budapest mission to immediately return home—but she refused. To her, the Jewish schoolgirls she taught were her "daughters." "If these children need me in the days of sunshine," she explained, "how much more will they need me in the days of darkness?" Later, her sister commented on Haining's refusal to flee to safety: "It was no surprise that she refused to come back. She would never have had a moment's happiness if she had come home and left the children." It was wrong, Haining declared, "to distinguish one child of one race and the child of another." Jesus said, "Let the little children come unto Me, and do not hinder them, for to such belongs the kingdom of heaven"—all children belonged to Jesus, she stated. As a British citizen, she was viewed as an enemy by the Nazi invaders, and an informer soon reported her opinions to the Gestapo.[6]

As Budapest's Jewish families were rounded up for deportation, she tried to reassure the children, and kept up a brave face. If her Jewish students were going to be deported to some terrible fate, Jane Haining was determined to go with them. She did—and the Nazis took her first. When the Gestapo came for her, they came in a car with a blaring siren. They searched her bedroom and her office, then they arrested her and took her away. She attempted to take her Bible with her, but one of the Gestapo agents ordered her to leave it behind, stating that she wouldn't need it where she was going. She was reportedly charged with eight crimes, which included helping Jewish children and crying for them. The children cried for *her* as they stood outside the school and watched her get into the Gestapo car. As a last act, she turned and lovingly smiled at them. "I still feel the tears in my eyes...," a surviving student later remembered. "I see the smile on her face as she bade farewell." She was sentenced to deportation, and was loaded into a cattle car with the Jews of Hungary whom she had come to serve and had grown to love. Her destination was a Nazi concentration camp.[7]

It was Auschwitz. Located about thirty-five miles west of the Polish city of Kraków, Auschwitz had been established on the site of a former Polish army post in 1940, and originally housed Polish slave laborers. After the German invasion of the Soviet Union in 1941, approximately fifteen thousand Soviet prisoners of war were sent to the camp, where almost all died. More than seventy thousand Poles also died there, along with twenty-one thousand Gypsies and twelve thousand others, most of whom were targeted for death by the Nazi state as subhuman undesirables. Those shocking numbers were dwarfed by the mass murder of Jews at Auschwitz—which totaled more than one million between 1940 and 1945. At the time Jane Haining arrived there in the spring of 1944, the huge, sprawling facility was nearing its final stage and consisted of several concentration camps, industrial and armament facilities that contributed to the German war effort, and support facilities. By then Adolf Hitler's Final Solution was at its peak: The tide of war had reversed itself and was surging against Germany, and the Nazi regime was frantically trying to destroy what remained of Europe's Jewish population.[8]

In the early summer of 1944, more than four thousand Hungarian Jews were killed at Auschwitz every day—and Jane Haining was among them. German authorities notified the Church of Scotland that Haining had died of illness; other evidence, however, revealed that she was executed with Hungarian Jewish women in a gas chamber at Auschwitz on August 16, 1944. If her experience at Auschwitz was typical for that time, she arrived at the facility's railway station with incoming Hungarian Jews from Budapest, then was herded into the back of a transport truck and taken to Auschwitz's processing center. There men and women prisoners were separated, with infants and small children remaining with the women. Everyone was required to turn over all valuables and remove their clothing. All prisoners, children included, had a serial number tattooed on the outside of their left forearm. Haining's number was 79467. "You are only numbers," an SS guard routinely told the newly tattooed prisoners. "A shot, and that number is gone. Don't try to escape." After a cursory examination by camp doctors, prisoners who were classified as able-bodied were assigned to labor camps, where they were worked to death or eventually executed in gas chambers.[9]

"On the way to heaven."

By the summer of 1944, most Jews were killed immediately upon arrival at Auschwitz, but as a political prisoner Haining was imprisoned for about two months before she was executed. If her experience was typical, she was issued wooden clog-type shoes and a striped, pajama-style prisoner uniform or the ragged clothes of an executed prisoner, and was housed in a filthy barracks that was infested with rats and illness. The sprawling Auschwitz complex was surrounded by a double barbed wire fence lit at night by searchlights, and kept under constant view by SS troops in watchtowers armed with machine guns. Prisoners were fed a starvation diet of meager vegetable broth, were awakened at four thirty a.m. for a grueling twelve-hour workday, and slept on wooden racks in rooms that were crowded far beyond their intended capacity. For Jews especially, the labor was intentionally so brutal that many prisoners quickly died of exhaustion. In the few weeks before her death, Haining was allowed to write a postcard to her superiors at the Church of Scotland. Her telling observation, which somehow got past Nazi censors, reflected her understanding of what lay ahead for her—in this life and afterward: "There is not much to report here on the way to heaven."[10]

Multiple gas chambers and crematoriums expertly designed by German engineers had been constructed at Auschwitz, and by mid-1944 were killing Jewish prisoners with shocking efficiency.

On at least one occasion, however, Jewish prisoners herded toward the gas chamber realized that they were about to be executed, and revolted—but were all shot to death. In another incident, the Auschwitz *Sonderkommando*—Jewish prisoners forced to move the dead from the gas chambers to the crematoriums—armed themselves with work tools and hand grenades smuggled in from the camp armaments factory and attacked their guards, hoping to fight their way out. They managed to kill several SS guards, but almost all were shot down, and several hundred other prisoners were executed in retaliation. Most Holocaust victims simply had no opportunity to revolt or hope of surviving if they tried.[11]

The German commanders who oversaw the Holocaust death camps kept meticulous records, which preserved a detailed account of the horrible experience endured by the Jews of Auschwitz and other prisoners—such as Jane Haining—when they were eventually overtaken by the Nazi Final Solution. Hundreds at a time, the women and children prisoners followed by the men, were herded through a cordon of SS guards and guard dogs into an undressing room adjacent to a gas chamber. There they were handed soap and towels, and were told to undress so they could take a shower— with instructions to neatly fold their clothes so they could easily retrieve them later. If anyone became suspicious and resisted, guards beat them with clubs. The gas chambers at Auschwitz were fitted with inoperable overhead shower nozzles, which were designed to deceive victims until the last moment and thus reduce the possibility of resistance. Typically, about two thousand people were crammed into the gas chamber. Then the door was closed and bolted, and the lights were turned off. From the roof above, an SS technician wearing a gas mask then dropped large tablets of Zyklon B—the fumigation poison—through an air-sealed opening into the room below. The tablets immediately emitted a deadly gas, which usually killed everyone in the gas chamber within five minutes.[12]

After thirty minutes the chamber was aired out, the door was opened, and prison laborers wearing gas masks dragged out the bodies, removed gold teeth from the dead for the Nazi treasury, and clipped the women's hair, which was used to make soft shoe coverings for German submarine crewmen. The bodies were carted to the crematorium, where they were burned in an oven, or they were placed in large piles outside and burned. Despite German efficiency, the disposal of the bodies could not keep up with the number of people gassed to death. In January 1945, Soviet forces reached the Polish city of Kraków and liberated Auschwitz. Before their arrival, the SS tried to kill as many Jews and others as possible, then put sixty thousand survivors on a forced march that killed more than fifteen thousand people. When Soviet troops captured the giant camp, they found only about seven thousand prisoners still alive. Some of Jane Haining's Jewish students somehow survived the Holocaust, and they never forgot her. "Those children who were in the home, they adored her," one recalled. "She was a real mother of her 'daughters.'" After Haining's death, the Bible she had been forced to leave behind was discovered at the Scottish school. In it was a bookmark, and on it—in her handwriting—was a Bible verse from the New Testament book of Mark: "Be not afraid, only believe."[13]

CHAPTER 26

IMRE BÁTHORY

Their headgear topped by their signature cock feathers, a battalion of Hungary's infamous Royal Gendarmes goose-steps its way on parade.

(CREDIT: YAD VASHEM)

"Where were you when your brother's blood was crying out to God?"
TWENTY-THREE-YEAR-OLD MARTIN WIESEL could not help looking nervous: he was racked by fear. He was seated with other passengers on a train rolling through the Hungarian countryside
toward Budapest, and two grim-looking police officers were moving from passenger to passenger, asking for identification papers.
Wiesel had good reason to be frightened: He was Jewish and the
policemen would likely send him to his death. It was April 1944,
and Hungary had been occupied by German forces for a month.
Wiesel knew that the Nazis were deporting Hungary's Jews to
death camps by the thousands—and that Nazi-like Arrow Cross
thugs were systematically executing Jews in mass shootings. An
eyewitness to one of the slaughters later recalled its horror:

> What I saw was worse than anything I had seen before,
> worse than the most frightening accounts I had ever wit-
> nessed. Two Arrow Cross men were standing on the
> embankment of the river, aiming and shooting a group
> of men, women and children into the Danube—one after
> another. On their coats was the Yellow Star. I looked at the
> Danube. It was neither blue nor gray, but red.[1]

Wiesel knew what could happen to him, and the two policemen working their way toward his seat were not ordinary traffic
police: they were Hungarian Royal Gendarmes—members of a
paramilitary group that helped enforce Nazi law. Their uniforms
were similar to German army uniforms, but instead of caps or hel-
mets they wore black dress hats topped by cock feathers. Already
their feathered headgear was a symbol of death for Jews, much like

the skull-and-crossbones insignia worn by the SS. Jews were disappearing in scores throughout Hungary, hauled off by the Gendarmes, who were known to beat even women and children with rifle butts and whips. Jews were no longer allowed even to travel by train, and now two cockaded Gendarmes were only feet away from Wiesel, carefully examining each passenger's identification card in their search for Jews. How could he possibly escape?[2]

Ironically, young Martin Wiesel had come to Hungary to keep from being killed in neighboring Romania, where he was born. In 1940, the year Hitler launched the German blitzkrieg across western Europe, a pro-Nazi government rose to power in Romania under General Ion Antonescu, a fascist military leader. Under Antonescu, Romania's Iron Guard—a thuggish force of pro-Nazi collaborators—looted Jewish homes, burned Jewish-owned businesses, and destroyed synagogues. Mass murder soon followed. On killing fields throughout the nation, Romanian troops slaughtered their Jewish countrymen. At one point more than three thousand Romanian Jews were ordered to a railway station, where they surrendered their valuables, turned in their house keys, boarded sealed railway cars, and were suffocated while on a trip to nowhere. Countless others were deported to Nazi death camps. Soviet forces would invade Romania in August 1944, prompting Romanians to overthrow Antonescu and switch sides to fight for the Allies. By then, however, more than 250,000 Romanian Jews would be dead. To escape the Holocaust in Romania, Wiesel had fled to Hungary—just before it was invaded by German forces.[3]

"I know that you are a Jew in trouble."
Now he sat on the train, trying not to tremble, while the Hungarian Gendarmes headed his way. Suddenly the train braked to a halt and the doors opened—American bombers had been pounding

munitions factories in Budapest for weeks and more bombs were now exploding nearby. The Gendarmes hurriedly waved all the passengers off the train and ordered them to take cover in a nearby ditch. Surely this was the opportunity for Wiesel to escape—but the policemen were too close and he had no opportunity to run. When the bombers were gone, the Gendarmes herded everyone back aboard and continued their identification check as the train resumed moving. Wiesel reclaimed his seat and nervously awaited his fate. Then a male passenger got up, moved to the seat opposite Wiesel's, and leaned forward. "I know that you are a Jew in trouble," he whispered, "don't worry."[4]

Wiesel looked at the man. He was middle-aged, with a self-confident bearing and the weathered face of a farmer. His name was Imre Báthory, and he *was* a farmer. He lived on Csepel Island, a thirty-mile-long island in the Danube south of Budapest. While much of the huge island remained agricultural, the area closest to Budapest was the site of oil refineries and aircraft manufacturing plants that supported the Nazi war effort. A few weeks earlier, in the wake of the German occupation of Hungary, American bombers based in Italy had begun making repeated bombing runs on the island's war industry sites, dropping hundreds of bombs. To protect them from stray bombs, Báthory had moved his wife and children to a place far away in the Hungarian countryside. He was aboard the train traveling back to Budapest when he noticed the dark-haired and obviously frightened young man, and figured out his dilemma. "I'll help you," he told Wiesel.[5]

When the feather-hatted Gendarmes reached the seats where Báthory and Wiesel were seated, the farmer confidently spoke up and engaged their attention. As he handed over his own identification card, Báthory calmly claimed Wiesel to be his son. He was sorry that his son had forgotten his identification card, Báthory explained, but he would vouch for him. Báthory's intervention endangered his own life: The Gendarmes were infamous for their barbarity. Charged with loading Jewish deportees into railway boxcars, they sometimes packed a single car with so many people that those who fainted were left standing even when unconscious. When checking people's identification papers, they sometimes stole their jewelry, even prying wedding bands off women's fingers. Why should such barbarians believe a simple farmer? But they did. After listening to Báthory's explanation, they handed back his identification card and moved on down the line, ignoring Wiesel as they checked other passengers. Soon they disappeared into the next car. Relieved, Báthory and Wiesel—Gentile and Jew—began a conversation. Báthory learned Wiesel's story, and Wiesel learned that Báthory was a Christian—a Protestant Evangelical. But why had Báthory been so willing to risk his life for a man he did not even know? The Nazi persecution of the Jews was sinful and ungodly, Báthory believed, and true Christians were obligated before God to oppose it. As for saving Wiesel's life, Báthory downplayed his heroics: He was only a human "vessel," he explained, "through which the Lord's purpose was fulfilled."[6]

When the train reached Csepel Island, Báthory invited Wiesel to go home with him. With his family waiting out the war in the distant countryside, there was plenty of room on the farm—and Wiesel could help with the chores. Báthory knew that he could be executed for helping a Jew, but he made the offer anyway—and Wiesel accepted. The two became close friends, and Báthory also agreed to take in Wiesel's uncle. In addition, he later gave shelter to a Jewish couple who needed refuge. His new Jewish friends remained in hiding at his farm until victorious Soviet forces occupied the Budapest area and the Nazis were gone. Then, Báthory's Jewish lodgers were finally free to emerge from hiding, and his family returned home. Wiesel and Báthory, however, remained lifelong friends. Once, long after the war, Báthory was asked why he was willing to endanger himself to save four Jewish strangers. His answer: "I know that when I stand before God on Judgement Day, I shall not be asked the question posed to Cain—where were you when your brother's blood was crying out to God?"[7]

CHAPTER 27

ANNA EHN

The same age as Ilona Katz when she was sent to a Nazi death camp, fourteen-year-old Polish Catholic Czeslawa Kwokaone was among the one and a half million children who died in the Holocaust. One million were Jewish.

(CREDIT: AUSCHWITZ–BIRKENAU MEMORIAL
AND MUSEUM)

"Jew-lover."

THIRTEEN-YEAR-OLD ANNA EHN was finally old enough to walk to church by herself. She was an Austrian girl who lived in Vienna with her family, and took her faith seriously enough to attend church alone. Despite Allied bombing raids that had reduced parts of picturesque Vienna to rubble by mid-1944, her parents obviously believed it was safe for her to make a short walk to church for an early-morning mass, and her mother had even sent along a snack. This morning, however, the walk to church changed Anna's life—and saved two others. As Anna walked independently along the sidewalk, just as any adult would do, a dark-haired, disheveled-looking, and raggedly dressed girl walked up to her and meekly asked if Anna had any food she could spare. Impulsively Anna handed the girl her snack, and—like typical adolescent girls—the two began to talk. Anna's new friend said her name was Ilona Katz, she too was thirteen years old, and, despite the German she spoke, she was Hungarian. She was also Jewish and starving.[1]

Ilona Katz was among the thousands of Hungarian Jews who had been deported to Austria instead of Nazi death camps after the Nazi takeover of Hungary in the spring of 1944. As the Soviet Red Army drove German forces out of the Soviet Union and across Poland toward Germany, the Nazis lost their supply of slave labor from the regions taken by the Soviets. The shortage of slave labor threatened to impair German war-related industries in Austria, which remained part of Greater Germany. In response to the crisis, the Nazis had diverted more than seventeen thousand Hungarian Jews to the country, several thousand to Vienna. There, the Jewish men were sent off to do heavy labor. The women and children were housed under guard in schools, factories, or vacant buildings, and were put to work in munitions factories and oil refineries, or were forced to clear rubble from the Allied bombing raids. Children Ilona's age or younger were among those forced to haul off rubble—a dangerous job that killed or injured many when unstable buildings collapsed.[2]

"Her deed was a lifesaving act for us."

"We went to bombed-out buildings right after the air raids," a Jew who had been a teenager at the time later remembered. "They used us to get into places where adults could not go. We had to carry out the corpses, the injured, and all the valuables. When we found only a limb or any other human body part, we had to carry those out too.... Several [children] died when they fell from somewhere. They were replaced with even younger children." As slave laborers, the captive Jews were fed a starvation diet or nothing at all, and children like Ilona begged and scrounged for food for themselves and their families. If caught, they were severely punished. "I was a little child...," recalled a Jewish woman. "A German lady passed by and I also started begging her to give me a piece of bread. When I wanted to go back the guard caught me and asked, 'Where have you been?' Then he noticed the bread in my hands. He took me to the shelter where there was a tight, small room full of garbage. He locked me in there [and] hit my head with his gun... Despite the fact that my head was bleeding I was locked in that storage. The door was closed and I was crying and begging the guards to let me out. I was extremely scared of the darkness. And when my mother came back from work she heard that I was elsewhere. She approached the guard and begged him to set me free since I was so young. The guard reluctantly complied, but with a warning: 'Tell her, if she dares to beg for food again something much worse will happen to her.'"[3]

Despite the danger many Austrians in Vienna, such as Anna and her family, reached out to the Jewish slave laborers brought into their midst in 1944. "We had to shovel the snow," one such laborer later recounted. "I and my cousin managed to escape and hide in the staircase of a bomb-damaged house, because we were very cold. After a while, one of the residents came home. She entered the lift and came back with milk and slices of bread with margarine. She gave us food and drink and asked us to place the milk bottle next to the lift afterward. Her deed was a lifesaving act for us, because we had already been completely drenched and frozen in the cold. Outside it was minus 15 degrees and the wind was cold."[4]

The day after she met her new Jewish friend, Anna Ehn went back to find her with more food. The two met again. She learned that Ilona had five brothers and sisters, and that the Katz family had been uprooted from its home in Hungary and brought to Vienna as slave laborers. All of them were facing hunger. Anna was deeply moved. In wartime there was little to spare, but she arranged to take food to Ilona every day. Day after day, week after week, the thirteen-year-old provided food for her Jewish friend and her family. One day Ilona greeted her with a frightening story. Her older sister had been injured in a bombing raid. She had been taken with other victims to the nearest medical facility—which had turned out to be a hospital for SS troops. Jewish slave laborers who were too ill or injured to work were shipped away to death camps. If hospital staffers realized that her sister was Jewish, she could disappear forever, as had so many others.[5]

Anna had a solution: She would go to the SS hospital to see Ilona's sister—and she would ask the hospital staff to release the girl into her care. Anna was unusually mature-acting for a thirteen-year-old, but both girls knew the plan was exceedingly dangerous. If SS soldiers at the hospital realized that Ilona's sister was Jewish and that Anna wanted to take her home, Anna would be labeled a "Jew-lover," and that could be deadly for her and her family. Still she went. Boldly and alone, Anna walked to the hospital, located Ilona's sister, talked to the hospital staff, and explained that she would take the girl home with her so she could recover without remaining in the hospital. Wartime hospitals in places like Vienna were crowded with air raid victims and beds were in constant demand, so perhaps Anna's request seemed reasonable. Whatever the reason, someone at the hospital agreed, and Anna escorted the injured Jewish girl out of harm's way, past the convalescing SS soldiers, away from the hospital, and to her home. There Ilona's sister remained until she recovered and went back to her family.[6]

Anna meanwhile continued to meet Ilona daily and bring her food. Then one day her Jewish friend failed to appear. Nor did she ever return. Soviet forces had entered Austria, and were advancing on Vienna. The Nazis hastily deported Vienna's Jewish slave laborers to Mauthausen concentration camp, which was located in upper Austria. It had been a camp for political prisoners and Soviet prisoners of war, but as Soviet forces overran Nazi concentration camps in Poland, Jewish survivors were sent to Mauthausen along with the Jewish slave laborers from Hungary. More than fourteen thousand Jews died in Mauthausen—but Ilona and her sister somehow survived. Anna Ehn would not learn that for decades. She too survived the war, grew to adulthood in postwar Austria, got married, and over her lifetime had children and grandchildren. Only then did she learn that the thirteen-year-old Jewish girl she had befriended on the street in Vienna had survived the Holocaust and was living in Israel—thanks in no small part to Anna Ehn's unprejudiced childhood heart.[7]

CHAPTER 28
ERNEST AND RENÉE LEPILEUR

American troops wade ashore under fire at Omaha Beach on D-Day, June 6, 1944. (CREDIT: NATIONAL ARCHIVES)

"They welcomed us like we were their own daughters."

JUNE THE SIXTH was a day that Ernest and Renée Lepileur would never forget. They were a French husband and wife living on the family farm near the city of Saint-Lô in Normandy, and like other Normans they had endured German military occupation for four years. Throughout all that time, as they lived under the threatening shadow of German uniforms, they yearned for *la libération de la France*—the day when Allied forces would invade France and free them from German occupation. They were overjoyed when they heard the long-awaited news: American, British, and Canadian troops had landed on the northwest coast of France—in Normandy—on D-Day, June 6, 1944. With the heartening news, however, came a new surge of fear: The fighting would surely come their way, making the German occupation troops even more alert. That could be deadly for the Lepileurs: German troops were already billeted on their farm—unaware that the Lepileurs were hiding two small Jewish children in their farmhouse.[1]

⸺

Their dangerous mission of hiding Jews had begun two years earlier in 1942, when Ernest Lepileur drove his horse-drawn covered cart to the train station in Saint-Lô. Given to wearing a traditional French beret, Lepileur was a tall, middle-aged man with a farmer's hands and a kindly, sun-wrinkled face. At the train station, he was met by a Catholic priest and two small, well-dressed girls: Janine and Suzy Fruchter, ages four and six. They were Jewish children from Paris, where their parents feared the family would be deported in the Nazi roundup of Parisian Jews. They had turned their children over to a priest, Father Louis Jeanne, who was working with the Jewish community in Paris to hide Jewish children from the Nazis. Father Jeanne had been born in Normandy and knew the Lepileur family. Believing the little girls would be safer on the Lepileur farm in the Norman countryside, he had made inquiries and the Lepileurs had volunteered to take the girls into safekeeping, even though they had three older children themselves.[2]

Janine and Suzy were bright, cheerful, and affectionate children, and as Lepileur's horse plodded along the back roads near Saint-Lô, pulling the cart homeward, the children quickly lost their fear and reveled in the country life they had never known in Paris. At the Lepileurs' aging stone farmhouse, the girls were greeted by the Lepileurs' twenty-three-year-old daughter Denise and her mother Renée Lepileur. A stocky, dark-haired homemaker, Madame Lepileur welcomed the girls with bowls of warm vegetable soup and bread with currant jam waiting on the kitchen table. "The farmhouse was lovely," Suzy recalled as an adult. "It was a wonderful time for us." The Lepileurs brought in a tutor to help Suzy keep up her schooling, but four-year-old Janine was interested only in the farm animals. "Because I was so small, I was allowed to ride on the donkey, and Mr. Lepileur would slip me a little coffee sweetened with sugar."[3]

"The Lepileurs brought light into our lives."

Ernest and Renée Lepileur became the grandparents that the Jewish girls had never known. Madame Lepileur doted on them, and Monsieur Lepileur made them Norman-style wooden clogs to wear. Denise Lepileur became the loving big sister who bathed them, brushed their hair, told them stories, and sang to them. The family told no one that the girls were Jewish: They told anyone who was curious that the little girls were distant relatives whose parents had sent them to the farm to escape the stress of wartime Paris. The girls were very knowledgeable about their Jewish heritage, and once Suzy chattered away to Ernest Lepileur about what she had learned from the Hebrew Bible—the Old Testament. Impressed, Lepileur listened attentively, then reassured her that God is loving and good. "The Lepileurs brought light into our lives," Suzy later explained, "with no regard for the risk they were taking."[4]

Then the Germans came. By the spring of 1944, the German high command expected an Allied invasion of France, even in Normandy, but believed the landing would occur near the port of Pas de Calais, at the narrowest point of the English Channel, which was far from Saint-Lô. Even so, that spring the Germans strengthened their defenses around Saint-Lô, a transportation center in Normandy, and German troops were billeted around the Lepileur farm. "The Germans moved onto the farm," Janine later remembered. "They killed our chickens and our rooster and ate them." German troops frequently passed back and forth through the farm without warning, which made the Lepileurs fear for the safety of the two girls. What if the Germans learned the children were Jewish? One day little Janine was playing outside the farmhouse when a patrol of German troops wandered into the yard. When Renée Lepileur saw the soldiers, she hurried outside to bring in the child—and what she encountered sent a bolt of fear through her body: Little Janine was sitting in the lap of a German soldier, who was singing to her in German. Perhaps the soldier missed his own children and was merely being friendly, but what if Janine happily began chattering about being Jewish as her sister had done with Ernest Lepileur? Suppressing her fright, Madame Lepileur politely retrieved the child from the soldier and carried her inside.[5]

In the early-morning darkness of D-Day, more than fifteen thousand American and British paratroopers landed on the Cotentin Peninsula in Normandy, seizing key crossroads and bridges for the seaborne invasion troops. Beginning at dawn on June 6, an armada of more than six thousand Allied warships and landing craft put approximately 156,000 Allied troops ashore on beaches code-named Omaha, Utah, Gold, Juno, and Sword. American troops suffered heavy fighting and serious casualties on Omaha Beach, but by day's end Allied forces were driving inland, and the area's German defenders were on the retreat. The Allied advance was soon stalled by heavy German reinforcements, however, whose stubborn defense transformed Normandy's hedgerow country into a bloody battlefield. Finally, at the end of July, Allied forces broke out of Normandy and began a rapid advance toward Paris—which brought savage fighting into the city of Saint-Lô and the surrounding countryside.[6]

Saint-Lô was a provincial capital, an agricultural marketplace, and a regional transportation center. Allied planners had deemed it a vital point that had to be captured for the Normandy Campaign to succeed—and its German defenders were equally determined to hold it. As the fighting approached, German troops commandeered the Lepileur farm and transformed the family's stone farmhouse into a command post—which made it a target for advancing American troops and supporting aircraft. The Germans gave the family twenty-four hours to pack up and leave. Hurriedly, the family fled, using their horse-drawn cart and the family bicycles. They spent the nights sleeping in fields, trying to stay ahead of the fighting. Once a German fighter aircraft strafed the road where they were fleeing along with other refugees, stitching it with a spray of bullets but missing the family. Later, just as they had crossed over a bridge, it was struck by a bomb and blown to pieces. The plan to protect Janine and Suzy by moving them away from the Nazi threat in Paris to pastoral Normandy had actually placed them in the midst of a bloody battle. Finally, after days and nights of traveling the back roads of Normandy, the family reached the safety of a friend's farmhouse far from the fighting.[7]

There, with German troops far away, the family—and their Jewish children—were out of harm's way. They remained there for weeks, waiting for news and hoping they could soon return home. On July 19, 1944, American troops captured the city of Saint-Lô after prolonged and savage fighting. At month's end, the Lepileurs made their way back to the family farm. What they found was shocking: The provincial capital of Saint-Lô was a mass of debris—now dubbed the Capital of Ruins—and the Lepileur farmhouse had been destroyed by the fighting. Much worse, the Lepileurs' seventeen-year-old son curiously examined an unexploded artillery shell he found in the farmyard, and was killed when it detonated. Sustained by their faith, Ernest and Renée Lepileur resumed their lives. With peace at hand in Normandy, they cleared the rubble from their farm and began the task of rebuilding their home, still caring for Janine and Suzy—who no longer had to worry about German troops suddenly appearing in the farmyard.[8]

By December 1944, Allied forces had liberated almost all of France, Belgium, and Luxembourg, and most of Holland. With the Germans gone, Janine and Suzy could return to Paris. There they were reunited with their parents, both of whom had managed to survive the German occupation. Neither girl would ever forget the "grandparents" and "big sister" who had protected them from the horrors of the Holocaust. Decades later Janine marveled at the sacrificial love she and her sister had received from the Lepileurs. "They welcomed us," she said, "like we were their own daughters."[9]

CHAPTER 29

RODRICK EDMONDS

When Master Sergeant Roddie Edmonds was ordered at gunpoint to surrender all Jewish soldiers under his command to his Nazi captors, he defiantly replied, "We're all Jews."

(CREDIT: RODDIEEDMONDS.COM)

"We are all Jews."

TWENTY-FIVE-YEAR-OLD RODDIE EDMONDS stood unflinching as a German officer pointed an army pistol at him point-blank and threatened to pull the trigger. A master sergeant in the US Army's 422nd Infantry Regiment, Edmonds was the senior noncommissioned officer at Stalag IX-A, a German prison camp where more than one thousand American prisoners of war were held captive in January of 1945. Earlier the camp's Nazi commander had ordered all American prisoners who were Jewish to assemble for a roll call so they could be identified and incarcerated together. In response, Sergeant Edmonds had ordered every American POW in the camp to assemble. The camp commander was incredulous—and incensed. "They cannot all be Jews!" he barked at Edmonds in English. Boldly the sergeant firmly replied, "We are all Jews." At that the Nazi officer drew his service pistol and aimed it at Edmonds, who was just inches away.[1]

A blond-headed mountain boy from Knoxville, Tennessee, Rodrick "Roddie" Edmonds had the stocky look of a college fullback. He had grown up in the Southern Bible Belt, and according to his son Chris, a Southern Baptist pastor, he surrendered his life to Jesus Christ before joining the army in 1941. "He just lived by the Golden Rule," the younger Edmonds said, "and tried to be a Good Samaritan." He rose quickly to the rank of master sergeant—which many troops called the "backbone" of the US Army—and saw combat at the Battle of the Bulge in December 1944. By then Allied forces had driven the German army out of almost all of France, through Belgium, and back into Germany.

American troops had almost outdistanced their supply line, and—believing the German army was in full retreat—the American high command allowed US troops to halt in the Ardennes region of Belgium to rest and recuperate. American military planners, however, had underestimated the strength and fighting ability of the German army.[2]

On December 16, 1944, Hitler launched a massive counterattack through Belgium and Luxembourg, unleashing more than two hundred thousand German troops and almost one thousand panzer tanks against unsuspecting American troops in the Ardennes. The American line bulged backward for sixty miles, giving the battle its name, and German forces spearheaded by elite SS troops initially made dramatic gains. American troops recovered and fought back, however, slowing the German advance until reinforcements rushed from throughout France could join the battle. By late January of 1945, German forces were on the retreat, out of fuel and pounded by American airpower. Hitler's mighty counteroffensive had failed, leaving Germany open to invasion by American and British forces from the west as Soviet forces advanced from the east. The Battle of the Bulge was the largest battle ever fought by the US military, involving almost one million American and German troops and costing sixty-seven thousand American and one hundred thousand German casualties.[3]

It also resulted in one of the largest mass surrenders of US troops in World War II. On the opening day of the German attack, two regiments of the US Army's 106th Infantry Division—the 422nd and the 423rd—were surrounded and cut off by the powerful German advance. After three days of fighting, the two regiments were almost out of ammunition, food, and medical supplies, and their commanding officers felt compelled to surrender. Almost seven thousand American soldiers became German prisoners of war. "The roads are littered with wrecked American vehicles," a German officer penned in his diary after the surrender. "Another column

passes. I count over a thousand men. Nearby there is another column of about 1,500, with about 50 officers." Sergeant Roddie
Edmonds was captured with the 422nd Infantry Regiment, but not
before demonstrating his leadership skills. "We were in combat on
the front lines for only a short period, but it was clear that Roddie
Edmonds was a man of great courage...," one of Edmonds's soldiers later recalled. "He did not throw his rank around. You knew
that he knew his stuff and he got across to you without being arro-
gant or inconsiderate. I admired him."[4]

After a bone-chilling trip in a freezing, overcrowded railway boxcar, Edmonds found himself as the senior noncommissioned officer in a German prison camp called Stalag IX-A, a
sprawling collection of wood and tarpaper buildings enclosed by
machine-gun towers and barbed wire located about thirty-five
miles southeast of Cologne. Almost immediately the camp's German commandant began taking action to identify the American
POWs who were Jewish. Unknown to Edmonds, Nazi policy was
to isolate Jewish prisoners of war for slave labor or deportation
to death camps. At other camps housing American prisoners of
war, the Nazis were already assembling Jewish GIs to serve as slave
laborers at Berga concentration camp—a Nazi-run slate mine
located near the Czechoslovakian border in eastern Germany.[5]

"If you shoot me, you will have to shoot all of us."

At Stalag IX-B—a sister camp to Stalag IX-A—American prisoners of war were ordered to identify their religion on what the
Germans falsely claimed to be a Red Cross personnel card. If a
prisoner refused to cooperate, he was threatened with beatings or
starvation. "When these cards had been filled out," a Jewish GI
later reported, "the German authorities insisted on the segrega-
tion of American prisoners of war who had indicated they were
Jewish." Over the protests of the senior American officer at Stalag
IX-B, 350 American prisoners of war were selected for deportation

to Berga—mainly those who had identified themselves as Jewish or who "looked Jewish" to the Germans, although a number of American "troublemakers" were also included.[6]

At Berga concentration camp, the American prisoners of war encountered the deadly conditions that the Nazis typically imposed on civilian Jews and others who were sent to slave labor camps. Fed a starvation diet, the men were forced every day to march two miles to the slate mine, sometimes trudging through deep snow without adequate winter clothing. Working in mine shafts more than 150 feet deep, they used sledgehammers to break up huge chunks of slate that had been dynamited from the mine walls for use in munitions. "Surviving was all you thought about," a Jewish American soldier later reported. "You were so worn down you didn't even think of all the death that was around you." Some American prisoners of war died of exhaustion. Some succumbed to lung congestion from the slate fumes or died of other illnesses. Others were shot to death by German guards. After the camp was overtaken by advancing Allied troops, the survivors were liberated and hospitalized.[7]

Sergeant Edmonds did not know what fate awaited the Jewish soldiers at Stalag IX-A if they were turned over to the Nazis, but rumors were circulating in the ranks that the Nazis were murdering Jews—and he was willing to risk his life to protect the Jewish soldiers under his command. So on January 27, 1945, when the camp commandant demanded that he assemble all the camp's Jewish soldiers, Edmonds ordered every American soldier in Stalag IX-A at that time to fall in on the camp parade ground. His explanation—"We are all Jews"—enraged the German commandant, but Edmonds defiantly stood his ground even when the officer trained his pistol on him.[8]

Unintimidated, Edmonds looked the officer in the face. "According to the Geneva Convention, we only have to give our name, rank and serial number," he said. "I can still hear the words he said to the German camp officer," Paul Stern, one of the Jewish soldiers in the ranks that day, recalled seventy years later. Germany had ratified the 1929 Geneva convention accords, which protected the rights of prisoners of war, but the Nazis routinely violated them—and the German officer threatened to shoot the sergeant on the spot if he did not give up the Jewish soldiers under his command. "If you shoot me," Edmonds replied evenly, "you will have to shoot all of us. And after the war you will be tried for war crimes." The two men stood face-to-face, only inches apart. It was a life-and-death moment. Then the German commandant turned and stomped away. The Jewish soldiers under Edmonds's command were saved, and on March 30, 1945, victorious American troops liberated Stalag IX-A. Back home in Tennessee, Roddie Edmonds pursued a career in sales, raised his family, was active in his church—and never mentioned his heroic act at Stalag IX-A. Only after his death in 1985 did his story surface. In 2015, he became the first American soldier to be named as Righteous Among the Nations by Israel's Yad Vashem.[9]

CHAPTER 30
PŘEMYSL PITTER

Přemysl Pitter saved countless Jewish children from the Holocaust, then, at war's end, ministered to Jewish children who had survived the Nazi death camps.
(CREDIT: NARODNI PEDAGOGICAL MUSEUM)

"Any doctrine that deifies the State is devilish."

ADOLF HITLER SEATED himself on a couch in the private quarters of his underground bunker in Berlin, and bit down on a small glass capsule filled with cyanide as he shot himself in the head with a 7.65mm Walther handgun. Beside him his longtime mistress and newly married wife, Eva Braun, also killed herself with a cyanide capsule. It was three thirty p.m. on Monday, April 30, 1945. The Nazi dictator who had brought death to millions of people, including six million Jews, and misery and suffering to millions more, was dead, and Nazi Germany died with him. Hitler had boasted that his Nazi empire would last for a thousand years, but despite its unprecedented horrors, it existed barely a dozen—and at the end it collapsed as rapidly as it had arisen. The German army's counter-attack at the Battle of the Bulge was Hitler's last desperate gamble, and it failed. In January of 1945, Soviet forces launched a massive offensive from the Eastern Front in Poland, unleashing 250,000 battle-hardened troops into Germany toward the Nazi capital of Berlin like a mighty, unstoppable tidal wave.[1]

Meanwhile, an equally irrepressible tide of American and British forces surged through Germany from the west. Germany's war industry and its sources of steel, coal, and oil were destroyed or captured, putting the Germany military in a chokehold, while American and British airpower destroyed the German air force—the Luftwaffe—and gave the Allies command of the skies. Despite a temporary setback in Holland, American and British forces crossed the Rhine river into Germany and were on the outskirts of Berlin by late April. General Dwight D. Eisenhower, the Allied commander, allowed Soviet forces to be the first to fight their way into the German capital. Berlin was transformed into a sea of fire, and Hitler was driven into the Führerbunker—the underground shelter beneath his offices in the battered German Chancellery. There, surrounded by approaching Soviet troops, with the muffled sounds of Russian artillery exploding overhead, Adolf Hitler helplessly witnessed the death of his dream of world conquest—which had proven a deadly nightmare for millions.[2]

One of his top generals recalled the appearance of the once-mighty German Führer near the end: "His fists raised, his cheeks flushed with rage, his whole body trembling, the man stood there in front of me, beside himself with fury and having lost all self-control.... He was almost screaming, his eyes seemed to pop out of his head and the veins stood out on his temples." By the end Hitler could do little more than rage: Nazi Germany's political and military power had suffered total ruin. Just before marrying his mistress in the bunker map room, Hitler dictated his last will and testament. In it he sarcastically and irrationally condemned the Jewish people he had so fervently attempted to exterminate. "Centuries will pass away," he stated, "but...the hatred will ever renew itself against those ultimately responsible whom we have to thank for everything: international Jewry and its helpers." Finally, as Soviet troops fought their way door-to-door toward his bunker, the fifty-six-year-old Hitler ate lunch with his bride, bade farewell to his top aides, and then committed suicide. As he had ordered, his body and his wife's were carried outside the bunker and burned so they could not be captured by his enemies. With Hitler dead, German military forces quickly surrendered. Four more months would be required for Allied forces to battle Imperial Japan into submission, but on May 8, 1945, the war in Europe officially ended.[3]

Some two hundred miles south of Berlin in Prague, Czechoslovakia, forty-four-year-old Přemysl Pitter learned the news of Hitler's death and the Nazi surrender with deep relief: For more than six years he had been hiding Jewish children from the Nazis. Tall, graying, with a receding hairline and a kindly face, Pitter had once expected to be shipped to a concentration camp himself; now the war was over and he had survived. But so many had not—especially within Europe's Jewish families. What would happen to their surviving children, who were now orphans? How many were still alive in the Nazi death camps? How would they get home? And who would take care of them? It was typical of Pitter to think of others more than himself—and to have a heart for the orphaned children of Europe's persecuted Jews. It was also typical of Pitter to try to do something to help—and he did.[4]

A native of Prague, Přemysl Pitter was an evangelical Christian who had committed his life to Jesus Christ as Lord and Savior. As a young man he had apprenticed as a printer, but had been drafted and forced to serve in the Austro-Hungarian Army alongside the Germans. He had no heart for it, and after the war he became a Christian, and helped establish a children's home in Prague's poorest neighborhood, which had many Jewish residents. After school, children who had destitution and despair awaiting them at home could come to Pitter's Milíč House, where they would be fed and could safely play, read, listen to music, learn crafts, or participate in gymnastics. "We forgot the poor conditions at home," a former student recalled long afterward. "Probably no one else in Europe built such a beautiful house for children. It was fantastic." In 1939, when Hitler ordered the invasion of Czechoslovakia, increasing numbers of Jewish children arrived at Pitter's children's home—and for more than afternoon recreation; they were seeking safety from the Nazis.[5]

"He reminded them that Jesus was Jewish too."

Nazi laws forbade them to attend public school, so at first Jewish children came to Milíč House to study. Eventually, however, as the Holocaust swept Czechoslovakia's Jews into deadly camps such as Theresienstadt, Treblinka, Majdanek, and Auschwitz, Jewish children came to Milíč House to hide. Some were left behind when their parents were taken, and were rescued by Pitter. Others were brought to the home by their parents to save them from deportation. With the help of a Swiss teacher named Olga Fierz, Pitter tried to provide a welcoming refuge for the Jewish children. "We all called him 'Uncle,'" a survivor recalled, "and we could turn to him with our fears or problems. When we gathered in the big room, he would talk to us, sometimes using the Bible as his starting point." Recalled another, "He told the Jewish children that the star they had to wear was something they could be proud of, and he reminded them that Jesus was Jewish too."[6]

Despite the risk, Pitter also befriended Jewish families in Prague who were under Nazi persecution, often bringing them food as conditions in Nazi-occupied Czechoslovakia worsened. As deportations increased, so did the danger to the Jewish children who were left behind. To protect them, Pitter sent them to safe houses in a rural area about fifty miles from Prague. He realized that he was under surveillance by the Gestapo, but he continued to shelter Jewish children anyway. One day Gestapo agents appeared at the children's home and took Pitter away to Gestapo headquarters. Ominously, Pitter was told to bring a suitcase with travel clothes. When he was gone, the Christian staff assembled and prayed for his safe return. During his interrogation by the local Gestapo chief, Pitter admitted that he was protecting Jewish children. Why, his interrogator asked, would he take such a risk for Jews? "From a human point of view," Pitter replied, "I'm sure you can understand why I'm helping these children." The Nazi stared at Pitter silently for a long moment, then said, "You may go." Back at the children's home, Pitter and the staff celebrated a miracle.[7]

An unknown number of Jewish children survived the Holocaust due to Pitter's efforts, and his outreach to Jewish children and others in need did not end with the war. As Nazi resistance collapsed, American and Soviet armies entered Czechoslovakia from opposite sides. Soviet forces occupied Prague on May 9, 1945, forcing the city's German defenders to surrender. Days earlier German troops in Prague had defeated an uprising by the Czech resistance at a cost of more than three thousand Czech civilians. When a newly formed Czech government was established, Přemysl Pitter was asked to locate and care for Jewish orphans from Czechoslovakia. He accepted the offer and pursued the task with typical zeal, soon locating hundreds of Jewish children orphaned by the Holocaust—and they were from Austria, Poland, the Ukraine, and elsewhere, as well as Czechoslovakia. They were housed in rambling abandoned homes that Pitter and the children called "castles."[8]

Most were youthful survivors of Nazi concentration camps. Their parents had died in gas chambers, and they had no homes awaiting them. Their appearance was shocking to the unprepared—skeletal bodies that resembled children. Typically, they were physically ill and weak—and psychologically traumatized. Most spoke in the whispered tones they had learned to use as frightened children in the camps. In Pitter's "castles" they received medical care, clothing, uninterrupted opportunities to sleep, and, for many, adequate food for the first time in years. At first some hid their food in their clothes, saving it for later in case there was no more. Eventually, however, under Pitter's loving care, they slowly began to emerge from the furtive, fearful attitudes that had helped them survive in death camps. "In the castles, we tried to free ourselves of the shock that we had suffered as children in concentration camps," one Jewish boy would later explain. "Peace and warmth and faith in human kindness returned—all of which we had lost entirely." Recalled another, "We didn't trust anybody after the war. Why should people be kind and good to us? And here we met Premysl Pitter, who was for us at that time a symbol of goodness, and he slowly won our hearts and minds. We trusted again."[9]

After a six-year German occupation, the war in Czechoslovakia had ended in a bloodbath—the Prague Uprising—which left countless Czechs vengeful and embittered when peace finally came. German civilians who had worked for the occupation government were killed in the streets; others were lynched on country roads. Thousands of German civilians were placed in an internment camp outside Prague, awaiting eventual return to Germany. Conditions in the camp were horrific. Unconcerned, many Czechs whose relatives had been killed by the Nazis believed it was time for the Germans among them to suffer. But not Pitter. He heard of conditions in the camp, went to see for himself—and was shocked by what he found. "Thousands of people were forced to sleep on the bare ground without blankets," he later reported. "The very sick and children lay in the blazing sun in unthinkable filth with flies crawling everywhere." Pitter too had cause to hate the Germans, but as a Christian he did not want to duplicate the sins of the Nazis—nor did he want the long-suffering Czech people to do so.[10]

He urged the Czech government to provide better treatment for the incarcerated German families. Such pleas did not endear him to Czech officials, who now functioned under the Soviet occupation army, and had little sympathy for their former enemies. Undeterred, Pitter began rescuing German orphans too— including the children of Nazis. Mixing non-Jewish German orphans and Jewish orphans seemed potentially disastrous. Instead, the children provided an extraordinary example of tolerance. Understandably, the Jewish children recoiled when they encountered German boys still wearing their Hitler Youth uniforms, but such fears disappeared along with the old clothing. Jewish children who had experienced the Nazi death camps were, some observed, "disturbingly independent, mature and unchildlike." Pitter, the devout Protestant, would later note that it had been the Jewish children—the Holocaust survivors—who proved most willing to put aside fear and hatred. "We children who had just come back from the camps had much more understanding and in a way even compassion," one of the Jewish orphans later observed. "I believe that when somebody has suffered so much, he can have another kind of relationship—even to the people who gave him so much trouble."[11]

Eventually most of Pitter's "castle children" were placed with new families, including more than seven hundred who were flown to Great Britain by the government at the urging of Britain's Jewish community. Přemysl Pitter, meanwhile, gained international recognition for his attempts to care for the lost children of the Holocaust. The admiration, however, was not shared by Czechoslovakia's new rulers. At war's end Soviet dictator Joseph Stalin refused to withdraw Soviet troops from most of the territory that the Russians had "liberated," and eastern European nations such as Czechoslovakia traded Nazi oppression for Communist oppression. Pitter continued to care for Czech orphans at Milíč House, but beginning in 1948, Czechoslovakia's Communist rulers insisted that he transform the home into an indoctrination center for Czech youth. Pitter refused, and was threatened with deportation to a uranium mine where he would work as a slave laborer. In 1951, he managed to escape to West Germany. There he again assisted refugees. Later he moved to Switzerland, authored several books, and worked for Radio Free Europe, which broadcast messages of freedom to the nations enslaved by Communism.[12]

Remembering the horrors of Adolf Hitler's Nazi Germany, he often expressed his concern about the shift of postwar Western culture from a Judeo-Christian consensus to a secular humanist perspective. The historic Judeo-Christian worldview accepted God as the authority over all things and the rightful center of human focus, while humanism claimed mankind to be the sole authority and preferred center of focus. In Pitter's opinion such a shift in worldview—from God-centered to man-centered—was nothing less than "modern Paganism." Without Jesus Christ, the

Bible taught, man's inherent sinful nature would inevitably draw him toward a darkened heart. As a former SS officer observed, "There is a darkness lurking in the soul of man that opens his heart to . . . the swastika." Pitter believed that such darkness lurked in the "modern Paganism" that was progressively being embraced by postwar Western culture and its governments.

He traveled, wrote, and spoke about the need to be vigilant— to evaluate all things, especially government leaders and policies— according to Judeo-Christian values. Always, until his death in 1976, he shared the lessons that he had learned from the Holocaust and the ungodly way it had devalued human life—including the right of children to life. "People and nations who sin against children," he predicted, "will eventually experience misery." Přemysl Pitter had experienced firsthand the horror and tragedy that had arisen when the German people and others abandoned biblical morality to embrace the state as savior and provider. The Holocaust that had victimized the innocent Jews of Europe, he believed, could happen again to Jews or others—if the Western world, like Nazi Germany, came to accept government as God. "Any doctrine that deifies the State is devilish," he warned, "and will eventually lead to national disaster."[13]

ACKNOWLEDGMENTS

At war's end, three European children study the wreckage of a German panzer tank. By then, two-thirds of Europe's Jews had perished in the Holocaust.

(CREDIT: IMPERIAL WAR MUSEUM)

No one writes a book alone. I am thankful to the many people who contributed to this one. My thanks to FaithWords executive editor Joey Paul, for his insight and direction on this book. I'm equally grateful to my literary agent, Steve Laube, for his valuable advice, and for recognizing the potential of this book from the beginning. Many thanks also to the team at FaithWords and Hachette Book Group in developing this title, especially to Becky Hughes and Luria Rittenberg, who provided skillful editorial assistance, and to Sadie Klein for her expert copyediting insights. The handsome jacket design is the work of Jody Waldrup. Sandra Tuttle, the gifted designer at NewMedia Digital in Myrtle Beach, crafted the book's map of Europe.

Researching and writing this book reminded me once more how deeply thankful I am for my dear friends Mort and Deborah Künstler and their daughter Jane, whose friendship and Jewish values have been a special blessing to me over the years. I'm also grateful to my friend and mentor the Reverend Randy Riddle for his constant encouragement, and to my close friends and prayer partners Mark Roach, Stoval Witte, and David Frost. Special thanks also to my pastor, Rick Adkins, and to family friend and prayer warrior Weeza Smith. I'm grateful too for the support I receive from the administration at Coastal Carolina University and from George Goldfinch and the advisory board of the CresCom Bank Center for Military & Veterans Studies. Special thanks too are due Elizabeth Smith Cannon for her timely French translation skills, and to her husband, Jesse, for sharing her time.

Numerous research and archival institutions graciously assisted the research for this work. I'm very grateful to Yad Vashem: The World Holocaust Remembrance Center in Jerusalem, and especially to Emanuel Saunders of the Yad Vashem Photo Archive. My sincere thanks to staff members at the United States Holocaust Memorial Museum in Washington, D.C., the Library of Congress, the National Archives, Deutsches-Bundesarchiv, the Imperial War Museum, Camp Vught National Memorial, Auschwitz-Birkenau Memorial and Museum, the Museum of Danish Resistance, the Rijksmuseum of Amsterdam, the Corrie ten Boom Museum, Marie de selliers and the Musée du Pays d'Ourthe-Amblève, Kobrin Photo Archive, Arkiv i Nordland, the United States Army Military History Institute, the Dwight D. Eisenhower Presidential Library and Museum, Goshen College, the National Pedagogical Museum, the National Museum of Denmark, and Kimbel Library at Coastal Carolina University. Special thanks are also due Trey Harris, Geoffrey and Else Ward, Johann Schediwy, Karl Marth, Dafna Itzkovich, Simon Viallon, Gili Diamant, Brian Yoder, Henrik Lundbak, the Reverend Chris Edmonds, and my friends at Conway Christian School. I owe a unique debt to my parents, Skip and Elizabeth Gragg, who sparked my lifelong love of history. I'm also very grateful for my brother Ted, and my cousins Bob, Charles, and Tony, who inspired my love of history—and for Connie, Sandra, Martha, and "Aunty" Delores for sharing them with me. And I am extremely thankful for the encouragement I have received from Deborah, Margaret, Joe, Jackie, Doug, Tina, John, Gail, Jimmy, Newt, and Mama-O. An award should go to my faithful family for enduring all my stories, repeatedly. Deep love and appreciation to Faith, Troy, Rachel, Jay, Elizabeth, Jon, Joni, Penny, Ryan, Skip, Matt, and Miranda—and to Kylah, Sophia, Cody, Jaxon, Gracie, Ashlyn, Ty, Jate, and Leyton. Always, my deepest love and appreciation to my wife, Cindy, who remains my cherished Proverbs 31 woman. Finally, I am grateful and eternally blessed by the abiding truth of Isaiah 53:5.

NOTES

Chapter 1. Feng Shan Ho

1. William L. Shirer, *The Rise and Fall of the Third Reich: A History of Nazi Germany,* New York: Simon & Schuster, 1960: 334–39; Robert T. Elson, *Prelude to War,* New York: Time-Life Books, 1977: 84–95.

2. John Toland, *Adolf Hitler: The Definitive Biography,* New York: Doubleday, 1976: 432–58; Shirer, *Rise and Fall of the Third Reich*: 334–39; Elson, *Prelude to War*: 84–95.

3. Feng-Shan Ho, *My Forty Years as a Diplomat,* edited and translated by Monto Ho, Pittsburgh: Dorrance Publishing, 2010: 2–9, 30–50, 117–26; Edmond Yee, *The Soaring Crane: The Story of Asian Lutherans in North America,* Minneapolis: Ausburg Fortress, 1998: 91–92; Manli Ho, "Feng Shan Ho," Center for Holocaust and Genocide Studies, University of Minnesota; "Chinese Visas in Vienna," Righteous Among the Nations, yadvashem.org; Jay Taylor, *The Generalissimo: Chiang Kai–Shek and the Struggle for Modern China,* Cambridge, MA: Harvard University Press, 2009: 101–6; Toland, *Adolf Hitler*: 410.

4. Joe O'Connor, "Miracle Man: How One Chinese Diplomat Saved Thousands of Jews from the Death Camps," *National Post,* November 1, 2011; Manli Ho, *Diplomat Rescuers and the Story of Feng Shan Ho,* Vancouver: Vancouver Holocaust Center, 1999: 2–23; "Chinese Visas in Vienna," Righteous Among the Nations.

5. Ian Kershaw, *Hitler: A Biography,* New York: W. W. Norton, 1998: 54–73, 113–28; Toland, *Adolf Hitler*: 3–27, 93–121.

6. Kershaw, *Hitler*: 54–73, 113–28; Fritz Redlich, *Hitler: Diagnosis of a Destructive Prophet,* New York: Oxford University Press, 2000: 22–29, 36–39, 42–48, 61–68; Toland, *Adolf Hitler*: 181–204.

7. Kershaw, *Hitler*: 144–49, 197–212; Toland, *Adolf Hitler*: 233–56, 329–38; Redlich, *Hitler*: 265–66.

8. Ho, *Forty Years as a Diplomat,* 30–49: "Chinese Visas in Vienna," Righteous Among the Nations; Yee, *Soaring Crane*: 91–92; Ho, *Diplomat Rescuers*: 2–23; Shirer, *Rise and Fall of the Third Reich*: 334–39; Elson, *Prelude to War*: 84–95; Felicity J. Rash, *The Language of Violence: Hitler's "Mein Kampf,"* New York: Peter Lang Publishing, 2006: 87.

9. *The Holocaust Chronicle: A History in Words and Pictures,* edited by David J. Hogan, Lincolnwood, IL: Publications International, 2003: 127; Elson,

Prelude to War: 84–95; Shirer, *Rise and Fall of the Third Reich*: 351; David Faber, *Munich 1938: Appeasement and World War II,* New York: Simon & Schuster, 2009: 152–56.

10. Judith Tydor Baumel, *The Holocaust Encyclopedia,* edited by Walter Laqueur, New Haven, CT: Yale University Press, 2001: 172–74; Hogan, *Holocaust Chronicle*: 132, 137, 142–47; Elson, *Prelude to War*: 84–95; Shirer, *Rise and Fall of the Third Reich*: 351; Henry L. Feingold, *The Politics of Rescue: The Roosevelt Administration and the Holocaust, 1938–1945,* New Brunswick, NJ: Rutgers University Press, 1970: 31–49, 127–135, 146–52, 163–72; Dennis R. Laffer, "The Jewish Trail of Tears: The Evian Conference of July 1938," graduate thesis, University of South Florida, 2011: 288–301; William L. Shirer, *Berlin Diary: The Journal of a Foreign Correspondent, 1934–1941,* New York: Alfred A. Knopf, 1941: 119–20.

11. "Chinese Visas in Vienna," Righteous Among the Nations; Ho, *Forty Years as a Diplomat*: 30–49; Yee, *Soaring Crane*: 91–92; Ho, *Diplomat Rescuers*: 2–23; Ho, "Feng Shan Ho"; Joe O'Connor, "Miracle Man: How One Chinese Diplomat Saved Thousands of Jews from the Death Camps," *National Post,* November 1, 2011.

12. Eric Metaxes, "Dr. Feng Shan Ho: A Lesser Known Christian Hero Who Changed the World," *Breakpoint,* October 16, 2015; May Zhou, "Ho Feng Shan: Man of Compassion, Courage," *China Daily USA,* April 24, 2015; Ho, *Forty Years as a Diplomat*: 30–49.

13. "Chinese Visas in Vienna," Righteous Among the Nations; Ho, *Forty Years as a Diplomat*: 30–49; Metaxes, "Dr. Feng Shan Ho"; Zhou, "Ho Feng Shan"; Yee, *Soaring Crane*: 91–92; O'Connor, "Miracle Man."

14. "Chinese Visas in Vienna," Righteous Among the Nations; Ho, *Forty Years as a Diplomat*: 30–49; Metaxes, "Dr. Feng Shan Ho"; Zhou, "Ho Feng Shan"; Yee, *Soaring Crane*: 91–92; Ho, *Diplomat Rescuers*: 2–23; Pierre Moulin, *Dachau, Holocaust, and US Samurais: Nisei Soldiers First in Dachau?,* Bloomington, IN: Authorhouse, 2007: 180–83; O'Connor, "Miracle Man."

15. "Chinese Visas in Vienna," Righteous Among the Nations; Ho, *Forty Years as a Diplomat*: 30–49; Metaxes, "Dr. Feng Shan Ho"; Zhou, "Ho Feng Shan"; Yee, *Soaring Crane*: 91–92; Ho, *Diplomat Rescuers*: 2–23; O'Connor, "Miracle Man."

16. "Chinese Visas in Vienna," Righteous Among the Nations; Ho, *Forty Years as a Diplomat*: 30–49; Metaxes, "Dr. Feng Shan Ho"; Zhou, "Ho Feng Shan"; Yee, *Soaring Crane*: 91–92; Ho, *Diplomat Rescuers*: 2–23; O'Connor, "Miracle Man."

17. "Chinese Visas in Vienna," Righteous Among the Nations; Ho, *Forty Years as a Diplomat*: 30–49; Metaxes, "Dr. Feng Shan Hoe"; Zhou, "Ho Feng Shan"; Yee, *Soaring Crane*: 91–92; Ho, *Diplomat Rescuers*: 18–23.

Chapter 2. Otto and Gertrud Mörike

1. Ron Devlin, "'Righteous Gentile' Harbored Jews in Wartime," *Morning Call*, March 19, 1995; Otto and Gertrude Mörike Collection, Landeskirchliches Archiv, Stuttgart; Max Krakauer, *Lights in Darkness,* Stuttgart: Calwer Verlag, 2007: 95; Alison Cook-Sather and John E. Moser, *Global Great Depression and the Coming of World War II,* New York: Paradigm Publishers, 2015: 39–46, 67–68, 77–84.

2. "Reverend Otto Mörike," Righteous Among the Nations, yadvashem.org; Ron Devlin, "'Righteous Gentile' Harbored Jews in Wartime"; Mörike Collection, Landeskirchliches Archiv; Krakauer, *Lights in Darkness*: 95; Hans M. Wuerth, "During Holocaust, Jews Were Helped by Righteous Gentiles," *Morning Call,* January 26, 2013.

3. "Reverend Otto Mörike," Righteous Among the Nations; Toland, *Adolf Hitler*: 88–89, 259–92, 328–88, 541–66; Shirer, *Rise and Fall of the Third Reich*: 222–27, 237–39, 270–73; Richard F. Hamilton and Holger H. Herwig, *The Origins of World War I,* Cambridge: Cambridge University Press, 2003: 3.

4. Hogan, *Holocaust Chronicle*: 55–64, 70–83, 119; Laffer, "The Jewish Trail of Tears": 288–301; Shirer, *Berlin Diary*: 119–20; Wuerth, "During Holocaust, Jews Were Helped by Righteous Gentiles"; Krakauer, *Lights in Darkness*: 95; Jean-Denis LaPlage, editor, *An Illustrated Dictionary of the Third Reich,* Jefferson, NC: McFarland, 2014: 39.

5. Mordecai Paldiel, *Churches and the Holocaust: Unholy Teaching, Good Samaritans and Reconciliation,* Jersey City, NJ: KTAV Publishing, 2006: 374; Peter Hoffman, *The History of the German Resistance, 1933–1945,* Montreal: McGill-Queen's, 1977: 13–15; Feingold, *Politics of Rescue:* 31–38; Wolfgang Gerlach, *And the Witnesses Were Silent: The Confessing Church and the Persecution of the Jews,* translated by Victoria J. Barnett, Lincoln: University of Nebraska Press, 2000: 161, 233; Victoria J. Barnett, *For the Soul of the People: Protestant Protest against Hitler,* New York: Oxford University Press, 1992: 139–42; Arthur C. Cochrane, *The Church's Confession under Hitler,* Philadelphia: Westminster Press, 1962: 237–42; Hans Rothfels, *The German Opposition to Hitler,* London: Oswald Wolff, 1961: 36–43.

6. Paldiel, *Churches and the Holocaust*: 374; Hoffman, *History of the German Resistance*: 13–15; Gerlach, *And the Witnesses Were Silent*: 161, 233; Barnett, *For the Soul of the People*: 139–42; Cochrane, *The Church's Confession under Hitler*: 237–42; Rothfels, *The German Opposition to Hitler*: 36–43; Shirer, *Rise and Fall of the Third Reich*: 240–41.

7. Paldiel, *Churches and the Holocaust*: 374; Hoffman, *History of the German Resistance*: 13–15; Gerlach, *And the Witnesses Were Silent*: 161, 233; Barnett,

For the Soul of the People: 139–42; Cochrane, *The Church's Confession under Hitler*: 237–42; Rothfels, *The German Opposition to Hitler*: 36–43.

8. *Preaching in Hitler's Shadow: Sermons of Resistance in the Third Reich,* edited by Dean G. Stroud, Grand Rapids, MI: William B. Eerdmans, 2013: 36–41; Gerlach, *And the Witnesses Were Silent*: 161, 233; Barnett, *For the Soul of the People*: 139–42; Paldiel, *Churches and the Holocaust*: 374; Cochrane, *The Church's Confession under Hitler*: 237–42; Hoffman, *History of the German Resistance*: 13–15; Rothfels, *The German Opposition to Hitler*: 36–43.

9. James Bentley, *Martin Niemöller, 1892–1984,* New York: Free Press, 1984: 129; Cochrane, *The Church's Confession under Hitler*: 237–42; Eric Metaxes, *Bonhoeffer: Pastor, Martyr, Prophet, Spy,* Nashville: Thomas Nelson, 2010: 222–27, 302–13; Gerlach, *And the Witnesses Were Silent*: 161, 233; Barnett, *For the Soul of the People*: 139–42; Paldiel, *Churches and the Holocaust*: 374; Hoffman, *History of the German Resistance*: 13–15; Rothfels, *The German Opposition to Hitler*: 36–43.

10. "Reverend Otto Mörike," Righteous Among the Nations; Devlin, "'Righteous Gentile' Harbored Jews in Wartime"; Mörike Collection, Landeskirchliches Archiv; Krakauer, *Lights in Darkness*: 95; Wuerth, "During Holocaust, Jews Were Helped by Righteous Gentiles."

11. Mörike Collection, Landeskirchliches Archiv; Krakauer, *Lights in Darkness*: 95; Wuerth, "During Holocaust, Jews Were Helped by Righteous Gentiles"; "Reverend Otto Mörike," Righteous Among the Nations; Devlin, "'Righteous Gentile' Harbored Jews in Wartime."

12. Wuerth, "During Holocaust, Jews Were Helped by Righteous Gentiles"; "Reverend Otto Mörike," Righteous Among the Nations; Devlin, "'Righteous Gentile' Harbored Jews in Wartime"; Mörike Collection, Landeskirchliches Archiv; Krakauer, *Lights in Darkness*: 95.

13. "Reverend Otto Mörike," Righteous Among the Nations; Wuerth, "During Holocaust, Jews Were Helped by Righteous Gentiles"; Devlin, "'Righteous Gentile' Harbored Jews in Wartime"; Mörike Collection, Landeskirchliches Archiv.

14. Feingold, *The Politics of Rescue*: 31–49, 127–35, 146–52, 163–72; Laffer, "The Jewish Trail of Tears": 288–301; Shirer, *Berlin Diary*: 119–20.

15. Alan Steinweis, *Kristallnacht 1938,* Cambridge, MA: Harvard University Press, 2009: 24–31, 42–58, 92–98; David M. Crowe, *The Holocaust: Roots, History and Aftermath,* Philadelphia: Westview Press, 2008: 124–47; LaPlage, *Illustrated Dictionary of the Third Reich*: 34, 64; Shirer, *Berlin Diary*: 119–20; Laffer, "The Jewish Trail of Tears": 288–301.

16. "Reverend Otto Mörike," Righteous Among the Nations; Wuerth, "During Holocaust, Jews Were Helped by Righteous Gentiles"; Devlin, "'Righteous Gentile' Harbored Jews in Wartime"; Mörike Collection, Landeskirchliches Archiv.

17. Wuerth, "During Holocaust, Jews Were Helped by Righteous Gentiles"; "Reverend Otto Mörike," Righteous Among the Nations; Devlin, " 'Righteous Gentile' Harbored Jews in Wartime"; Mörike Collection, Landeskirchliches Archiv; Krakauer, *Lights in Darkness*: 95.

18. "Reverend Otto Mörike, "Righteous Among the Nations; Wuerth, "During Holocaust, Jews Were Helped by Righteous Gentiles"; Devlin, " 'Righteous Gentile' Harbored Jews in Wartime"; Mörike Collection, Landeskirchliches Archiv.

19. Wuerth, "During Holocaust, Jews Were Helped by Righteous Gentiles"; Devlin, " 'Righteous Gentile' Harbored Jews in Wartime"; Mörike Collection, Landeskirchliches Archiv; Krakauer, *Lights in Darkness*: 95; "Reverend Otto Mörike," Righteous Among the Nations.

Chapter 3. Francis Foley

1. Mordecai Paldiel, *Diplomat Heroes of the Holocaust*, Jersey City: KTAV Publishing, 2007: 8–17; "Frank Foley: The Quiet Briton," *Inside Out*, BBC Homepage, 24 September 2014; Mordecai Paldiel, *The Righteous Among the Nations: Rescuers of Jews during the Holocaust*, New York: HarperCollins, 2007: 117–18; "Francis Foley," Righteous Among the Nations, yadvashem.org; "Berlin Honors a True British Hero," *Deutsche Welle*, December 25, 2004; Owen Bowcott, "The Spy Left Out in the Cold," *London Guardian*, September 21, 2007.

2. Paldiel, *Righteous Among the Nations*: 117–18; "Francis Foley," Righteous Among the Nations; Bowcott, "The Spy Left Out in the Cold"; Michael Smith, *Foley: The Spy Who Saved 10,000 Jews*, London: Hodder & Stoughton, 1999: 5–11.

3. Ezra Mendelsohn, *Studies in Contemporary Jewry*, vol. 3 of *Jews and Other Ethnic Groups in a Multi-Ethnic World*, New York: Oxford University Press, 1987: 3:313; Anthony Cave Brown, *Bodyguard of Lies*, Guildford, UK: Lyons Press, 1975: 161; Giles MacDonogh, *1938: Hitler's Gamble*, New York: Basic Books, 2009: 84–85; Smith, *Foley*: 38–43; "Francis Foley," Righteous Among the Nations.

4. "The Spy Hero of Stourbridge: Frank Foley," *Worcestershire Life*, February 18, 2010; Smith, *Foley*: 73–79; Paldiel, *Righteous Among the Nations*: 117–18; "Francis Foley," Righteous Among the Nations.

5. Mendelsohn, *Studies in Contemporary Jewry*: 3:313; Brown, *Bodyguard of Lies*: 161; MacDonogh, *1938: Hitler's Gamble*: 84–85; Smith, *Foley*: 5–11, 38–43, 73–79.

6. "Francis Foley," Righteous Among the Nations; Peter Longerich, *Heinrich Himmler*, New York: Oxford University Press, 2012: 225–38, 242–48; Nikolaus Wachsmann, *KL: A History of the Nazi Concentration Camps*, New York: Farrar, Straus and Giroux, 2015: 97–109, 126–42.

7. Mendelsohn, *Studies in Contemporary Jewry*: 3:313; Brown, *Bodyguard of Lies*: 161; MacDonogh, *1938: Hitler's Gamble*: 84–85; Smith, *Foley*: 73–79; Paldiel, *Righteous Among the Nations*: 117–18; "Francis Foley," Righteous Among the Nations.

8. Smith, *Foley*: 73–79; Paldiel, *Righteous Among the Nations*: 117–18; "Francis Foley," Righteous Among the Nations; Bowcott, "The Spy Left Out in the Cold."

Chapter 4. Geertruida Wijsmuller

1. "Geertruida Wijsmuller," Righteous Among the Nations, yadvashem.org; Judith Tydor Baumel-Schwartz, *Never Look Back: The Jewish Refugee Children in Britain, 1938–1945,* West Lafayette, IN: Purdue University Press, 2012: 61–67, 107–18; Shirer, *Rise and Fall of the Third Reich*: 365, 963, 978; Truus Wijsmuller-Meijer, *Geen tijd voor tranen,* Amsterdam: P. N. van Kampen, 1964: 4–8, 34–42.

2. Miriam Keesing, "The Children of Tante Truus," *Dokin Stichting Duitse Oorlogskindren in Nederland,* 1 May 2010; "Geertruida Wijsmuller," Righteous Among the Nations; *The Kindertransport in Britain, 1938–39: New Perspectives,* edited by Andrea Hammel and Bea Lewkowicz, Amsterdam: Rodopi, 2012: 8–18.

3. Deborah Hodge, *Rescuing the Children: The Story of the Kindertransport,* Plattsburgh, NY: Tundra Books, 2012: 33–35; "Mrs. Geertruida Wijsmuller-Meijer," *AJR Information* 33, no. 11 (November 1978): 11; Fiona Hurley, "Auntie Truus: A Holocaust Savior to Thousands of Children," Saavyauntie.com; Keesing, "Children of Tante Truus"; Baumel-Schwartz, *Never Look Back*: 107–18; Shirer, *Rise and Fall of the Third Reich*: 963, 978; Wijsmuller-Meijer, *Geen tijd voor tranen*: 4–8; "Geertruida Wijsmuller," Righteous Among the Nations.

4. "German Church Leader Testifies against Eichmann at Jerusalem Trial," *Jewish Telegraphic Agency,* May 17, 1961; Baumel, *Holocaust Encyclopedia*: 162–63; Hogan, *Holocaust Chronicle,* 122–29; Shirer, *Rise and Fall of the Third Reich*: 963, 978; Martin Gilbert, *The Holocaust: A History of the Jews of Europe During the Second World War,* New York: Henry Holt, 1985; Ina Lazereva and Adam Luck, "His Body Spasmed...Then My Nazi Tormentor Was Dead," *Daily Mail,* January 20, 2015; Ad van Liempt, *Hitler's Bounty Hunters: The Betrayal of the Jews,* Oxford: Berg, 2005: 131, 225.

5. "German Church Leader Testifies against Eichmann at Jerusalem Trial," *Jewish Telegraphic Agency,* May 17, 1961; "Geertruida Wijsmuller," Righteous Among the Nations; "Mrs. Geertruida Wijsmuller-Meijer," *AJR Information*: Hurley, "Auntie Truus: A Holocaust Savior to Thousands of Children."

6. Keesing, "Children of Tante Truus"; Baumel-Schwartz, *Never Look Back:* 107–18; Shirer, *Rise and Fall of the Third Reich*: 963, 978; Wijsmuller-Meijer, *Geen tijd voor tranen*: 4–8; Gilbert, *The Holocaust*: 94, 120, 284; Alle G. Hoekema, "Dutch Mennonites and German Jewish Refugee Children, 1938–1945," *Mennonite Quarterly Review* 87 (April 2013): 133–35; Hodge, *Rescuing the Children*: 33–35.

7. Lucy Ward, "Kindertransport: 'To My Dying Day, I Will Be Grateful to This Country,'" *Telegraph*, March 18, 2016; "Geertruida Wijsmuller," Righteous Among the Nations; Alexander Gordon and Olga Levy Drucker, quoted in *Into the Arms of Strangers: Stories of the Kindertransport,* directed by Mark Jonathan Harris, Warner Bros., 2000.

8. Baumel-Schwartz, *Never Look Back*: 61–67, 107–18; Shirer, *Rise and Fall of the Third Reich*: 365, 963, 978; Wijsmuller-Meijer, *Geen tijd voor tranen*: 34–42; "Geertruida Wijsmuller," Righteous Among the Nations; Gilbert, *The Holocaust*: 94, 120, 284; Hoekema, "Dutch Mennonites and German Jewish Refugee Children, 1938–1945": 133–35; Hodge, *Rescuing the Children*: 33–35; Daphne L. Meijer, "Unknown Children: The Last Train from Westerbork," *Children and the Holocaust,* Washington, DC: United States Holocaust Memorial Museum, 2004: 98–99; Jacob Presser, *Ashes in the Wind: The Destruction of Dutch Jewry,* Detroit: Wayne State University Press, 1982: 8, 342, 407–12.

9. Baumel-Schwartz, *Never Look Back*: 107–18; "Geertruida Wijsmuller," Righteous Among the Nations; Gilbert, *The Holocaust*: 120, 284; Hoekema, "Dutch Mennonites and German Jewish Refugee Children, 1938–1945": 133–35; Hodge, *Rescuing the Children*: 33–35; Meijer, "Unknown Children": 98–99; Presser, *Ashes in the Wind*: 407–12.

10. Jonathan Wittenberg, "Kindertransport Revealed," *Jewish Chronicle*, December 2, 2011; "Geertruida Wijsmuller," Righteous Among the Nations; Gilbert, *The Holocaust*: 120, 284; Hoekema, "Dutch Mennonites and German Jewish Refugee Children, 1938–1945": 133–35; Hodge, *Rescuing the Children*: 33–35; Meijer, "Unknown Children": 98–99; Presser, *Ashes in the Wind*: 407–12.

11. Hoekema, "Dutch Mennonites and German Jewish Refugee Children, 1938–1945": 133–35; Hodge, *Rescuing the Children*: 33–35; Meijer, "Unknown Children": 98–99; Presser, *Ashes in the Wind*: 407–12; Wittenberg, "Kindertransport Revealed"; "Geertruida Wijsmuller," Righteous Among the Nations; Gilbert, *The Holocaust*: 120, 284.

12. Bernard Wasserstein, *The Ambiguity of Virtue: Gertrude van Tijn and the Fate of the Dutch Jews,* Cambridge, MA: Harvard University Press, 2014: 83–85; Wittenberg, "Kindertransport Revealed"; Ward, "Kindertransport: 'To My Dying Day, I Will Be Grateful to This Country.'"

Chapter 5. Heinrich Grüber

1. "Pastor Grüber's Office," *Widerstand: Evangelische Christinnen Und Christen Im Nationalsozialismus,* Bildnachweise; "Heinrich Grüber," Righteous Among the Nations, yadvashem.org.

2. Ruth Hanna Sachs, *Coming Together,* vol. 1 of *White Rose Hisotry,* Lehi, UT: Exclamation! Publishing, 2002: 291–92; "Heinrich Grüber," Righteous Among the Nations; Hartmut Ludwig Page, *An der Seite der Entrechteten und Schwachen: Zur Geschichte des Büro Pfarrer Grüber,* Berlin: Logos Verlag, 2009: 1–23.

3. "Heinrich Grüber," Righteous Among the Nations; Page, *An der Seite der Entrechteten und Schwachen*: 1–23.

4. "Pastor Grüber's Office," *Widerstand: Evangelische Christinnen*; Page, *An der Seite der Entrechteten und Schwachen*: 1–23; "Heinrich Grüber," Righteous Among the Nations.

5. Page, *An der Seite der Entrechteten und Schwachen*: 15–23; "Heinrich Grüber," Righteous Among the Nations; "Testimony of Heinrich Grueber," Adolf Eichmann Trial, session 42, 5 May 1961, Adolf Eichmann Trial Collection, Steven Spielberg Film and Video Archives, US Holocaust Memorial Museum; "The Trial of Adolf Eichmann," session 41, part 3, Nizkor Project, nizkor.org.

6. "Heinrich Grüber," Righteous Among the Nations; "Testimony of Heinrich Grueber," Adolf Eichmann Trial Collection; "The Trial of Adolf Eichmann," Nizkor Project; Gilbert, *The Holocaust*: 543–44; Guy Walters, *Hunting Evil: The Nazi War Criminals Who Escaped and the Quest to Bring Them to Justice,* New York: Broadway Books, 2009: 70–74.

7. "Testimony of Heinrich Grueber," Adolf Eichmann Trial Collection; "The Trial of Adolf Eichmann," Nizkor Project; Gilbert, *The Holocaust*: 543–44; Walters, *Hunting Evil*: 70–74; Luke 10:25–37.

8. "Pastor Grüber's Office," *Widerstand: Evangelische Christinnen*; Page, *An der Seite der Entrechteten und Schwachen*: 1–23; "Heinrich Grüber," Righteous Among the Nations.

9. "Heinrich Grüber," Righteous Among the Nations; "Pastor Grüber's Office," *Widerstand: Evangelische Christinnen*; Page, *An der Seite der Entrechteten und Schwachen*: 1–23; "Testimony of Heinrich Grueber," Adolf Eichmann Trial Collection.

10. "Heinrich Grüber," Righteous Among the Nations; "Pastor Grüber's Office," *Widerstand: Evangelische Christinnen*; Page, *An der Seite der Entrechteten und Schwachen*: 1–23.

11. Yahuda Bauer and Nili Keren, *A History of the Holocaust,* Danbury, CT: Franklin Watts, 1982: 159–60; Baumel, *Holocaust Encyclopedia*: 606–10.

12. Bauer and Keren, *History of the Holocaust:* 110–13, 115–19, 227–29; Shirer, *Rise and Fall of the Third Reich:* 41–49; Baumel, *Holocaust Encyclopedia:* 148–49; Wachsmann, *KL: History of Nazi Concentration Camps:* 41–49, 55–62, 176–83, 200–22; Gerald Reitlinger, *The S.S.: Alibi of a Nation, 1922–1945,* New York: Viking Press, 1957: 260–63

13. "Heinrich Grüber," Righteous Among the Nations; "Pastor Grüber's Office," *Widerstand: Evangelische Christinnen;* Page, *An der Seite der Entrechteten und Schwachen:* 1–23; "Testimony of Heinrich Grueber," Adolf Eichmann Trial Collection.

14. "Heinrich Grüber," Righteous Among the Nations; "Pastor Grüber's Office," *Widerstand: Evangelische Christinnen;* Baumel, *Holocaust Encyclopedia:* 137, 505; "Testimony of Heinrich Grueber," Adolf Eichmann Trial; Wachsmann, *KL: History of Nazi Concentration Camps:* 9–18.

15. "Heinrich Grüber," Righteous Among the Nations; "Pastor Grüber's Office," *Widerstand: Evangelische Christinnen;* "Testimony of Heinrich Grueber," Adolf Eichmann Trial Collection.

16. Wachsmann, *KL: History of Nazi Concentration Camps:* 430–39; "Heinrich Grüber," Righteous Among the Nations; "Pastor Grüber's Office," *Widerstand: Evangelische Christinnen;* Genesis 41:52 "Testimony of Heinrich Grueber," Adolf Eichmann Trial Collection.

17. "Heinrich Grüber," Righteous Among the Nations; "Pastor Grüber's Office," *Widerstand: Evangelische Christinnen;* Hebrews 12:1; "Testimony of Heinrich Grueber," Adolf Eichmann Trial Collection.

18. "Heinrich Grüber," Righteous Among the Nations; "Pastor Grüber's Office," *Widerstand: Evangelische Christinnen;* Guy Walters, "Don't Be Fooled, Eichmann Was a Monster," *Telegraph,* October 31, 2015; Richard Philbrick, "Religion on Upswing in East Germany," *Chicago Daily Tribune,* September 29, 1962; "Lutheran Pastor Who Aided Jews under Hitler Dies," *Pittsburgh Press,* November 30, 1975; "Testimony of Heinrich Grueber," Adolf Eichmann Trial Collection.

Chapter 6. Nicholas Winton

1. Shirer, *Rise and Fall of the Third Reich:* 420–28, 444–45, 448–54; Elson, *Prelude to War:* 206–10; Patrick Crowhurst, *Hitler and Czechoslovakia in World War II: Domination and Retaliation,* London: I. B. Tauris, 2013: 110–12; Faber, *Munich:* 433–39.

2. Faber, *Munich:* 410–24; Crowhurst, *Hitler and Czechoslovakia:* 89–96; Shirer, *Rise and Fall of the Third Reich:* 420–28, 444–45, 448–54; Elson, *Prelude to War:* 206–10.

3. Faber, *Munich:* 1–7; Shirer, *Rise and Fall of the Third Reich:* 420–28, 448–54; Elson, *Prelude to War:* 206–10.

4. Faber, *Munich*: 410–24; Crowhurst, *Hitler and Czechoslovakia*: 32–36; Shirer, *Rise and Fall of the Third Reich*: 448–54; Elson, *Prelude to War*: 206–10.

5. Faber, *Munich*: 437–40; Crowhurst, *Hitler and Czechoslovakia*: 32–36; Shirer, *Rise and Fall of the Third Reich*: 448–54; Elson, *Prelude to War*: 208–10.

6. "Nicholas Winton," Righteous Among the Nations, yadvashem.org; Emily Langer, "Nicholas Winton, Rescuer of Children during the Holocaust, Dies at 106," *Washington Post*, July 1, 2015.

7. Joseph Frager, "Nicholas Winton: Triumph over Evil," *Arutz Sheva*, July 8, 2015; Robert D. McFadden, "Nicholas Winton, Rescuer of 669 Children from Holocaust, Dies at 106," *New York Times*, July 1, 2015; "Nicholas Winton," Righteous Among the Nations.

8. "Nicholas Winton," Righteous Among the Nations; Langer, "Nicholas Winton, Rescuer of Children during the Holocaust, Dies at 106"; Baumel, *Holocaust Encyclopedia*: 77–82; Hogan, *Holocaust Chronicle*: 135, 145, 179.

9. Baumel, *Holocaust Encyclopedia*: 78–81; "Nicholas Winton," Righteous Among the Nations; Gary Levine, "Inner Greatness: How Nicholas Winton and Doreen Warriner Saved the World," *Naples Herald*, July 7, 2015; Doreen Warriner, "Winter in Prague," *Slavonic and East European Review* 62, no. 2 (April 1984): 209–40.

10. Baumel, *Holocaust Encyclopedia*: 78–81; "Nicolas Winton," Righteous Among the Nations; Crowhurst, *Hitler and Czechoslovakia*: 59–63; Langer, "Nicholas Winton, Rescuer of Children during the Holocaust, Dies at 106."

11. "Nicholas Winton," Righteous Among the Nations; Susan Cohen, "Winter in Prague: The Humanitarian Mission of Doreen Warriner," *AJR Journal* 2, no. 8 (August 2011): 3; Linda Rabben, *Give Refuge to the Stranger: The Past, Present, and Future of Sanctuary,* Walnut Creek, CA: Left Coast Press, 2011: 102–8.

12. "Nicholas Winton," Righteous Among the Nations; Langer, "Nicholas Winton, Rescuer of Children during the Holocaust, Dies at 106."

13. "Nicholas Winton," Righteous Among the Nations; Frager, "Nicholas Winton: Triumph over Evil"; McFadden, "Nicholas Winton, Rescuer of 669 Children from Holocaust, Dies at 106"; Levine, "Inner Greatness: How Nicholas Winton and Doreen Warriner Saved the World"; Langer, "Nicholas Winton, Rescuer of Children during the Holocaust, Dies at 106."

14. Frager, "Nicholas Winton: Triumph over Evil"; McFadden, "Nicholas Winton, Rescuer of 669 Children from Holocaust, Dies at 106"; Levine, "Inner Greatness: How Nicholas Winton and Doreen Warriner Saved the World"; Langer, "Nicholas Winton, Rescuer of Children during the Holocaust, Dies at 106"; "Nicholas Winton," Righteous Among the Nations.

15. Neil Tweetie, "The Unsung British Hero with His Own Schindler's List," *Telegraph*, March 17, 2013; John Miles, "Winton's Children: Saved from

the Holocaust," *Newsweek*, July 3, 2015; "Nicholas Winton," Righteous Among the Nations.

16. Tweetie, "The Unsung British Hero with His Own Schindler's List"; Miles, "Winton's Children: Saved from the Holocaust"; "Nicholas Winton," Righteous Among the Nations.

17. Tweetie, "The Unsung British Hero with His Own Schindler's List"; Miles, "Winton's Children: Saved from the Holocaust"; "Nicholas Winton," Righteous Among the Nations.

18. Tweetie, "The Unsung British Hero with His Own Schindler's List"; Miles, "Winton's Children: Saved from the Holocaust"; "Nicholas Winton," Righteous Among the Nations; Stephen Addison, "Nicholas Winton, the 'British Schindler,' Dies at 106," Reuters, July 1, 2015.

Chapter 7. Jan Karski

1. Richard Hargreaves, *Blitkrieg Unleashed: The German Invasion of Poland,* Mechanicsburg, PA: Stackpole Books, 2008: 97–104; B. H. Liddell Hart, *History of the Second World War,* New York: Da Capo Press, 1999: 27–32; David Irving, *Hitler's War,* New York: Viking, 1964: 12–28.

2. Shirer, *Rise and Fall of the Third Reich*: 468–502, 958–63; Robert Wernick, *Blitzkrieg,* New York: Time-Life, 1977: 18–23; Irving, *Hitler's War*: 12–28.

3. "The Program for the Complete Elimination of Jewry," *Nazi Conspiracy and Aggression,* Washington, DC: US Government Printing Office, 1948: 1:390; "Testimony of Otto Ohlendorf," Nuremberg Trials, National Archives Records Administration, Case 9 Transcripts, RG 238, Entry 92, Box 1, vol. 2, p. 510.

4. Shirer, *Rise and Fall of the Third Reich*: 956–59; Irving, *Hitler's War*: 12–28; Roger Manvell and Heinrich Fraenkel, *Heinrich Himmler: The Sinister Life of the Head of the SS and Gestapo,* London: Greenhill Books, 2007: 85; Baumel, *Holocaust Encyclopedia*: 279; Hogan, *Holocaust Chronicle*: 149–51.

5. Shirer, *Rise and Fall of the Third Reich*: 956–59; *The Nazi Elite,* edited by Ronald Smelser and Rainer Zitelmann, New York: NYU Press, 1993: 155–64; Manvell and Fraenkel, *Heinrich Himmler*: 119–20.

6. Jan Karski, *Story of a Secret State: My Report to the World,* Washington, DC: University of Georgetown Press, 2010: xxii–xxx, 6–10, 304, 360–64; "Jan Karski," Righteous Among the Nations, yadvashem.org.

7. Katyn Forest Massacre Collection, General Records of the Department of State, National Archives and Records Administration, Record Group 59, Central Decimal File, 1940–1944, box 2919, folder 740.00116; E. Thomas Wood and Stansilaw M. Jankowski, *Karski: How One Man Tried to Stop the Holocaust,* Hoboken, NJ: John Wiley & Sons, 1994: 151–56, 170–73, 199–203; Baumel, *Holocaust Encyclopedia*: 279; Hogan, *Holocaust Chronicle*: 149–51; "Jan Karski," Righteous Among the Nations.

8. *The Jew in the Modern World: A Documentary History,* edited by Paul Mendes-Flohr and Jehuda Reinharz, London: Oxford University Press, 1995: 684; Baumel, *Holocaust Encyclopedia*: 279; Hogan, *Holocaust Chronicle*: 149–51; "Jan Karski," Righteous Among the Nations.

9. Michael Kaufman, "Jan Karski Dies at 86; Warned West about Holocaust," *New York Times,* July 15, 2000; "Jan Karski," Righteous Among the Nations; Karski, *Story of a Secret State*: 360–64.

10. "Jan Karski, 1991," 1990–1991 Medal Recipients, wallenburg.umich.edu; "Jan Karski," Righteous Among the Nations; Karski, *Story of a Secret State*: 360–64.

11. "Jan Karski," Righteous Among the Nations; Karski, *Story of a Secret State*: 360–64; "Jan Karski, 1991," 1990–1991 Medal Recipients.

12. "Jan Karski," Righteous Among the Nations; Karski, *Story of a Secret State*: 360–64; "Jan Karski, 1991," 1990–1991 Medal Recipients.

13. "Account of Karski's Conversation with President Roosevelt," *Jan Karski: Humanity's Hero,* Polish Museum of History Exhibit and Official Website; "Jan Karski," Righteous Among the Nations.

14. Karski, *Story of a Secret State*: 362–64; "Jan Karski," Righteous Among the Nations.

15. Kaufman, "Jan Karski Dies at 86: Warned West about Holocaust"; Karski, *Story of a Secret State*: 64.

16. Karski, *Story of a Secret State*: 64; Joseph Brunner, "American Involvement in the Nuremburg War Crimes Trial Process," *Michigan Journal of History* 1, no. 4 (Winter, 2004): 1–3; William J. Bosch, *Judgment on Nuremberg: American Attitudes toward the Major German War-Crime Trials*, Chapel Hill: University of North Carolina Press, 1970: 75.

17. Brunner, "American Involvement in the Nuremburg War Crimes Trial Process,": 1–3; Bosch, *Judgment on Nuremberg*: 75.

18. Robert L. Beir, *Roosevelt and the Holocaust,* Fort Lee, NJ: Barricade Books, 2006: 220; Renee Ghert-Zand, "Holocaust Whistle-Blower Honored by Georgetown," *Times of Israel*, April 23, 2014.

Chapter 8. Józef and Wiktoria Ulma

1. "Józef and Wiktoria Ulma," Righteous Among the Nations, www.yadvashem.org; Wlodzimierz Redzioch, "They Gave Up Their Lives," *Catholic Sunday Weekly,* November 10, 2015; Barbara Nowak, "The Quiet Heroism," *Visit Rzeszow* 14 (September 2012): 54–56; "Story of Polish Family Slain with Jews They Tried to Save," *Zenit*, April 16, 2011.

2. "Józef and Wiktoria Ulma," Righteous Among the Nations; Redzioch, "They Gave Up Their Lives"; Nowak, "The Quiet Heroism": 54–56; "Story of Polish Family Slain with Jews They Tried to Save."

3. "Story of Polish Family Slain with Jews They Tried to Save"; "Józef and Wiktoria Ulma," Righteous Among the Nations; Redzioch, "They Gave Up Their Lives"; Nowak, "The Quiet Heroism": 55–56.

4. "Józef and Wiktoria Ulma," Righteous Among the Nations; Bauer and Keren, *History of the Holocaust*: 296; Redzioch, "They Gave Up Their Lives"; Nowak, "The Quiet Heroism": 54–56; "Story of Polish Family Slain with Jews They Tried to Save."

5. "Józef and Wiktoria Ulma," Righteous Among the Nations; Hershel and Abraham Edelheit, *A World in Turmoil: An Integrated Chronology of the Holocaust and World War II*, New York: Greenwood Publishing, 1991: 311; Raul Hilberg, *The Destruction of European Jews*, New Haven, CT: Yale University Press, 2003: 502–6; Andrzej Paczkowski, *The Spring Will Be Ours: Poland and the Poles from Occupation to Freedom*, University Park: Pennsylvania State University Press, 1985: 55; Nowak, "The Quiet Heroism": 56; "Story of Polish Family Slain with Jews They Tried to Save."

Chapter 9. Max Liedtke

1. "Max Liedtke," Righteous Among the Nations, yadvashem.org.

2. Ibid.; John Jacob Hartman and Jacek Krochmal, *I Remember Every Day . . . : The Fates of the Jews of Przemyśl during World War II*, Przemyśl: Towarzystwo Przyjaciót Nauk w Przemyślu, 2003: 275–78.

3. Israel Gutman, Sara Bender, Daniel Fraenkel, and Jacob Borut, *Lexikon der Gerechten unter den Völkern: Deutsche und Österreicher*, Göttingen: Wallstein Verlag, 2005: 65, 182–84; Hilberg, *Destruction of the European Jews*: 133, 334–35; Norman Davies, *No Simple Victory: World War II in Europe, 1939–1945*, New York: Penguin Books, 2008: 236–37; Yitsak Arad, *The Holocaust in the Soviet Union*, Lincoln: University of Nebraska Press, 2009: 279; *The Nazi Germany Sourcebook: An Anthology of Texts*, edited by Roderick Stackelberg and Sally A. Winkle, New York: Routledge, 2002: 344; "Max Liedtke," Righteous Among the Nations.

4. "Albert Battel," Righteous Among the Nations, yadvashem.org; Hogan, *Holocaust Chronicle*: 242, 269; "Max Liedtke," Righteous Among the Nations; Hartman and Krochmal, *I Remember Every Day*: 275; Wolfgang Curilla, *Der Judenmord in Polen und die deutsche Ordnungspolizei 1939–1945*, Paderborn: Schöningh, 2010: 253; Shirer, *Rise and Fall of the Third Reich*, 662–63; Sönke Neitzel and Harald Welzer, *Soldiers: German POWs on Fighting, Killing, and Dying*, New York: Alfred A. Knopf, 2012: 187.

5. "Max Liedtke," Righteous Among the Nations; Hartman and Krochmal, *I Remember Every Day*: 275; "Albert Battel," Righteous Among the Nations.

6. "Max Leidtke," Righteous Among the Nations; Hartman and Krochmal, *I Remember Every Day*: 275; "Albert Battel," Righteous Among the Nations.

7. "Max Liedtke," Righteous Among the Nations; Hartman and Krochmal, *I Remember Every Day*: 275; "Albert Battel," Righteous Among the Nations.

8. "Max Liedtke," Righteous Among the Nations; Hartman and Krochmal, *I Remember Every Day*: 275; "Albert Battel," Righteous Among the Nations.

9. "Max Liedtke," Righteous Among the Nations; Hartman and Krochmal, *I Remember Every Day*: 275; "Albert Battel," Righteous Among the Nations.

10. Sarah Gordon, *Hitler, Germans and the "Jewish Question,"* Princeton, NJ: Princeton University Press, 1984: 280; "Max Liedtke," Righteous Among the Nations; Hartman and Krochmal, *I Remember Every Day*: 275; "Albert Battel," Righteous Among the Nations; Davies, *No Simple Victory*: 236–37; Arad, *Holocaust in the Soviet Union*: 279; Shirer, *Rise and Fall of the Third Reich*: 662–63; Neitzel and Welzer, *Soldiers*: 187; Curilla, *Der Judenmord in Polen*: 253; Yisrael Gutman, *The Jews of Warsaw, 1939–1943: Ghetto, Underground, Revolt,* Bloomington: Indiana University Press, 1982: 285–88.

11. "Max Leidtke," Righteous Among the Nations; Hartman and Krochmal, *I Remember Every Day*: 275; "Albert Battel," Righteous Among the Nations.

Chapter 10. Julius Madritsch

1. Julius Madritsch Oral History Interview, Oskar Schindler/Imperial War Museum Collection, Record Group 50.147–0011, United States Holocaust Memorial Museum; Julius Madritsch, *Menschen in Not!,* Vienna, 1963: 1–28; "Julius Madritsch," Righteous Among the Nations, yadvashem.org.

2. Martin Gilbert, *The Righteous: The Unsung Heroes of the Holocaust,* New York: Henry Holt, 2002: 221–25; Julius Madritsch Oral History Interview, Oskar Schindler Collection; Madritsch, *Menschen in Not!*: 6–28; "Julius Madritsch," Righteous Among the Nations.

3. Hogan, *Holocaust Chronicle*: 196, 221–22; Bernard Offen, *My Hometown Concentration Camp: A Survivor's Account of Life in the Kraków Ghetto and Płaszów Concentration Camp,* Portland, OR: Vallentine Mitchell, 2008: 20–23; Wachsmann, KL: *History of the Nazi Concentration Camps*: 200, 201; Julius Madritsch Oral History Interview, Oskar Schindler Collection; Madritsch, *Menschen in Not!*: 6–28; "Julius Madritsch," Righteous Among the Nations.

4. Hogan, *Holocaust Chronicle*: 196, 221–22; Offen, *A Survivor's Account*: 20–23; Wachsmann, KL: *History of the Nazi Concentration Camps*: 200, 201; Julius Madritsch Oral History Interview, Oskar Schindler Collection; Madritsch, *Menschen in Not!*: 6–22; "Julius Madritsch," Righteous Among the Nations.

5. David Crowe, *Oskar Schindler: The Untold Story of His Life, Wartime Activities and the True Story behind the List,* New York: Westview Press, 2004: 155–57; Lewis Fagen Oral History Interview, Oskar Schindler/Imperial War Museum Collection, Record Group 50.147–0003, United States Holocaust Memorial Museum; Madritsch, *Menschen in Not!*: 11–28; Gilbert, *The Righteous*: 221–25; "Julius Madritsch," Righteous Among the Nations.

6. Gilbert, *The Righteous*: 221–25; Crowe, *Oskar Schindler*: 191–93; Robin O'Neil, *Oskar Schindler: Stepping Stone to Life,* Salisbury, UK: Susaneking, 2007: 1–20; "Oswald Bosko," Righteous Among the Nations, yadvashem .org; Madritsch, *Menschen in Not!*: 14–28; "Julius Madritsch," Righteous Among the Nations.

7. "Oswald Bosko," Righteous Among the Nations"; Madritsch, *Menschen in Not!*: 14–28; "Julius Madritsch," Righteous Among the Nations.

8. Margot Norris, *Writing War in the Twentieth Century,* Charlottesville: University of Virginia Press, 2000: 123; Martin Winstone, *The Holocaust Sites of Europe: An Historic Guide,* London: I. B. Tauris, 2010: 236; William Hauben, *From the Flames: Miracles and Wonders of Survival,* New York: Writer's Club Press, 2000: 28; Ryszard Kotarba, *A Historical Guide to the German Camp at Płaszów, 1942–1945,* Warsaw: Institute of National Remembrance, 2014: 5–11; "Oswald Bosko," Righteous Among the Nations; Madritsch, *Menschen in Not!*: 14–28; "Julius Madritsch," Righteous Among the Nations.

9. Regina Nelken Testimony, Official Transcript of the Trial of Amon Goeth, Holocaust Education and Research Archive Team, www .HolocaustResearchProject.org; "The Trial of Amon Goeth," part 3, 26 September 1946, Holocaust Education and Archive Research Team, www .holocaustresearchproject.org; "Julius Madritsch," Righteous Among the Nations.

10. "Julius Madritsch," Righteous Among the Nations; Regina Nelken Testimony, Official Transcript of the Trial of Amon Goeth; "Trial of Amon Goeth," part 3, 26 September 1946; Norris, *Writing War in the Twentieth Century*: 121–34; Winstone, *The Holocaust Sites of Europe*: 236; Hauben, *From the Flames*: 28; Kotarba, *Historical Guide to the German Camp at Płaszów*: 5–11; Madritsch, *Menschen in Not!*: 20–28.

11. Regina Nelken Testimony, Official Transcript of the Trial of Amon Goeth; "Trial of Amon Goeth," part 3, 26 September 1946; Norris, *Writing War in the Twentieth Century*: 121–34; Winstone, *The Holocaust Sites of Europe*: 236; Hauben, *From the Flames*: 28; Kotarba, *Historical Guide to the German Camp at Płaszów*: 5–11; Madritsch, *Menschen in Not!*: 20–28; "Julius Madritsch," Righteous Among the Nations.

12. "Julius Madritsch," Righteous Among the Nations; Regina Nelken Testimony, Official Transcript of the Trial of Amon Goeth; "Trial of Amon Goeth," part 3; Norris, *Writing War in the Twentieth Century*: 121–34; Winstone, *The Holocaust Sites of Europe*: 236; Hauben, *From the Flames*: 28; Kotarba, *Historical Guide to the German Camp at Płaszów*: 5–11; Madritsch, *Menschen in Not!*: 20–28.

13. Crowe, *Oskar Schindler*: 372–73; Thomas Keneally, *Searching for Schindler: A Memoir,* New York: Doubleday, 2007: 135–36; O'Neil, *Oskar Schindler*: 8–20; "Julius Madritsch," Righteous Among the Nations; Regina Nelken Testimony, Official Transcript of the Trial of Amon Goeth; "Trial of Amon

Goeth," part 3, 26 September 1946; Norris, *Writing War in the Twentieth Century*: 121–34; Winstone, *The Holocaust Sites of Europe*: 236; Hauben, *From the Flames*: 28; Kotarba, *Historical Guide to the German Camp at Płaszów*: 5–11; Madritsch, *Menschen in Not!*: 20–28.

Chapter 11. Hans Christen Mamen

1. "Hans Christen Mamen," Righteous Among the Nations, yadvashem.org; Else and Geoff Ward, "Hans Christen Mamen: Courier of Our Lord," www .wwiinorge.com/our-stories/hans-christen-mamen; Tom Landos, "Tribute to the Rev. Hans Christen Mamen," *Capitol Words* 150, no. 53 (April 22, 2004): 610; Robert Edwards, *The Winter War: Russia's Invasion of Finland, 1939–40*, New York: Open Road, 2011: 76–85, 155–70, 200–24; Gerhart L. Weinberg, *A World at Arms: A Global History of World War II*, Cambridge: Cambridge University Press, 1994: 103–8; *Hitler's Forgotten Armies: Combat in Norway and Finland*, edited by Bob Carruthers, Barnsley, UK: Pen and Sword Books, 2012: 22–28.

2. "Testimony of Hans Christen Mamen," *Neighboring Nations: Saving the Lives of Norwegian and Danish Jews,* Jewish Museum of Sweden, judiskamuseet .se; "Hans Christen Mamen," Righteous Among the Nations; Ward, "Hans Christen Mamen: Courier of Our Lord"; Landos, "Tribute to the Rev. Hans Christen Mamen": 610; Ragnar Ulstein, "The Rescue of Approximately 1,000 Jews in Norway During the Second World War," Holocaust Encyclopedia, ushmm.org/learn/holocaust-encyclopedia.

3. Hart, *History of the Second World War*: 52–59; Weinberg, *World at Arms*: 103–8; Carruthers, *Hitler's Forgotten Armies*: 22–28.

4. Geirr H. Haarr, *The German Invasion of Norway: April 1940*, Annapolis, MD: Naval Institute Press, 2009: 5–8, 44–53; Weinberg, *World at Arms*: 103–8; Carruthers, *Hitler's Forgotten Armies*: 22–28; Shirer, *Rise and Fall of the Third Reich*: 673–78, 681–700; Hart, *History of the Second World War*: 52–59.

5. Shirer, *Rise and Fall of the Third Reich*: 673–78, 681–700; Hart, *History of the Second World War*: 52–59; Haarr, *German Invasion of Norway*: 5–8, 44–53; Weinberg, *World at Arms*: 103–8; Carrthers, *Hitler's Forgotten Armies*: 22–28.

6. "Norway," Holocaust Encyclopedia, US Holocaust Memorial Museum, ushmm.org; Philip Friedman, *Roads to Extinction: Essays on the Holocaust*, Lansing: University of Michigan Press, 1980: 66, 287; Samuel Abrahamsen, *Norway's Response to the Holocaust*, New York: Holocaust Library, 1991: 4, 81; "Hans Christen Mamen," Righteous Among the Nations.

7. Mordecai Paldiel, *The Path of the Righteous: Gentile Rescuers of Jews during the Holocaust*, Hoboken, NJ: KTAV Publishing, 1993: 367–68; "Testimony of Hans Christen Mamen," *Neighboring Nations*; "Hans Christen Mamen," Righteous Among the Nations; Ward, "Hans Christen Mamen: Courier of Our Lord"; Ulstein, "Rescue of Approximately 1,000 Jews in Norway"; Landos, "Tribute to the Rev. Hans Christen Mamen": 610.

8. "Testimony of Hans Christen Mamen," *Neighboring Nations*; "Hans Christen Mamen," Righteous Among the Nations; Ward, "Hans Christen Mamen: Courier of Our Lord"; Landos, "Tribute to the Rev. Hans Christen Mamen," 610; Paldiel, *Path of the Righteous*: 367–68; Ulstein, "Rescue of Approximately 1,000 Jews in Norway."

9. Paldiel, *Path of the Righteous*: 367–68; Ulstein, "Rescue of Approximately 1,000 Jews in Norway"; "Testimony of Hans Christen Mamen," *Neighboring Nations*; "Hans Christen Mamen," Righteous Among the Nations; Ward, "Hans Christen Mamen: Courier of Our Lord"; Landos, "Tribute to the Rev. Hans Christen Mamen": 610.

10. "Testimony of Hans Christen Mamen," *Neighboring Nations*; "Hans Christen Mamen," Righteous Among the Nations; Ward, "Hans Christen Mamen: Courier of Our Lord"; Landos, "Tribute to the Rev. Hans Christen Mamen": 610; Paldiel, *Path of the Righteous*: 367–68; Ulstein, "Rescue of Approximately 1,000 Jews in Norway."

11. "Testimony of Hans Christen Mamen," *Neighboring Nations*; "Hans Christen Mamen," Righteous Among the Nations; Ulstein, "Rescue of Approximately 1,000 Jews in Norway"; Ward, "Hans Christen Mamen: Courier of Our Lord"; Paldiel, *Path of the Righteous*: 367–68; Landos, "Tribute to the Rev. Hans Christen Mamen": 610.

12. Ulstein, "Rescue of Approximately 1,000 Jews in Norway"; Paldiel, *Path of the Righteous*: 367–68; "Testimony of Hans Christen Mamen," *Neighboring Nations*; "Hans Christen Mamen," Righteous Among the Nations; Ward, "Hans Christen Mamen: Courier of Our Lord"; Landos, "Tribute to the Rev. Hans Christen Mamen": 610.

13. Paldiel, *Path of the Righteous*: 367–68; "Testimony of Hans Christen Mamen," *Neighboring Nations*; "Hans Christen Mamen," Righteous Among the Nations; Ulstein, "Rescue of Approximately 1,000 Jews in Norway"; Landos, "Tribute to the Rev. Hans Christen Mamen": 610.

14. Ward, "Hans Christen Mamen: Courier of Our Lord"; Landos, "Tribute to the Rev. Hans Christen Mamen": 610; Ulstein, "Rescue of Approximately 1,000 Jews in Norway"; "Testimony of Hans Christen Mamen," *Neighboring Nations*; "Hans Christen Mamen," Righteous Among the Nations; Paldiel, *Path of the Righteous*: 367–68.

15. "Testimony of Hans Christen Mamen," *Neighboring Nations*; "Hans Christen Mamen," Righteous Among the Nations; Ward, "Hans Christen Mamen: Courier of Our Lord"; Paldiel, *Path of the Righteous*: 367–68; Landos, "Tribute to the Rev. Hans Christen Mamen": 610; Ulstein, "Rescue of Approximately 1,000 Jews in Norway"; Baumel, *Holocaust Encyclopedia*: 449–51.

16. "Testimony of Hans Christen Mamen," *Neighboring Nations*; "Hans Christen Mamen," Righteous Among the Nations; Ward, "Hans Christen

Mamen: Courier of Our Lord"; Ulstein, "Rescue of Approximately 1,000 Jews in Norway"; Paldiel, *Path of the Righteous*: 367–68; Landos, "Tribute to the Rev. Hans Christen Mamen": 610; Baumel, *Holocaust Encyclopedia*: 449–51.

17. "Hans Christen Mamen," Righteous Among the Nations; Ward, "Hans Christen Mamen: Courier of Our Lord"; Paldiel, *Path of the Righteous*: 367–68; Ulstein, "Rescue of Approximately 1,000 Jews in Norway"; Landos, "Tribute to the Rev. Hans Christen Mamen": 610.

Chapter 12. Gilleleje Lutheran Church

1. Stephen Foehr, "Zealand: Heart and Soul of Denmark," *Islands: An International Magazine* 6, no. 2 (March/April 1986): 61–68.

2. Shirer, *Rise and Fall of the Third Reich*: 694–99; Hart, *History of the Second World War*: 51–54; *History of World War II*, vol. 1, edited by Peter Mavrikis, London: Marshall Cavendish, 2005: 1:276–84; David Lampe, *Hitler's Savage Canary: A History of the Danish Resistance in World War II*, Barnsley, UK: Frontline Books, 2010: 23–25, 34–39, 100–11.

3. Hart, *History of the Second World War*: 51–54; Mavrikis, *History of World War II*: 1:276–84; Lampe, *Hitler's Savage Canary*: 23–25, 34–39, 100–11.

4. "The Rescue of Denmark's Jews," Righteous Among the Nations, yadvashem .org; Leo Goldberger, *The Rescue of the Danish Jews: Moral Courage Under Stress*, New York: NYU Press, 1987: xxi; *Antisemitism, Christian Ambivalence and the Holocaust*, edited by Kevin P. Spicer, Bloomington: Indiana University Press, 2007: 4–6; Sofic Lene Bak, *Nothing to Speak Of: Wartime Experiences of the Danish Jews, 1943–1945*, Copenhagen: Danish Jewish Museum, 2011: 39–40; Lampe, *Hitler's Savage Canary*: 67–78; Baumel, *Holocaust Encyclopedia*: 145–48.

5. Bak, *Nothing to Speak Of*: 202–3, 252; Lampe, *Hitler's Savage Canary*: 67–78; Baumel, *Holocaust Encyclopedia*: 145–48; Shirer, *Rise and Fall of the Third Reich*: 694–99; Rupert Butler, *Legions of Death: The Nazi Enslavement of Eastern Europe*, London: Hamlyn Publications, 1983: 214–18.

6. Mette and Steven Jensen, *Denmark and the Holocaust*, Copenhagen: Kobenhaven Institute for International Studies, 2003: 45; Bak, *Nothing to Speak Of*: 202–3, 252; Lampe, *Hitler's Savage Canary*: 67–78; Baumel, *Holocaust Encyclopedia*: 145–48; Shirer, *Rise and Fall of the Third Reich*: 694–99; Rupert Butler, *Legions of Death*: 214–18; Spicer, *Antisemitism, Christian Ambivalence and the Holocaust*: 5; Acts 5:29.

7. Bo Lidegaard, *Countrymen: The Untold Story of How Denmark's Jews Escaped the Nazis*, New York: Alfred A. Knopf, 2013: 278–92; Russell Martin, *Beethoven's Hair: An Extraordinary Historical Odyssey and a Scientific Mystery Solved*, New York: Broadway Books, 2000: 95–99; Gilbert, *The Righteous*: 257–58; "October 1943: The Rescue of the Danish Jews from Annihilation," Archives, Museum of Danish Resistance, Copenhagen; Christian Tortzen, *Gilleleje, Oktober 1943: Under jodernes flugt for nazismen*,

Copenhagen: Fremad, 1970: 251–59; "Gilleleje 1943," produced by Eliane Attias Sofie, Jewish Federation Council of Greater Los Angeles, 1970; "Rescue of Denmark's Jews," Righteous Among the Nations.

8. Gilbert, *The Righteous*: 257–58; Lidegaard, *Countrymen*: 278–92; Martin, *Beethoven's Hair*: 95–99; "October 1943: The Rescue of the Danish Jews from Annihilation"; Tortzen, *Gilleleje, Oktober 1943*: 251–59; "Gilleleje 1943"; "Rescue of Denmark's Jews," Righteous Among the Nations.

9. Lidegaard, *Countrymen*: 278–92; Martin, *Beethoven's Hair*: 95–99; "October 1943: The Rescue of the Danish Jews from Annihilation"; Tortzen, *Gilleleje, Oktober 1943*: 251–59; Gilbert, *The Righteous*: 257–58; "Gilleleje 1943"; "Rescue of Denmark's Jews," Righteous Among the Nations.

10. Gilbert, *The Righteous*: 257–58; Lidegaard, *Countrymen*: 278–92; Martin, *Beethoven's Hair*: 95–99; "October 1943: The Rescue of the Danish Jews from Annihilation"; Tortzen, *Gilleleje, Oktober 1943*: 251–59; "Gilleleje 1943"; "Rescue of Denmark's Jews," Righteous Among the Nations.

11. Martin, *Beethoven's Hair*: 95–99; "October 1943: The Rescue of the Danish Jews from Annihilation"; Tortzen, *Gilleleje, Oktober 1943*: 251–59; "Gilleleje 1943"; Gilbert, *The Righteous*: 257–58; Lidegaard, *Countrymen*: 278–92; "Rescue of Denmark's Jews," Righteous Among the Nations.

12. Gilbert, *The Righteous*: 257–58; Lidegaard, *Countrymen*: 278–92; Martin, *Beethoven's Hair*: 95–99; "October 1943: The Rescue of the Danish Jews from Annihilation"; Tortzen, *Gilleleje, Oktober 1943*: 251–59; "Gilleleje 1943"; "Rescue of Denmark's Jews," Righteous Among the Nations.

13. Martin, *Beethoven's Hair*: 95–99; Gilbert, *The Righteous*: 257–58; Lidegaard, *Countrymen*: 278–92; "October 1943: The Rescue of the Danish Jews from Annihilation"; Tortzen, *Gilleleje, Oktober 1943*: 251–59; "Gilleleje 1943"; "Rescue of Denmark's Jews," Righteous Among the Nations.

14. Martin, *Beethoven's Hair*: 95–99; Gilbert, *The Righteous*: 257–58; Lidegaard, *Countrymen*: 278–92; "October 1943: The Rescue of the Danish Jews from Annihilation"; Tortzen, *Gilleleje, Oktober 1943*: 251–59; "Gilleleje 1943"; Leni Yahil, *The Rescue of Danish Jewry: Test of a Democracy*, Philadelphia: Jewish Publication Society of America, 1969: 258; "Rescue of Denmark's Jews," Righteous Among the Nations.

15. Gilbert, *The Righteous*: 257–58; Lidegaard, *Countrymen*: 278–92; "October 1943: The Rescue of the Danish Jews from Annihilation"; Tortzen, *Gilleleje, Oktober 1943*: 251–59; "Gilleleje 1943"; Yahil, *Rescue of Danish Jewry*: 258–60; "Names and Numbers of Righteous Among the Nations per Country," Righteous Among the Nations, yadvashem.org.

Chapter 13. Joseph Peeters

1. "Joseph Peeters," Righteous Among the Nations, yadvashem.org; "Father Peeters: Pastor of Comblain-au-Pont," La Maison du Souvenir d'Oupeye,

maisondusouvenir.be/abbe_peeters.php; "Joseph Albert Peeters," Hommages, Bel-Memorial, bel-memorial.org; J. Fabre, *L'abbé Joseph Peeters: curé de Comblain-au-Pont,* Liège: Catholic Intellectual Center of Belgium, 1957: 17–24, 79–92.

2. Larry Zuckerman, *The Rape of Belgium: The Untold Story of World War I,* New York: New York University Press, 2004: 29–31; Jean-Michel Veranneman, *Belgium in the Second World War,* Barnsley, UK: Pen and Sword Books, 2014: 151–56; Shirer, *Rise and Fall of the Third Reich:* 644–61, 728–42.

3. Zuckerman, *Rape of Belgium:* 29–31; Veranneman, *Belgium in the Second World War:* 151–56; Shirer, *Rise and Fall of the Third Reich:* 644–61, 728–42; Alan F. Wilt, *War from the Top: German and British Decision Making during World War II,* Bloomington: Indiana University Press, 1990: 139.

4. *Hitler's Europe Ablaze: Occupation, Resistance, and Rebellion during World War II,* edited by Philip Cooke and Ben H. Shepherd, New York: Skyhorse Publishing, 2014: 43–56; Zuckerman, *Rape of Belgium:* 29–31; Veranneman, *Belgium in the Second World War:* 151–56; Shirer, *Rise and Fall of the Third Reich:* 644–61, 728–42; Wilt, *War from the Top:* 140–46; Paldiel, *Churches and the Holocaust:* 131–38.

5. *Encyclopedia of the Holocaust,* edited by Robert Rozett and Shmuel Spector, London: Routledge Publishing, 2000: 338–39; *Belgium and the Holocaust: Jews, Belgians and Germans,* edited by Dan Michman, Jerusalem: Daf-Noy Press, 1998: 521–34; René Henry, *L'Almanach de Notre Terroir,* Liège, Belg.: Dricol Editions, 1998: 346; Baumel, *Holocaust Encyclopedia:* 55–60; Paldiel, *Churches and the Holocaust:* 131–37.

6. "Joseph Peeters," Righteous Among the Nations; "Father Peeters: Pastor of Comblain-au-Pont"; Fabre, *L'abbé Joseph Peeters:* 79–92, 145–49, 155–62; "Joseph Albert Peeters," Hommages, Bel-Memorial.

7. "Joseph Peeters," Righteous Among the Nations; Fabre, *L'abbé Joseph Peeters:* 145–49, 155–62; Yvonne de Ridder Files, *The Quest for Freedom: A Story of Belgian Resistance in World War II,* Santa Barbara, CA: Fithian Press, 1991: 79–83; Herman Bodson, *Downed Allied Airmen and the Evasion of Capture: The Role of Local Resistance Networks in World War II,* Jefferson, NC: McFarland, 2001: 21–28.

8. "Joseph Peeters," Righteous Among the Nations; "Father Peeters: Pastor of Comblain-au-Pont"; Fabre, *L'abbé Joseph Peeters:* 79–92, 145–49, 155–62; "Joseph Albert Peeters," Hommages, Bel-Memorial.

9. Fabre, *L'abbé Joseph Peeters:* 145–49, 155–62; "Joseph Peeters," Righteous Among the Nations; "Joseph Albert Peeters," Hommages, Bel-Memorial; "Father Peeters: Pastor of Comblain-au-Pont."

10. "Joseph Peeters," Righteous Among the Nations; "Father Peeters: Pastor of Comblain-au-Pont"; Fabre, *L'abbé Joseph Peeters:* 155–62; "Joseph Albert Peeters," Hommages, Bel-Memorial.

11. Paldiel, *Churches and the Holocaust*: 147; Romans 8:28, 38–39; Fabre, *L'abbé Joseph Peeters*: 155–62; "Joseph Albert Peeters," Hommages, Bel-Memorial; "Father Peeters: Pastor of Comblain-au-Pont"; "Joseph Peeters," Righteous Among the Nations.

Chapter 14. Madeleine Rouffart

1. Simon Gronowski, *L'enfant du 20e convoi,* Liège, Belg.: Luc Pire, 2005: 71–79, 121–28; "Madeleine Rouffart, Renacle Rouffart, Robert Maistriau, Jean Franklemon, George Livshitz," Righteous Among the Nations, yadvashem .org; Simon Gronowski, "Auschwitz and Forgiveness," Michelvanderburg .com.

2. Jim Curtis, "Escaping the Train from Auschwitz: Catholics and the Holocaust," *Catholic Medical Quarterly* 63, no. 3: (August 2013): 45–46; "Madeleine Rouffart," Righteous Among the Nations; Gronowski, *L'enfant du 20e convoi*: 71–79.

3. Baumel, *Holocaust Encyclopedia*: 56–59; Curtis, "Escaping the Train from Auschwitz": 25; "Madeleine Rouffart," Righteous Among the Nations; Gronowski, *L'enfant du 20e convoi*: 71–79.

4. "Madeleine Rouffart," Righteous Among the Nations; Gronowski, *L'enfant du 20e convoi*: 71–79; Curtis, "Escaping the Train from Auschwitz": 25.

5. Gronowski, *L'enfant du 20e convoi*: 71–79; Curtis, "Escaping the Train from Auschwitz": 25; "Madeleine Rouffart," Righteous Among the Nations.

6. Gronowski, *L'enfant du 20e convoi*: 142–49, 160–169; Curtis, "Escaping the Train from Auschwitz": 25; "Madeleine Rouffart," Righteous Among the Nations.

7. Curtis, "Escaping the Train from Auschwitz": 25; "Madeleine Rouffart," Righteous Among the Nations; Gronowski, *L'enfant du 20e convoi*: 71–79.

8. Althea Williams and Sarah Ehrlich, "Escaping the Train to Auschwitz," *BBC Magazine*, April 20, 2013: 3–5; Curtis, "Escaping the Train from Auschwitz": 25; "Madeleine Rouffart," Righteous Among the Nations; Gronowski, *L'enfant du 20e convoi*: 71–79.

9. Marion Schreiber, *The Twentieth Train: The True Story of the Ambush of the Death Train to Auschwitz,* New York: Grove Press, 2000: 17–18, 32–33, 210–11, 241–42; Ian Black, "The Heroes of Mechelen," *Guardian*, June 19, 2003.

10. Schreiber, *The Twentieth Train*: 210–11, 241–42; Black, "The Heroes of Mechelen"; Curtis, "Escaping the Train from Auschwitz": 25; "Madeleine Rouffart," Righteous Among the Nations; Gronowski, *L'enfant du 20e convoi*: 142–49.

11. Black, "The Heroes of Mechelen"; Schreiber, *The Twentieth Train*: 210–11, 241–42; "Madeleine Rouffart," Righteous Among the Nations; Gronowski, *L'enfant du 20e convoi*: 142–49, 160–69.

12. Black, "The Heroes of Mechelen"; Schreiber, *The Twentieth Train*: 241–42; "Madeleine Rouffart," Righteous Among the Nations; Gronowski, *L'enfant du 20e convoi*: 142–49, 160–69.

13. "Madeleine Rouffart," Righteous Among the Nations; Schreiber, *The Twentieth Train*: 241–42; Gronowski, *L'enfant du 20e convoi*: 142–49, 160–69.

14. "Madeleine Rouffart," Righteous Among the Nations; Schreiber, *The Twentieth Train*: 241–42; Gronowski, *L'enfant du 20e convoi*: 142–49, 160–69.

15. Black, "The Heroes of Mechelen"; "Madeleine Rouffart," Righteous Among the Nations; Schreiber, *The Twentieth Train*: 241–42; Gronowski, *L'enfant du 20e convoi*: 142–49, 160–69.

16. "Madeleine Rouffart," Righteous Among the Nations; Schreiber, *The Twentieth Train:* 241–42; Gronowski, *L'enfant du 20e convoi*: 142–49, 160–69.

17. "Madeleine Rouffart," Righteous Among the Nations; Schreiber, *The Twentieth Train*: 241–42; Gronowski, *L'enfant du 20e convoi*: 142–49, 160–69; Althea Williams, "A Child in Time: Surviving Auschwitz," *History Today* 63, no. 4 (April 2013): 52–54; Sanhedrin 4:1 (22a), *Jerusalem Talmud*, New York: Walter De Gruyter, 2005.

Chapter 15. Bastiaan Jan Ader

1. Johanna-Ruth Dobschiner, *Selected to Live,* London: Hodder & Stoughton, 2006: 5–18; Don Stephens, "Johanna-Ruth Dobschiner: A Survivor of the Holocaust," jewishroots.net; "Hansie Douglas: Holocaust Chronicler Who Was the Only One of Her Family to Escape with Her Life," *Herald*, August 16, 2002; Sense de Jong, "Stories of Domie and Hansie," sensedejong .newsmake.net; Don Stephens, *War and Grace: Short Biographies from the World Wars,* Darlington, UK: EP Books, 2005: 81–89.

2. Ronald E. Powaski, *Lightning War: Blitzkrieg in the West, 1940,* Edison, NJ: Castle Books, 2006: 78–82; Shirer, *Rise and Fall of the Third Reich*: 682, 720–23; Werner Warmbrunn, *The Dutch under German Occupation,* Stanford, CA: Stanford University Press, 1972: 11–34.

3. Powaski, *Lightning War*: 78–82; Shirer, *Rise and Fall of the Third Reich*: 682, 720–23; Hart, *History of the Second World War*: 66–68; Mavrikis, *History of World War II*: 181–85; Warmbrunn, *The Dutch under German Occupation*: 31–34; Wilt, *War from the Top*: 67–70.

4. Warmbrunn, *The Dutch under German Occupation*: 62–68; Baumel, *Holocaust Encyclopedia*: 437–43; Gilbert, *The Holocaust*: 140–3, 375–78.

5. Dobschiner, *Selected to Live*: 52–71, 111–19; Stephens, "Johanna-Ruth Dobschiner: A Survivor"; "Hansie Douglas: Holocaust Chronicler Who Was the Only One of Her Family to Escape with Her Life"; Stephens, *War and Grace*: 87–89.

6. Stephens, "Johanna-Ruth Dobschiner: A Survivor"; "Hansie Douglas: Holocaust Chronicler Who Was the Only One of Her Family to Escape with Her Life"; Dobschiner, *Selected to Live*: 52–71, 111–19.

7. Stephens, "Johanna-Ruth Dobschiner: A Survivor"; "Hansie Douglas: Holocaust Chronicler Who Was the Only One of Her Family to Escape with Her Life"; Dobschiner, *Selected to Live*: 111–19.

8. "Hansie Douglas: Holocaust Chronicler Who Was the Only One of Her Family to Escape with Her Life"; Dobschiner, *Selected to Live*: 111–19; Stephens, "Johanna-Ruth Dobschiner: A Survivor."

9. "Hansie Douglas: Holocaust Chronicler Who Was the Only One of Her Family to Escape with Her Life"; Dobschiner, *Selected to Live*: 111–19; Stephens, "Johanna-Ruth Dobschiner: A Survivor."

10. Alexander Dumbadze, *Bas Jan Ader: Death Is Elsewhere,* Chicago: University of Chicago Press, 2013: 24–25; "Bastiaan Jan Adder," Righteous Among the Nations, yadvashem.org; Henry Havard, *Picturesque Holland: A Journey in the Provinces of Friesland, Groningen, Drenthe, Overyssel, Guelders and Limbourg,* London: Richard Bentley, 1876: 126–29; Stephens, *War and Grace*: 86–89.

11. Dumbadze, *Bas Jan Ader*: 24–25; "Bastiaan Jan Adder," Righteous Among the Nations; Stephens, *War and Grace*: 83–89; J. A. Ader-Appels, *Een Groninger Pastorie in de Storm,* Franeker, Neth.: Van Wijnen, 1990: 7–18, 37–51.

12. "Service to Commemorate the 100th Birthday of the Rev. B. J. Ader," Nieuwbeerta Dutch Reformed Church, December 27, 2009; Dumbadze, *Bas Jan Ader*: 24–25; "Bastiaan Jan Adder," Righteous Among the Nations; Stephens, *War and Grace*: 79–96; Ader-Appels, *Een Groninger Pastorie in de Storm*: 37–51, 78–90.

13. "Hansie Douglas: Holocaust Chronicler Who Was the Only One of Her Family to Escape with Her Life"; Dobschiner, *Selected to Live*: 52–71, 111–19; Stephens, "Johanna-Ruth Dobschiner: A Survivor."

14. "Bastiaan Jan Adder," Righteous Among the Nations; Stephens, *War and Grace*: 87–89; Ader-Appels, *Een Groninger Pastorie in de Storm*: 78–90; "The Execution of Bas Ader, Pastor and Resistance Fighter," *Historiek*, November 20, 2014; "Hansie Douglas: Holocaust Chronicler Who Was the Only One of Her Family to Escape with Her Life"; Dobschiner, *Selected to Live*: 511–19; Stephens, "Johanna-Ruth Dobschiner: A Survivor."

Chapter 16. The Ten Boom Family

1. Corrie ten Boom, *In My Father's House: The Years Before the Hiding Place,* Old Tappan, NJ: Fleming H. Revell, 1976: 178; "Corrie ten Boom," Righteous Among the Nations, yadvashem.org; "Corrie ten Boom," United States Holocaust Memorial Museum, Holocaust Encyclopedia, ushmm.org.

2. "Corrie ten Boom," Righteous Among the Nations; Matthew 25:40; Ten Boom, *In My Father's House*: 175; Corrie ten Boom with John and Elizabeth Sherrill, *The Hiding Place: The Triumphant True Story of Corrie ten Boom*, Old Tappan, NJ: Fleming H. Revell, 1971: 77–78, 86–88, 128–40.

3. "Corrie ten Boom," Righteous Among the Nations; Ten Boom, *In My Father's House*: 36–49; Ten Boom, *Hiding Place*: 86–88, 128–40; Patricia Ferreira, "Corrie ten Boom: A Dutch Savior," International Raoul Wallenberg Foundation, raoulwallenberg.net.

4. "Corrie ten Boom," Righteous Among the Nations; Ten Boom, *In My Father's House*: 36–49; Ten Boom, *Hiding Place*: 86–88, 128–40; Ferreira, "Corrie ten Boom: A Dutch Savior."

5. "Corrie ten Boom," Righteous Among the Nations; Ferreira, "Corrie ten Boom: A Dutch Savior"; Ten Boom, *In My Father's House*: 36–49; Ten Boom, *Hiding Place*: 128–40, 152.

6. "Corrie ten Boom," Righteous Among the Nations; Ferreira, "Corrie ten Boom: A Dutch Savior"; Ten Boom, *Hiding Place*: 174–79, 194–205, 210–19; Ten Boom, *In My Father's House*: 11; Hogan, *Holocaust Chronicle*: 412, 444, 499, 539; "Camp Vught," Camp Vught National Memorial, nmkampvught.nl; "History," Ravensbrück Women's Concentration Camp, ravensbrueck.de.

7. Ten Boom, *Hiding Place*: 174–79, 194–206, 210–19; "Corrie ten Boom," Righteous Among the Nations; Hogan, *Holocaust Chronicle*: 444, 499, 539; Gilbert, *The Holocaust*: 806; Wachsmann, *KL: History of Nazi Concentration Camps*: 232–36.

8. Ten Boom, *Hiding Place*: 194–206, 210–19; "Corrie ten Boom," Righteous Among the Nations.

9. Ten Boom, *Hiding Place*: 194–203, 212, 227; "Corrie ten Boom," Righteous Among the Nations.

10. Ten Boom, *Hiding Place*: 239–49; "Corrie ten Boom," Righteous Among the Nations; Corrie ten Boom with Jamie Buckingham, *Tramp for the Lord*, Grand Rapids, MI: Fleming H. Revell, 1974: 56–58; "Corrie ten Boom," *New York Times*, April 17, 1983.

Chapter 17. Jean Henri Weidner

1. Shirer, *Rise and Fall of the Third Reich*: 742–45; Williamson Murray and Allan R. Millett, *A War to Be Won: Fighting the Second World War*, Cambridge, MA: Harvard University Press, 2000: 71–73.

2. Wernick, *Blitzkrieg*: 117–19, 183–89, 194–99; Shirer, *Rise and Fall of the Third Reich*: 742–45; Murray and Millett, *A War to Be Won*: 71–73.

3. "Swastika Flag Flies over the Eiffel Tower," Holocaust Encyclopedia, US Holocaust Memorial Museum; Wernick, *Blitzkrieg*: 194–99; Shirer, *Rise and Fall of the Third Reich*: 742–45.

4. "The Holocaust in France," yadvashem.org; Hanna Diamond, *Fleeing Hitler: France 1940,* Oxford: Oxford University Press, 2007: 2–10, 21–28, 216–18; "Swastika Flag Flies over the Eiffel Tower."

5. "Jean Weidner," Righteous Among the Nations, yadvashem.org; Shirer, *Rise and Fall of the Third Reich*: 742–45; Murray and Millett, *A War to Be Won*: 71–73; "The Holocaust in France"; Diamond, *Fleeing Hitler*: 21–28, 216–18; "Swastika Flag Flies over the Eiffel Tower."

6. "Jean Weidner," Righteous Among the Nations; "The Life and Times of John Weidner: I Had No Choice," Weidner Foundation, weidnerfoundation .org; Herbert Ford, *Flee the Captor,* Hagerstown, MD: Southern Publishing, 1966: 17–23, 151–59, 287–94; *The Courage to Care,* edited by Carol Rittner and Sondra Myers, New York: New York University Press, 1986: 58–59.

7. Wilona Karimabadi, "Running from Death: The Story of Adventist Holocaust Rescuer John Weidner," *Adventist Review,* June 26, 2008; "The Life and Times of John Henry Weidner," Weidner Foundation; Ford, *Flee the Captor*: 17–23, 151–59, 287–94; Ritter and Myers, *Courage to Care*: 58–59; "Jean Weidner," Righteous Among the Nations; Leviticus 19:17.

8. Ritter and Myers, *Courage to Care*: 58–59; Karimabadi, "Running from Death"; "The Life and Times of John Weidner," Weidner Foundation; Ford, *Flee the Captor*: 151–59, 287–94; "Jean Weidner," Righteous Among the Nations.

9. Ritter and Myers, *Courage to Care*: 58–59; Karimabadi, "Running from Death"; "Life and Times of John Weidner," Weidner Foundation; Ford, *Flee the Captor*: 151–59, 287–94; "Jean Weidner," Righteous Among the Nations.

10. Ritter and Myers, *Courage to Care*: 58–59; Karimabadi, "Running from Death"; "Life and Times of John Weidner," Weidner Foundation; Ford, *Flee the Captor*: 151–59, 287–94; "Jean Weidner," Righteous Among the Nations.

11. Karimabadi, "Running from Death"; "Life and Times of John Weidner," Weidner Foundation; Ritter and Myers, *Courage to Care*: 58–59; Ford, *Flee the Captor*: 287–94; "Jean Weidner," Righteous Among the Nations.

12. Ford, *Flee the Captor*: 287–94; Karimabadi, "Running from Death"; "Life and Times of John Weidner," Weidner Foundation; Ritter and Myers, *Courage to Care*: 58–59; Arnold Charitan, *Tenements,* New York: iUniverse, 2007: 53.

13. "Jean Weidner," Righteous Among the Nations; Charitan, *Tenements*: 53; Karimabadi"; "Life and Times of John Weidner," Weidner Foundation; Ritter and Myers, *Courage to Care*: 58–59; Ford, *Flee the Captor*: 287–94; Myrna Oliver, "John Weidner, Hero of the Holocaust, Dies," *Los Angeles Times,* May 23, 1994.

Chapter 18. André Trocmé

1. André Trocmé, *Jesus and the Non-Violent Revolution,* Rifton, NY: Plough Publications, 2011: v–xii, 5–6; "André and Magda Trocmé," Righteous Among the Nations, yadvashem.org; Baumel, *Holocaust Encyclopedia*: 217–21.

2. Julian Jackson, *France: The Dark Years, 1940–1944,* New York: Oxford University Press, 2001: 150–55, 217–21, 317–22, 377–79; Gilbert, *The Holocaust*: 123–26, 482; Trocmé, *Jesus and the Non-Violent Revolution*: xii; "André and Magda Trocmé," Righteous Among the Nations; Romans 13:1; Acts 5:29.

3. Trocmé, *Jesus and the Non-Violent Revolution*: xii, 28; Philip P. Hallie, *Lest Innocent Blood Be Shed: The Story of the Village of Le Chambon and How Goodness Happened There*, New York: Harper & Row, 1994: xx, 22–24, 51–53; "André and Magda Trocmé," Righteous Among the Nations; Abstract, André and Magda Trocmé Papers, Peace Collection, Swathmore College; *Weapons of the Spirit*, produced by Pierre Sauvage, Chambon Foundation; Justin Young, "Andre Trocme and Le Chambon: The Preciousness of Human Life," unpublished thesis, University of California–Santa Barbara, 2005: 4–5.

4. Anik Fraud, "Le Plateau Vierais-Lignon, 1939–44: Un Histoire," Lieu de Mémoire au Chambon-sur-Lignon: 6–32; Pierre Sauvage, "Ten Questions about Righteous Conduct in Le Chambon and Elsewhere during the Holocaust," US Holocaust Memorial Council Conference, Elie Wiesel, chairman, Washington, DC, September 19, 1984; Allison Stark Draper, *Pastor André Trocmé: Spiritual Leader of the French Village Le Chambon,* New York: Rosen Publishing, 2001: 22–26, 70.

5. Malcolm Gladwell, *David and Goliath: Underdogs, Misfits, and the Art of Battling Giants,* New York: Little, Brown, 2013: 263–69; Christopher Chalamet, *Revivalism and Social Christianity: The Prophetic Faith of Henri Nick and André Trocmé,* Eugene, OR: Pickwick Publications, 2013: 152–56; Peter Grose, *A Good Place to Hide: How One French Village Saved Thousands of Lives during World War II,* New York: Pegasus Books, 2015: 95–98, 151–59; *Weapons of the Spirit*, produced by Pierre Sauvage; Draper, *Pastor André Trocmé*: 22–26, 70; Trocmé, *Jesus and the Non-Violent Revolution*: xii, 28, 102–3, 149–60; Hallie, *Lest Innocent Blood Be Shed*: xx, 111–19, 222–28; "André and Magda Trocmé," Righteous Among the Nations.

6. Gladwell, *David and Goliath*: 263–69; Chalamet, *Revivalism and Social Christianity*: 152–56; Grose, *Good Place to Hide*: 95–98, 151–59; *Weapons of the Spirit*, produced by Pierre Sauvage; Draper, *Pastor André Trocmé*: 22–26, 70; Trocmé, *Jesus and the Non-Violent Revolution*: xii, 149–60; Hallie, *Lest Innocent Blood Be Shed*: xx, 111–19, 222–28; "André and Magda Trocmé," Righteous Among the Nations; *Churchill: A Major New Assessment of His Life in Peace and War,* edited by Robert Blake and William Roger Louis, New York: Oxford University Press, 1993: 337.

7. Rick Atkinson, *An Army at Dawn: The War in North Africa, 1942–1943,* New York: Henry Holt, 2003: 23–28, 114–19, 161–69; Draper, *Pastor André Trocmé*: 22–26, 70; Gladwell, *David and Goliath*: 263–69; Chalamet,

Revivalism and Social Christianity: 152–56; Grose, *Good Place to Hide*: 95–98, 151–59; Trocmé, *Jesus and the Non-Violent Revolution*: xii, 149–60; Hallie, *Lest Innocent Blood Be Shed*: xx, 222–28; "André and Magda Trocmé," Righteous Among the Nations; *Weapons of the Spirit*, produced by Pierre Sauvage.

8. Draper, *Pastor André Trocmé*: 22–26, 70; Gladwell, *David and Goliath*: 263–69; Chalamet, *Revivalism and Social Christianity*: 152–56; Grose, *Good Place to Hide*: 95–98, 151–59; Trocmé, *Jesus and the Non-Violent Revolution*: xii, 149–60; Hallie, *Lest Innocent Blood Be Shed*: xx, 111–19, 222–28; "André and Magda Trocmé," Righteous Among the Nations; *Weapons of the Spirit*, produced by Pierre Sauvage.

9. Proverbs 25:21; Draper, *Pastor André Trocmé*: 22–26, 70; Gladwell, *David and Goliath*: 263–69; Chalamet, *Revivalism and Social Christianity*: 152–56; Grose, *Good Place to Hide*: 95–98, 151–59; Trocmé, *Jesus and the Non-Violent Revolution*: v–xi, 149–160; Hallie, *Lest Innocent Blood Be Shed*: xx, 81–85; "André and Magda Trocmé," Righteous Among the Nations; *Weapons of the Spirit,* produced by Pierre Sauvage; Marilyn Ham, *A Mighty Fortress: Hymn Arrangements for Solo Piano*, Fort Lauderdale FL: FJH Sacred Piano Library, 2003.

10. Draper, *Pastor André Trocmé*: 22–26, 70; Gladwell, *David and Goliath*: 263–69; Chalamet, *Revivalism and Social Christianity*: 152–56; Grose, *Good Place to Hide*: 95–98, 151–59; Trocmé, *Jesus and the Non-Violent Revolution*: xii, 149–60; Hallie, *Lest Innocent Blood Be Shed*: 111–19, 222–28; "André and Magda Trocmé," Righteous Among the Nations; *Weapons of the Spirit*, produced by Pierre Sauvage.

11. Robert Thomas Jr., "Magda Trocmé, 94, Is Dead; Sheltered Victims of Nazis," *New York Times*, October 19, 1996; "André and Magda Trocmé," Righteous Among the Nations; Draper, *Pastor André Trocmé*: 22–26, 70; Gladwell, *David and Goliath*: 263–69; Chalamet, *Revivalism and Social Christianity*: 152–56; Grose, *Good Place to Hide*: 95–98, 151–59; Hallie, *Lest Innocent Blood Be Shed*: 222–28; *Weapons of the Spirit*, produced by Pierre Sauvage; Trocmé, *Jesus and the Non-Violent Revolution*: xii. Acts 5:29.

Chapter 19. Lois Gunden

1. Mary Jean Gunden, "Lois Gunden: A Righteous Gentile," *Mennonite* 16, no. 9 (September 2013): 12–16; "Lois Gunden Clemens," *Elkhart Truth*, August 29, 2005; Esther 4:14.

2. "Women of Valor: Lois Gunden," Righteous Among the Nations, yadvashem; Gunden, "Lois Gunden: A Righteous Gentile": 12–16; "Lois Gunden Clemens"; Nicholas Wapshott, *The Sphinx: Franklin Roosevelt, the Isolationists, and the Road to World War II*, New York: W. W. Norton, 2015: 4–7, 256–62, 337–41.

3. "Women of Valor: Lois Gunden," Righteous Among the Nations; Gunden, "Lois Gunden: A Righteous Gentile": 12–16; Julien Licourt, "The Camp at Rivesaltes Is the Tower of Babel," *Le Figero*, October 16, 2015; Hogan, *Holocaust Chronicle*: 204; Mary Jean Gunden and Jodi J. Beyeler, eds., "Letters from Lois," *Goshen College Bulletin*, Fall 2013: 22–27; John David Unruh, *In the Name of Christ: A History of the Mennonite Central Committee and Its Service, 1920–1951,* Scottsdale AZ: Herald Publishing, 1952: 46–47.

4. "Women of Valor: Lois Gunden," Righteous Among the Nations; Gunden, "Lois Gunden: A Righteous Gentile": 12–16; Licourt, "The Camp at Rivesaltes Is the Tower of Babel"; Gunden and Beyeler, "Letters from Lois": *Bulletin*, 22–27; Unruh, *In the Name of Christ*: 46–47.

5. "Women of Valor: Lois Gunden," Righteous Among the Nations; Mary Gunden, "Lois Gunden: A Righteous Gentile": 12–16; Licourt, "The Camp at Rivesaltes Is the Tower of Babel"; Gunden and Beyeler, "Letters from Lois": 22–27; Unruh, *In the Name of Christ*: 46–47.

6. "Women of Valor: Lois Gunden," Righteous Among the Nations; Gunden, "Lois Gunden: A Righteous Gentile": 12–16; Gunden and Beyeler, "Letters from Lois": 22–27; Unruh, *In the Name of Christ*: 46–47.

7. "Women of Valor: Lois Gunden," Righteous Among the Nations; Gunden, "Lois Gunden: A Righteous Gentile": 12–16; Gunden and Beyeler, "Letters from Lois": 22–27; Unruh, *In the Name of Christ*: 46–47.

8. "Women of Valor: Lois Gunden," Righteous Among the Nations; Gunden, "Lois Gunden: A Righteous Gentile": 12–16; Gunden and Beyeler, "Letters from Lois": 22–27; Unruh, *In the Name of Christ*: 46–47.

9. "Women of Valor: Lois Gunden," Righteous Among the Nations; Gunden, "Lois Gunden: A Righteous Gentile": 12–16; Licourt, "The Camp at Rivesaltes Is the Tower of Babel"; Gunden and Beyeler, "Letters from Lois": 22–27.

10. "Interview with Paul F. Du Vivier," Foreign Affairs Oral History Collection, Manuscripts Division, Library of Congress; Erin Rhoda, "Why One Maine Man Is Grateful for Prisoner Swaps: The Germans Had His Parents," *Arguably*, June 13, 2014; "Women of Valor: Lois Gunden," Righteous Among the Nations; Gunden, "Lois Gunden: A Righteous Gentile": 12–16; Gunden and Beyeler, "Letters from Lois": 22–27; Unruh, *In the Name of Christ*: 46–47.

11. "Women of Valor: Lois Gunden," Righteous Among the Nations; Gunden, "Lois Gunden: A Righteous Gentile": 12–16; Gunden and Beyeler, "Letters from Lois": 22–27; Unruh, *In the Name of Christ*: 46–47; *Breaking Bread Together,* edited by Elaine Sommers Rich, Eugene, OR: Wipf and Stock, 2007: 187.

Chapter 20. Princess Alice of Battenberg

1. Shirer, *Rise and Fall of the Third Reich*: 289, 469, 739, 816–25; Baumel, *Holocaust Encyclopedia*: 265–69, 704–7; Gilbert, *The Holocaust*: 141–56, 287–89; Mark Mazower, *Inside Hitler's Greece: The Experience of Occupation, 1941–44*, New Haven, CT: Yale University Press, 1993: 235–42.

2. Hugo Vickers, *Alice: Princess Andrew of Greece,* New York: St. Martin's Press, 2002: 22–28, 71–76, 112–19, 171–81; "Princess Alice of Battenberg," Righteous Among the Nations, yadvashem.org; Mary Greene, "The Other Queen Mother," *Daily Mail*, August 17, 2012; "The Duke of Edinburgh," The Official Website of the British Monarchy, royal.gov.uk; Somdeep Sen, "Princess Alice of Battenberg," The International Raoul Wallenberg Foundation, raoulwallenberg.net.

3. Vickers, *Alice*: 22–28, 71–76, 112–19, 171–81; "Princess Alice of Battenberg," Righteous Among the Nations; Greene, "The Other Queen Mother"; "Duke of Edinburgh"; Sen, "Princess Alice."

4. Sarah Helm, "Duke Will Tip-Toe to His Mother's Grave," *Independent*, September 17, 1994; Vickers, *Alice*: 22–28, 71–76; "Princess Alice of Battenberg," Righteous Among the Nations; Greene, "The Other Queen Mother"; "Duke of Edinburgh"; Sen, "Princess Alice."

5. "Princess Alice of Battenberg," Righteous Among the Nations; Vickers, *Alice*: 171–81, 291–305, 310–18; "Princess Alice of Battenberg," Righteous Among the Nations; Matthew 25:40; Greene, "The Other Queen Mother"; "Duke of Edinburgh"; Sen, "Princess Alice"; Helm, "Duke Will Tip-Toe to His Mother's Grave.

6. "Princess Alice of Battenberg," Righteous Among the Nations; Vickers, *Alice*: 291–305, 310–18; Greene, "The Other Queen Mother"; "Duke of Edinburgh"; Sen, "Princess Alice"; Helm, "Duke Will Tip-Toe to His Mother's Grave."

7. "Princess Alice of Battenberg," Righteous Among the Nations; Vickers, *Alice*: 291–305, 310–18; Greene, "The Other Queen Mother"; "Duke of Edinburgh"; Sen, "Princess Alice"; Helm, "Duke Will Tip-Toe to His Mother's Grave."

8. "Princess Alice of Battenberg," Righteous Among the Nations; Vickers, *Alice*: 291–305, 310–18; Greene, "The Other Queen Mother"; "Duke of Edinburgh"; Sen, "Princess Alice"; Helm, "Duke Will Tip-Toe to His Mother's Grave."

9. Rafael Medoff, "Three Graves in Jerusalem," Jewish News Service, April 29, 2013; "Princess Alice of Battenberg," Righteous Among the Nations; Vickers, *Alice*: 291–305, 310–18; Greene, "The Other Queen Mother"; "Duke of Edinburgh"; Sen, "Princess Alice"; Helm, "Duke Will Tip-Toe to His Mother's Grave."

Chapter 21. Daniil Tymchyna

1. "Hieromonk Daniil Tymchyna," Righteous Among the Nations, yadvashem .org; Timothy Snyder, *Bloodlands: Europe between Hitler and Stalin,* New York: Basic Books, 2010: vii, 2–14, 59–67, 379–401.

2. Michael Jones, *Total War: From Stalingrad to Berlin,* London: John Murray Publishing, 2011: 6–18; David M. Glantz, *Operation Barbarossa: Hitler's Invasion of Russia, 1941,* London: History Group, 2009: 4–18; Snyder, *Bloodlands*: 59–67, 379–401; Shirer, *Rise and Fall of the Third Reich*: 960–63.

3. David Stahel, *Operation Barbarossa and Germany's Defeat in the East,* Cambridge: Cambridge University Press, 2009: 153–67; Timothy Snyder, "Hitler vs. Stalin: Who Killed More?" *New York Review of Books,* March 10, 2011; Michael Berenbaum, *The World Must Know: The History of the Holocaust as Told in the United States Holocaust Memorial Museum,* Washington, DC: Holocaust Memorial Museum, 1993: 91–99; *The Shoah in Ukraine: History, Testimony, Memorialization,* edited by Ray Brandon and Wendy Lower, Bloomington: Indiana University Press, 2009: 290–99; Lisa Cooper, *A Forgotten Land: Growing Up in the Jewish Pale; Based on the Recollections of Pearl Unikow Cooper,* Jerusalem: Urim Publications, 2013: 142–49.

4. Stahel, *Operation Barbarossa*: 153–67; Snyder, "Hitler vs. Stalin: Who Killed More?"; Berenbaum, *The World Must Know*: 91–99; Brandon and Lower, *The Shoah in Ukraine*: 290–99; Cooper, *Forgotten Land*: 142–49; Shirer, *Rise and Fall of the Third Reich*: 937.

5. Jones, *Total War*: 6–18; Glantz, *Operation Barbarossa*: 4–18; Snyder, *Bloodlands*: 379–401, 408–12; Shirer, *Rise and Fall of the Third Reich*: 960–63; Stahel, *Operation Barbarossa*: 153–67; Snyder, "Hitler vs. Stalin: Who Killed More?"; Berenbaum, *The World Must Know*: 91–99; Brandon and Lower, *The Shoah in the Ukraine*: 290–99; Cooper, *Forgotten Land*: 142–49.

6. *Holocaust in the Ukraine,* edited by Boris Zabarko, Portland, OR: Vallentine Mitchell, 2005: xxiv–xxvii; Baumel, *Holocaust Encyclopedia*: 645–53; "Holocaust in the Ukraine, 1941," Holocaust Encyclopedia, US Holocaust Memorial Museum; Wendy Lower, *Nazi Empire-Building and the Holocaust in Ukraine,* Chapel Hill: University of North Carolina Press, 2005: 81–86.

7. "Babi Yar: Witness and Survivor Accounts of the Mass Murder in Kiev," Holocaust Education Archive and Research Team, holocaustresearchproject. org; Baumel, *Holocaust Encyclopedia*: 645–53; Lower, *Nazi Empire-Building and the Holocaust in Ukraine*: 81–86; Gilbert, *The Holocaust*: 206.

8. Robert E. Conot, *Justice at Nuremberg,* New York: Harper & Row, 1983: 232; Shirer, *Rise and Fall of the Third Reich*: 961.

9. "Hieromonk Daniil Tymchyna," Righteous Among the Nations; Baumel, *Holocaust Encyclopedia*: 645–53.

10. "Hieromonk Daniil Tymchyna," Righteous Among the Nations; Vladislav Davidzun, "Andrey Sheptytsky Welcomed Nazis to the Ukraine: That's Not the Whole Story," *Tablet Magazine*, December 12, 2014; Steve Lippman, "Righteous Gentile or Nazi Supporter?" *Jewish Week*, April 9, 2012; Matthew Matuszak, "Holocaust Survivor Praises Sheptytsky," *Ukrainian Weekly*, October 28, 2007.

11. "Testimony of Oded Amarant," Righteous Among the Nations, yadvashem .org; "Hieromonk Daniil Tymchyna," Righteous Among the Nations; Matuszak, "Holocaust Survivor Praises Sheptytsky"; Lippman, "Righteous Gentile or Nazi Supporter?"

12. "Testimony of Oded Amarant," Righteous Among the Nations; "Hieromonk Daniil Tymchyna," Righteous Among the Nations; Matuszak, "Holocaust Survivor Praises Sheptytsky"; Lippman, "Righteous Gentile or Nazi Supporter?"

13. "Testimony of Oded Amarant," Righteous Among the Nations; "Hieromonk Daniil Tymchyna," Righteous Among the Nations; Matuszak, "Holocaust Survivor Praises Sheptytsky"; Lippman, "Righteous Gentile or Nazi Supporter?"

14. Matuszak, "Holocaust Survivor Praises Sheptytsky"; "Testimony of Oded Amarant," Righteous Among the Nations; "Hieromonk Daniil Tymchyna," Righteous Among the Nations; Lippman, "Righteous Gentile or Nazi Supporter?"

15. Matuszak, "Holocaust Survivor Praises Sheptytsky"; "Testimony of Oded Amarant," Righteous Among the Nations; "Hieromonk Daniil Tymchyna," Righteous Among the Nations; Lippman, "Righteous Gentile or Nazi Supporter?"

16. Jones, *Total War*: 6–18; Glantz, *Operation Barbarossa*: 4–18; Stahel, *Operation Barbarossa and Germany's Defeat in the East*: 153–67; Baumel, *Holocaust Encyclopedia*: 586–91.

17. Shirer, *Rise and Fall of the Third Reich*: 914–19; Stahel, *Operation Barbarossa and Germany's Defeat in the East*: 153–67; Jones, *Total War*: 6–18; Glantz, *Operation Barbarossa*: 4–18; Baumel, *Holocaust Encyclopedia*: 586–91.

18. "Hieromonk Daniil Tymchyna," Righteous Among the Nations; "Mykola and Maria Dyuk," Righteous Among the Nations, www.yadvashem.org; "Testimony of Oded Amarant," Righteous Among the Nations; Lippman, "Righteous Gentile or Nazi Supporter?"

Chapter 22. Iosif and Anna Nazaruk

1. "Testimony of Hinka Goldfarb Weizman," Righteous Among the Nations, www.yadvashem.org; "Iosif and Anna Nazaruk," Righteous Among the Nations, yadvashem.org; "Kobrin," International Jewish Cemetery Project, International Association of Jewish Genealogical Societies; *The Encyclopedia*

of Jewish Life before and during the Holocaust, edited by Shmuel Spector and Geoffrey Wigoder, New York: NYU Press, 2001: 48, 138; David Ashkenazi, "Kobryn, Belarus," www.jewishgen.org.

2. *The Book of Kobrin: The Scroll of Life and Destruction,* edited by Betzalel Shwartz, San Francisco: Holocaust Center of Northern California, 1992: 383–83; Christopher R. Browning, *Ordinary Men: Reserve Police Battalion 101 and the Final Solution in Poland,* New York: HarperCollins, 1992: 12–20.

3. Edelheit and Edelheit, *A World in Turmoil:* 224–36; Gilbert, *The Holocaust:* 279–82; Pierre James, *The Murderous Paradise: German Nationalism and the Holocaust,* Westport, CT: Greenwood Publishing, 2001: 5; Robert Gerwarth, *Hitler's Hangman: The Life of Heydrich,* New Haven, CT: Yale University Press, 2011: 209.

4. David Downing, *The Nazi Death Camps,* Pleasantville, NY: World Almanac Library, 2006: 4–20; "Concentration Camp System in Depth," Holocaust Encyclopedia, US Holocaust Memorial Museum, ushmm.org; Wachsmann, *KL: History of Nazi Concentration Camps:* 292.

5. Andrea Simon, *Bashert: A Granddaughter's Holocaust Quest,* Jackson: University Press of Mississippi, 2002: 34–42, 153–59, 259; Felix Ackermann, "The Spirit of Lukiskes," *Journal of Belarusian Studies* 7, no. 3 (2015): 60–69; Snyder, *Bloodlands:* 235–50; Waitman Wade Beorn, *Marching into Darkness: The Wehrmacht and the Holocaust in Belarus,* Cambridge, MA: Harvard University Press, 2014: 98–105.

6. Gilbert, *The Holocaust:* 239; Simon, *Bashert:* 34–42, 153–59; Ackermann, "Spirit of Lukiskes": 60–69; Snyder, *Bloodlands:* 235–50; Beorn, *Marching into Darkness:* 98–105.

7. "Testimony of Hinka Goldfarb Weizman," Righteous Among the Nations; "Iosif and Anna Nazaruk," Righteous Among the Nations.

8. "Testimony of Hinka Goldfarb Weizman," Righteous Among the Nations; "Iosif and Anna Nazaruk," Righteous Among the Nations.

9. "Testimony of Hinka Goldfarb Weizman," Righteous Among the Nations; "Iosif and Anna Nazaruk," Righteous Among the Nations.

10. "Testimony of Hinka Goldfarb Weizman," Righteous Among the Nations; "Iosif and Anna Nazaruk," Righteous Among the Nations.

11. Spector and Wigoder, *Encyclopedia of Jewish Life:* 196, 332; Zeev Barmatz, *Heroism in the Forest: The Jewish Partisans of Belarus,* Glil Yam, Israel: Kotarim Publishing, 2013: 78–81; "Testimony of Hinka Goldfarb Weizman," Righteous Among the Nations; "Iosif and Anna Nazaruk," Righteous Among the Nations.

12. "Testimony of Hinka Goldfarb Weizman," Righteous Among the Nations; "Iosif and Anna Nazaruk," Righteous Among the Nations.

Chapter 23. Anton Schmid

1. "Anton Schmid," Righteous Among the Nations, yadvashem.org; Wolfram Wette, *Feldwebel Anton Schmid: Ein Held der Humanität*, Frankfurt: S. Fischer, 2003: 2–8, 13–19, 102–28; Rainer Mayerhofer, "Feldwebel Anton Schmid," *Weiner Zeitung*, May 27, 2013; Lonka Kozybracka, "Report about Anton Schmid," Righteous Among the Nations, yadvashem.org; Anton Schmid to Steffi Schmid, 13 April 1942, Anton Schmid Collection, Shoah Resource Center, International School for Holocaust Studies; *Final Letters: From the Yad Vashem Archive,* edited by Yehudit Kleinman and Dafni Reuven, London: Weidenfeld and Nicholson, 1991: 102–4.

2. Prit Buttar, *Between Giants: The Battle for the Baltics in World War II,* Oxford: Osprey Publishing, 2013: 105–11, 126–32, 142–49; Baumel, *Holocaust Encyclopedia*: 663–67; Shirer, *Rise and Fall of the Third Reich*: 962–64.

3. Kazimierz Sakowicz, *Ponary Diary, 1941–1943: A Bystander's Account of a Mass Murder,* edited by Yitzhak Arad, translated by Laurence Weinbaum, New Haven, CT: Yale University Press, 2005: 22–27; Shivaun Woolfson, *Holocaust Legacy in Post-Soviet Lithuania: People, Places and Objects,* London: Bloomsbury Publishing, 2014: 62–69; Hogan, *Holocaust Chronicle,* 480; Simon Wiesenthal, *The Murderers among Us: The Simon Wiesenthal Memoirs,* edited by Joseph Wechsberg, New York: McGraw-Hill, 1967: 61–68, 71–76, 220–29, 243–87; Roger Cohen, "New Model for Soldiers in Germany," *New York Times,* May 9, 2000; Wolfram Wette, *The Wehrmacht: History, Myth, Reality,* Cambridge, MA: Harvard University Press, 2006: 280–84; Hannah Arendt, *Eichmann in Jerusalem: A Report on the Banality of Evil,* New York: Viking, 1963: 230–32; "Anton Schmid," Righteous Among the Nations.

4. Woolfson, *Holocaust Legacy*: 62–69; Hogan, *Holocaust Chronicle*: 480; Cohen, "New Model for Soldiers in Germany"; Wette, *Wehrmacht*: 280–84; "Anton Schmid," Righteous Among the Nations.

5. Cohen, "New Model for Soldiers in Germany"; Wette, *Wehrmacht*: 280–84; "Anton Schmid," Righteous Among the Nations.

6. "Anton Schmid," Righteous Among the Nations; Wette, *Feldwebel Anton Schmid*: 234–46, 277–91; Mayerhofer, "Feldwebel Anton Schmid"; Kozybracka, "Report about Anton Schmid," Righteous Among the Nations; Anton Schmid to Steffi Schmid, 13 April 1942, Anton Schmid Collection; Kleinman and Reuven, *Final Letters: From the Yad Vashem Archive*: 102–4; Cohen, "New Model for Soldiers in Germany."

7. "Anton Schmid," Righteous Among the Nations; Mayerhofer, "Feldwebel Anton Schmid"; Kozybracka, "Report about Anton Schmid," Righteous Among the Nations; Anton Schmid to Steffi Schmid, 13 April 1942, Anton Schmid Collection; kleinman and Reuven, *Final Letters: From the Yad Vashem Archive*: 102–4; Cohen, "New Model for Soldiers in Germany."

8. Mayerhofer, "Feldwebel Anton Schmid"; Kozybracka, "Report about Anton Schmid," Righteous Among the Nations; Anton Schmid to Steffi Schmid, 13 April 1942, Anton Schmid Collection; kleinman and Reuven, *Final Letters: From the Yad Vashem Archive*: 102–4; Cohen, "New Model for Soldiers in Germany"; "Anton Schmid," Righteous Among the Nations.

Chapter 24. Aldo Brunacci

1. "Aldo Brunacci," Righteous Among the Nations, yadvasehm.org; Barry Meier, "In Assisi, a Survivor Recalls Rescue from the Holocaust," *New York Times*, November 27, 1998; Paldiel, *Righteous Among the Nations*: 285–88; Hogan, *Holocaust Chronicle*: 420, 489.
2. Martin Gilbert, *The Second World War: A Complete History*, New York: Henry Holt, 1989: 149–51, 318–23, 434–42, 485–93; Christopher Hibbert, *Mussolini*, New York: St. Martin's Press, 2008: 201–23, 311–29.
3. Baumel, *Holocaust Encyclopedia*: 329–39; William C. Simpson, *A Vatican Lifeline: Allied Fugitives, Aided by the Italian Resistance, Foil the Gestapo in Nazi-Occupied Rome, 1944*, London: Pen and Sword, 1995: 50–68, 78–79, 121–29; Gordon Thomas, *The Pope's Jews: The Vatican's Secret Plan to Save Jews from the Nazis*, New York: St. Martin's Press, 2012: 15–17, 61–68, 81–88, 107, 124–29, 133–38, 251–66, 271–79; Paldiel, *Righteous Among the Nations*: 285–88.
4. "Aldo Brunacci," Righteous Among the Nations; Robert Monyhan and Delia Gallagher, "The Secret Letter," *Inside the Vatican* (January 2004): 74–76.
5. Nicola Caracciolo, *Uncertain Refuge: Italy and the Jews During the Holocaust*, Urbana: University of Illinois Press, 1995: 126–28; Lisa Belig, "Assisi Honors Friends of Jews," *Jewish Floridian*, March 26, 1982; "Aldo Brunacci," Righteous Among the Nations; Paldiel, *Path of the Righteous*: 358; Meier, "In Assisi, a Survivor Recalls Rescue from the Holocaust."
6. "Honor Townspeople of Assisi Who Saved Jews in World War II," Jewish Telegraphic Agency, March 16, 1982; "Aldo Brunacci," Righteous Among the Nations; Josef Raischl and Andre Cirino, *Three Heroes of Assisi in World War II*, Phoenix, AZ: Vesuvius Press, 2014: 59–67, 79–81, 114–18.
7. Raischl and Cirino, *Three Heroes of Assisi*: 8–12, 81; "Brizi Family," Righteous Among the Nations, yadvashem.org; Belig, "Assisi Honors Friends of Jews"; Monyhan and Gallagher, "The Secret Letter": 74–76; Paldiel, *Path of the Righteous*: 356–58.
8. Victor Gaetan, "Following Francis' Footsteps: How Assisi Protected Jews During World War II," *National Catholic Register*, March 6, 2016; Raischl and Cirino, *Three Heroes of Assisi*: 8–12, 81; Paldiel, *Righteous Among the Nations*: 285–88; "Aldo Brunacci Family," Righteous Among the Nations; Belig, "Assisi Honors Friends of Jews"; Paldiel, *Path of the Righteous*: 358.
9. Gaetan, "Following Francis' Footsteps"; Raischl and Cirino, *Three Heroes of Assisi*: 8–12, 81; Paldiel, *Righteous Among the Nations*: 285–88; "Aldo

Brunacci," Righteous Among the Nations; Belig, "Assisi Honors Friends of Jews"; Paldiel, *Path of the Righteous*: 358.

10. "Aldo Brunacci," Righteous Among the Nations; Gaetan, "Following Francis' Footsteps"; Raischl and Cirino, *Three Heroes of Assisi*: 8–12, 81; Paldiel, *Righteous Among the Nations*: 285–88; Belig, "Assisi Honors Friends of Jews"; Paldiel, *Path of the Righteous*: 358.

11. Paldiel, *Righteous Among the Nations*: 285–88; Raischl and Cirino, *Three Heroes of Assisi*: 8–12, 81; "Aldo Brunacci," Righteous Among the Nations; Belig, "Assisi Honors Friends of Jews"; Paldiel, *Path of the Righteous*: 358.

12. Gilbert, *The Second World War*: 491–509, 648–58, 667–74; Hibbert, *Mussolini*: 331–38, 383–98.

13. Meier, "In Assisi, a Survivor Recalls Rescue from the Holocaust"; Monyhan and Gallagher, "The Secret Letter": 74-76; Belig, "Assisi Honors Friends of Jews"; Paldiel, *Righteous Among the Nations*: 288; "Father Brunacci: Hero of the Holocaust," *NPR Morning Edition,* March 26, 2004.

Chapter 25. Jane Haining

1. "Jane Haining," Righteous Among the Nations, yadvashem.org; "Jane Haining: Scotland's Schindler," *Independent,* December 20, 2008; Louis Bulow, "Jane Haining: Rescuer of Jews," annefrank.dk; Billy Kay, *The Scottish World: A Journey into the Scottish Diaspora,* Edinburgh: Mainstream Publishing, 2008: 121–29.

2. Amy Lester, "Evolution of the Scottish Mission in Budapest," reformatus .hu; "Jane Haining," Righteous Among the Nations; "Time to Honour Our Overlooked Holocaust Martyr ," *Herald,* February 1, 2009; Lynley Smith, *From Matron to Martyr: One Woman's Ultimate Sacrifice for the Jews,* Mustang, OK: Tate Publishing, 2012: 406; "Jane Haining: Scotland's Schindler"; Kay, *Scottish World*: 121–29; Bulow, "Jane Haining: Rescuer of Jews."

3. "Jane Haining," Righteous Among the Nations; Lester, "Evolution of the Scottish Mission in Budapest"; "Time to Honour Our Overlooked Holocaust Martyr"; Smith, *From Matron to Martyr*: 406; "Jane Haining: Scotland's Schindler"; Kay, *Scottish World*: 121–29; Bulow, "Jane Haining: Rescuer of Jews."

4. Deborah S. Cornelius, *Hungary in World War II: Caught in a Cauldron,* New York: Fordham University Press, 2011: 294–301, 324–44; Baumel, *Holocaust Encyclopedia*: 314–21; Hilberg, *Destruction of European Jews*: 940–43, 948–68, 971–74, 1030, 1039–56; Shirer, *Rise and Fall of the Third Reich*: 839–42, 972–73.

5. Cornelius, *Hungary in World War II*: 294–301, 324–44; Baumel, *Holocaust Encyclopedia*: 314–21; Hilberg, *Destruction of European Jews*: 971–74, 1030, 1039–56; Shirer, *Rise and Fall of the Third Reich*: 839–42, 972–73.

6. "Jane Haining," Righteous Among the Nations; Lester, "Evolution of the Scottish Mission in Budapest"; "Time to Honour Our Overlooked

Holocaust Martyr"; Smith, *From Matron to Martyr*: 406; "Jane Haining: Scotland's Schindler"; Kay, *Scottish World*: 121–29; Bulow, "Jane Haining: Rescuer of Jews"; Matthew 19:14 (ESV).

7. "Jane Haining," Righteous Among the Nations; Lester, "Evolution of the Scottish Mission in Budapest"; "Time to Honour Our Overlooked Holocaust Martyr"; Smith, *From Matron to Martyr*: 406; "Jane Haining: Scotland's Schindler"; Kay, *Scottish World*: 121–29; Bulow, "Jane Haining: Rescuer of Jews."

8. Yisrael Gutman and Michael Berenbaum, *Anatomy of the Auschwitz Death Camp*, Bloomington: Indiana University Press, 1994: 6–12, 19–22, 30–37; "Tattoos and Numbers: The System of Identifying Prisoners at Auschwitz," Holocaust Encyclopedia, US Holocaust Memorial Museum; Gilbert, *The Holocaust*: 121–23, 239–44, 291–98.

9. Gutman and Berenbaum, *Anatomy of the Auschwitz Death Camp*: 163–72, 231–44; Gilbert, *The Holocaust*: 291–98, 309–21, 340–49, 437–40; Hilberg, *Destruction of the European Jews*: 1016–22, 1030; "Jane Haining," Righteous Among the Nations; Smith, *From Matron to Martyr*: 406.

10. Gutman and Berenbaum, *Anatomy of the Auschwitz Death Camp*: 163–72, 231–44; Gilbert, *The Holocaust*: 291–98, 309–21, 340–49, 437–40; "Jane Haining," Righteous Among the Nations; Smith, *From Matron to Martyr*: 406; Hilberg, *Destruction of the European Jews*: 1030.

11. Gutman and Berenbaum, *Anatomy of the Auschwitz Death Camp*: 163–72, 231–44; Gilbert, *The Holocaust*: 340–49, 437–40; "Jane Haining," Righteous Among the Nations; Smith, *From Matron to Martyr*: 406; Hilberg, *Destruction of the European Jews*: 955–62, 977–83, 1031–39.

12. Shirer, *Rise and Fall of the Third Reich*: 970–73; Baumel, *Holocaust Encyclopedia*: 716–18; Gilbert, *The Holocaust*: 530–36, 678–83, 693–97; Hilberg, *Destruction of the European Jews*: 936–44, 1037–41.

13. Gilbert, *The Holocaust*: 782–93; Gutman and Berenbaum, *Anatomy of the Auschwitz Death Camp*: 163–72, 231–44; "Jane Haining," Righteous Among the Nations; "Time to Honour Our Overlooked Holocaust Martyr"; Smith, *From Matron to Martyr*: 406; "Jane Haining: Scotland's Schindler"; Bulow, "Jane Haining: Rescuer of Jews"; Mark 5:36.

Chapter 26. Imre Báthory

1. "Imre Báthory," Righteous Among the Nations, yadvashem.org; Randolph L. Braham, *The Politics of Genocide: The Holocaust in Hungary*, Detroit: Wayne State University Press, 2000: 136–39; Sheryl Ochayon, "The Shoes on the Danube Promenade," The International School for Holocaust Studies, yadvashem.org.

2. "Imre Báthory," Righteous Among the Nations; Cecil D. Eby, *Hungary at War: Civilians and Soldiers in World War II*, University Park: Pennsylvania

State University Press, 1998: 357–58; Tibor Timothy Vajda, *In the Whirlwind of History: Struggle on and Keep the Faith,* New York: iUniverse, 2005: 189; Alex Kershaw, *The Envoy: The Epic Rescue of the Last Jews of Europe in the Desperate Closing Months of World War II,* Cambridge, MA: Da Capo Press, 2010: 144–51.

3. *The Destruction of Romanian and Ukrainian Jews during the Antonescu Era,* edited by Randolph L. Braham, Ann Arbor: University of Michigan Press, 2008: 74–82; "Romania," Holocaust Encyclopedia, US Holocaust Memorial Museum, ushmm.org; "World War II Mass Grave of Jews Murdered by Romanian Soldiers Is Uncovered in Remote Forest," *Daily Mail,* November 5, 2010; Radu Ioanid, *The Sword of the Archangel: Fascist Ideology in Romania,* New York: Columbia University Press, 1990: 211–26.

4. "Imre Báthory," Righteous Among the Nations.

5. Eby, *Hungary at War:* 357–58; Vajda, *In the Whirlwind of History:* 189; "Imre Báthory," Righteous Among the Nations.

6. Eby, *Hungary at War:* 357–58; Vajda, *In the Whirlwind of History:* 189; "Imre Báthory," Righteous Among the Nations.

7. "Holocaust Survivors and Victims Database," US Holocaust Memorial Museum, ushmm.org; John Erickson, *Stalin's War with Germany,* vol. 2 of *The Road to Berlin,* London: Orion Publishing, 1998: 642–48; Avril Alba, *The Holocaust Museum: Sacred Secular Space,* New York: St. Martin's Press, 2015: 48; Paldiel, *Path of the Righteous:* 377; *The Writer Uprooted: Contemporary Jewish Exile Literature,* edited by Alvin H. Rosenfeld, Bloomington: Indiana University Press, 2008: 185–86; "Imre Báthory," Righteous Among the Nations.

Chapter 27. Anna Ehn

1. "Anna Ehn," Righteous Among the Nations, yadvashem.org.

2. Randolph L. Braham, *The Destruction of Hungarian Jewry: A Documentary Account,* New York: Pro Arte Publishing, 1963: 998; King Frojimovics and Eva Kovacs, "Jews in a 'Judenrein' City: Hungarian Jewish Slave Laborers in Vienna (1944–1945)," *Hungarian Historical Review* 4, no. 3: 711–48; István Hargittai, *Our Lives: Encounters of a Scientist,* Budapest: Akademiai Klado, 2004: 55; *Hogan, Holocaust Chronicle:* 516, 610; Shirer, *Rise and Fall of the Third Reich:* 1106–17; Eleonore Lappin, "The Death Marches of Hungarian Jews through Austria in the Spring of 1945," yadvashem.org; Baumel, "Anna Ehn," Righteous Among the Nations; Baumel, *Holocaust Encyclopedia:* 49, 320–321, 409–10.

3. "Anna Ehn," Righteous Among the Nations; Braham, *Destruction of Hungarian Jewry:* 998; Frojimovics and Kovacs, "Jews in a 'Judenrein' City": 711–48; Hargittai, *Our Lives:* 55; Lappin, "Death Marches of Hungarian Jews"; Baumel, *Holocaust Encyclopedia:* 409–10.

4. "Anna Ehn," Righteous Among the Nations; Baumel, *Holocaust Encyclopedia*: 49.
5. "Anna Ehn," Righteous Among the Nations; Baumel, *Holocaust Encyclopedia*: 49.
6. "Anna Ehn," Righteous Among the Nations; Erwin Bartmann, *Für Volk and Führer: The Memoir of a Veteran of the First SS Panzer Division Leibstandarte SS Adolf Hitler,* translated by Derik Hammond, Solihull, UK: Helion Publishing, 2013: 134–36.
7. "Anna Ehn,"Righteous Among the Nations.

Chapter 28. Ernest and Renée Lepileur

1. "Ernest and Renée Lepileur," Righteous Among the Nations, yadvashem.org; Christopher Argyle, *Chronology of World War II: The Day by Day Illustrated Record 1939–45,* London: Marshal Cavendish, 1980: 157–60.
2. "Ernest and Renée Lepileur," Righteous Among the Nations; Michel Emilla, "A Place Dedicated to Denise Lepileur-Levallois," *Ouest France*, March 10, 2014; François Gillot, "My Parents Were Gassed; A Manchegan Family Saved Me," d-day.tendanceouest.com; "Denise Lepileur-Levallois," *Anonymous, Just and Persecuted by the Nazis*, AJPN.org.
3. "Ernest and Renée Lepileur," Righteous Among the Nations; Emilla, "A Place Dedicated to Denise Lepileur-Levallois"; Gillot, "My Parents Were Gassed"; "Denise Lepileur-Levallois," *Anonymous, Just and Persecuted by the Nazis.*
4. "Ernest and Renée Lepileur," Righteous Among the Nations; Emilla, "A Place Dedicated to Denise Lepileur-Levallois"; Gillot, "My Parents Were Gassed"; "Denise Lepileur-Levallois," *Anonymous, Just and Persecuted by the Nazis.*
5. "Ernest and Renée Lepileur," Righteous Among the Nations; Emilla, "A Place Dedicated to Denise Lepileur-Levallois"; Gillot, "My Parents Were Gassed"; "Denise Lepileur-Levallois," *Anonymous, Just and Persecuted by the Nazis.*
6. Oberst Walter Gaul, "The German Air Force, Luftwaffe, and the Invasion of Normandy, 1944," Navy Department Archives, US Naval History and Heritage Command, history.navy.mil; Anthony Beevor, *D-Day: The Battle for Normandy,* New York: Viking, 2009: 282–89; Stephen Ambrose, *D-Day, June 6, 1944: The Climactic Battle of World War II,* New York: Simon & Schuster, 1994: 166–68; Cornelius Ryan, *The Longest Day: June 6, 1944,* New York: Simon & Schuster, 1959: 182–96, 233–54; Vince Milano and Bruce Conner, *Normandiefront: D-Day to St. Lô Through German Eyes,* Stroud UK: Spellmount Press, 2011: 283; Martin Blumenson, *Breakout and Pursuit: The U.S. Army in the European Theater,* Washington, DC: United States Army Center of Military History, 1961: 155–86.
7. Beevor, *D-Day*: 282–89; Ambrose, *D-Day*: 166–68; Ryan, *The Longest Day*: 182–96, 233–254; Milano and Conner, *Normandiefront*: 283;

Blumenson, *Breakout and Pursuit*: 155–86; "Ernest and Renée Lepileur," Righteous Among the Nations; Emilla, "A Place Dedicated to Denise Lepileur-Levallois"; Gillot, "My Parents Were Gassed"; "Denise Lepileur-Levallois," *Anonymous, Just and Persecuted by the Nazis.*

8. Ryan, *The Longest Day*: 182–96, 233–54; Milano and Conner, *Normandie-front*: 283; Blumenson, *Breakout and Pursuit*: 155–86; Beevor, *D-Day*: 282–89; Ambrose, *D-Day*: 166–68; "Ernest and Renée Lepileur," Righteous Among the Nations; Emilla, "A Place Dedicated to Denise Lepileur-Levallois"; Gillot, "My Parents Were Gassed"; "Denise Lepileur-Levallois," *Anonymous, Just and Persecuted by the Nazis.*

9. "Ernest and Renée Lepileur," Righteous Among the Nations.

Chapter 29. Rodrick Edmonds

1. "Roddie Edmonds," Righteous Among the Nations, yadvashem.org; John Kline, "A Return to Stalag IX-A," Indianamilitary.org; "Stalag IXA Ziegenhain," Gendenkstattenportal zu Orden der Erinnerung in Europa, memorialmuseums.org; "My Father Kept a Cape in His Closet," Righteous Among the Nations, yadvashem.org.

2. "Roddie Edmonds," Righteous Among the Nations; Kieren Corcoran, "We Are All Jews," *Daily Mail*, December 2, 2015; Stanley Weintraub, *11 Days in December: Christmas at the Bulge, 1944,* New York: New American Library, 2006: 27–42, 140–49.

3. Charles MacDonald, *A Time for Trumpets: The Untold Story of the Battle of the Bulge,* London: Perennial, 1985: 116–24, 331–39; Max Hastings, *Armageddon: The Battle for Germany, 1944–1945,* New York: Vintage Books, 2005: 210–34; Roger Cohen, *Soldiers and Slaves: American Soldiers Trapped by the Nazis' Final Gamble,* New York: Anchor Books, 2006: 71–79; Mitchell G. Bard, *Forgotten Victims: The Abandonment of Americans in Hitler's Camps,* Boulder, CO: Westview Press, 1994: 83–86.

4. MacDonald, *Time for Trumpets*: 116–24, 331–39; Hastings, *Armageddon*: 210–34; Cohen, *Soldiers and Slaves*: 71—79; Bard, *Forgotten Victims*: 83–86; "Roddie Edmonds," Righteous Among the Nations; "My Father Kept a Cape in His Closet," Righteous Among the Nations; Corcoran, "We Are All Jews"; Sam Sokol, "Yad Vashem Honors American GI Who Told Nazis, 'We Are All Jews,' " *Jerusalem Post*, December 2, 2015; John Shearer, "Son Shares Details of Dad Roddie Edmonds' Life Following Revelations of His WWII Actions," *Knoxville News-Sentinel*, January 2, 2016.

5. "Roddie Edmonds," Righteous Among the Nations; Kline, "A Return to Stalag IX-A"; "Stalag IXA Ziegenhain."

6. Kline, "A Return to Stalag IX-A"; "Stalag IXA Ziegenhain"; Flint Whitlock, *Given Up for Dead: American GIs in the Nazi Concentration Camp at Berga,*

New York: Basic Books, 2005: 122–49; David Chuter, *War Crimes: Confronting Atrocity in the Modern World,* London: Lynn Rienner, 2003: 60–69, 265–69; J. W. Nessworthy Diary, 30 March 1945, "Thirty-one Days in Stalag IX-A," craxford-family.co.uk; Roddie Edmonds," Righteous Among the Nations.

7. Kline, "A Return to Stalag IX-A"; "Stalag IXA Ziegenhain"; Whitlock, *Given Up for Dead*: 122–49; Chuter, *War Crimes*: 265–69; Nessworthy Diary, 30 March 1945; "Sergeant Roddie Edmonds," roddieedmonds.com.

8. "Roddie Edmonds," Righteous Among the Nations; "My Father Kept a Cape in His Closet," Righteous Among the Nations; Corcoran, "We Are All Jews"; Sokol, "Yad Vashem Honors American GI Who Told Nazis, 'We Are All Jews' "; Shearer, "Son Shares Details of Dad Roddie Edmonds' Life Following Revelations of His WWII Actions."

9. "Roddie Edmonds," Righteous Among the Nations; "My Father Kept a Cape in His Closet," Righteous Among the Nations; Corcoran, "We Are All Jews"; Sokol, "Yad Vashem Honors American GI Who Told Nazis, 'We Are All Jews' "; Shearer, "Son Shares Details of Dad Roddie Edmonds' Life Following Revelations of His WWII Actions"; "American Named Righteous Among the Nations by Yad Vashem," Press Room, yadvashem.org.

Chapter 30. Přemysl Pitter

1. Hugh Trevor-Roper, *The Last Days of Hitler,* Chicago: University of Chicago Press, 1992: 46–49, 60–68, 201–9, 230–48; Traudl Jung, *Until the Final Hour: Hitler's Last Secretary,* edited by Melissa Müller, New York: Arcade Publishing, 2002: 152–64, 184–89; Joachim Fest, *Inside Hitler's Bunker: The Last Days of the Third Reich,* New York: St. Martin's Press, 2004: 1–8, 130–38, 158–64; James P. O'Donnell, *The Bunker: The History of the Reich Chancellery Groups,* New York: Da Capo, 1978: 230–38; Shirer, *Rise and Fall of the Third Reich*: 1103, 1106–40; Kershaw, *Hitler*: 947–49.

2. Kershaw, *Hitler*: 947–49; Trevor-Roper, *Last Days of Hitler*: 46–49, 60–68; Jung, *Until the Final Hour*: 152–64, 184–89; Fest, *Inside Hitler's Bunker*: 1–8, 130–38, 158–64; O'Donnell, *The Bunker*: 230–38; Shirer, *Rise and Fall of the Third Reich*: 1103, 1106–40.

3. Trevor-Roper, *Last Days of Hitler*: 46–49, 60–68, 201–9, 230–48; Kershaw, *Hitler*: 947–49; Jung, *Until the Final Hour*: 152–64, 184–89; Fest, *Inside Hitler's Bunker*: 130–38, 158–64; O'Donnell, *The Bunker*: 230–38; Shirer, *Rise and Fall of the Third Reich*: 1106–40.

4. "Přemysl Pitter," Righteous Among the Nations, yadvashem.org; Teresa Stepkova, "Premysl Pitter," holocaust.cz; David Vaughn, "Přemysl Pitter: The Good Fundamentalist," Radio Prague's website, January 16, 2011, radio.cz/en/section/books/premysl-pitter-the-good-fundamentalist; Baumel, *Holocaust Encyclopedia*: 82.

5. Wolf Oschlies, "Premysl Pitter (1895–1976): Retter tschechischer, jüdischer und deutscher Kinder," Zukunft braucht Erinnerung website, October 4, 2004, zukunft-braucht-erinnerung.de/premysl-pitter/; *Zukunet Erinnerurrung*, October 4, 2004; "Přemysl Pitter," Righteous Among the Nations; Stepkova, "Premysl Pitter"; Vaughn, "Přemysl Pitter: The Good Fundamentalist";

6. "Přemysl Pitter," Righteous Among the Nations; Oschlies, "Premysl Pitter (1895–1976): Retter Tschechischer, Jüdischer und Deutscher Kinder"; Stepkova, "Premysl Pitter"; Vaughn, "Přemysl Pitter: The Good Fundamentalist"; Baumel, *Holocaust Encyclopedia*: 82.

7. "Přemysl Pitter," Righteous Among the Nations; Oschlies, "Premysl Pitter (1895–1976): Retter Tschechischer, Jüdischer und Deutscher Kinder"; Stepkova, "Premysl Pitter"; Vaughn, "Přemysl Pitter: The Good Fundamentalist"; Baumel, *Holocaust Encyclopedia*: 82.

8. "Přemysl Pitter," Righteous Among the Nations; Oschlies, "Premysl Pitter (1895–1976): Retter Tschechischer, Jüdischer und Deutscher Kinder"; Stepkova, "Premysl Pitter"; "Přemysl Pitter: The Good Fundamentalist"; Jenni Frazer, "What Happened to the Jewish Orphans Brought to Britain in 1945?" *Telegraph*, February 6, 2016; Holly Case, "Innocents Lost: On Postwar Orphans," *Nation*, October 12, 2011; "The Orphans Who Survived the Nazi Camps," BBC News, news.bbc.co.uk; Baumel, *Holocaust Encyclopedia*: 82.

9. "Přemysl Pitter," Righteous Among the Nations; Oschlies, "Premysl Pitter (1895–1976): Retter Tschechischer, Jüdischer und Deutscher Kinder"; Stepkova, "Premysl Pitter"; Vaughn, "Premysl Pitter: The Good Fundamentalist"; Frazer, "What Happened to the Jewish Orphans Brought to Britain in 1945?"; Case, "Innocents Lost: On Postwar Orphans"; "Orphans Who Survived the Nazi Camps"; Baumel, *Holocaust Encyclopedia*: 82.

10. Oschlies, "Premysl Pitter (1895–1976): Retter Tschechischer, Jüdischer und Deutscher Kinder"; Stepkova, "Premysl Pitter"; Vaughn, "Přemysl Pitter: The Good Fundamentalist"; Frazer, "What Happened to the Jewish Orphans Brought to Britain in 1945?"; Case, "Innocents Lost: On Postwar Orphans"; "Orphans Who Survived the Nazi Camps"; "Přemysl Pitter," Righteous Among the Nations.

11. "Přemysl Pitter: The Good Fundamentalist"; Oschlies, "Premysl Pitter (1895–1976): Retter Tschechischer, Jüdischer und Deutscher Kinder"; Stepkova, "Premysl Pitter"; Frazer, "What Happened to the Jewish Orphans Brought to Britain in 1945?"; Case, "Innocents Lost: On Postwar Orphans"; "Orphans Who Survived the Nazi Camps"; "Přemysl Pitter," Righteous Among the Nations.

12. Oschlies, "Premysl Pitter (1895–1976): Retter Tschechischer, Jüdischer und Deutscher Kinder"; Stepkova, "Premysl Pitter"; Vaughn, "Přemysl

Pitter: The Good Fundamentalist"; Frazer, "What Happened to the Jewish Orphans Brought to Britain in 1945?"; Case, "Innocents Lost: On Postwar Orphans"; "Orphans Who Survived the Nazi Camps"; "Přemysl Pitter," Righteous Among the Nations.

13. "Olga Fierzova and Premysl Pitter," Displaced Persons/Return to Life, US Holocaust Memorial Museum, ushmm.org; Oschlies, "Premysl Pitter (1895–1976): Retter Tschechischer, Jüdischer und Deutscher Kinder"; Stepkova, "Premysl Pitter"; Vaughn, "Přemysl Pitter: The Good Fundamentalist"; Frazer, "What Happened to the Jewish Orphans Brought to Britain in 1945?"; Case, "Innocents Lost: On Postwar Orphans"; "Orphans Who Survived the Nazi Camps"; "Přemysl Pitter," Righteous Among the Nations.

BIBLIOGRAPHY

Abrahamsen, Samuel. *Norway's Response to the Holocaust*. New York: Open Library, 1991.

Ackermann, Felix. "The Spirit of Lukiskes." *Journal of Belarusian Studies* 7, no. 3 (2015): 62–67.

Ader-Appels, J. A. *Een Groninger Pastorie in de Storm*. Franeker, Neth.: Van Wijnen, 1990.

Alba, Avril. *The Holocaust Museum: Sacred Secular Space*. New York: St. Martin's Press, 2015.

Ambrose, Stephen E. *D-Day, June 6, 1944: The Climactic Battle of World War II*. New York: Simon & Schuster, 1994.

Arad, Yitsak. *The Holocaust in the Soviet Union*. Translated by Ora Cummings. Lincoln: University of Nebraska Press, 2009.

Arendt, Hannah. *Eichmann in Jerusalem: A Report on the Banality of Evil*. New York: Viking, 1963.

Argyle, Christopher. *Chronology of World War II: The Day by Day Illustrated Record 1939–45*. London: Marshal Cavendish, 1980.

Atkinson, Rick. *An Army at Dawn: The War in North Africa, 1942–1943*. New York: Henry Holt, 2003.

Bak, Sofie Lene. *Nothing to Speak Of: Wartime Experiences of the Danish Jews 1943–1945*. Translated by Virginia Raynolds Laursen. Copenhagen: Danish Jewish Museum, 2011.

Bard, Mitchell G. *Forgotten Victims: The Abandonment of Americans in Hitler's Camps*. Boulder, CO: Westview Press, 1994.

Barmatz, Zeev. *Heroism in the Forest: The Jewish Partisans of Belarus*. Translated by Anna Mowszowski. Glil Yam, Israel: Kotarim Publishing, 2013.

Barnett, Victoria J. *For the Soul of the People: Protestant Protest against Hitler*. New York: Oxford University Press, 1992.

Bartmann, Erwin. *Für Volk and Führer: The Memoir of a Veteran of the 1st SS Panzer Division Leibstandarte SS Adolf Hitler*. Translated by Derik Hammond. Solihull, UK: Helion Publishing, 2013.

Bauer, Yahuda, and Nili Keren. *A History of the Holocaust*. Danbury, CT: Franklin Watts, 1982.

Baumel, Judith Tydor. *The Holocaust Encyclopedia*. Edited by Walter Laqueur. New Haven, CT: Yale University Press, 2001.

Baumel-Schwartz, Judith Tydor. *Never Look Back: The Jewish Refugee Children in Britain, 1938–1945*. West Lafayette, IN: Purdue University Press, 2012.

Beevor, Antony. *D-Day: The Battle for Normandy.* New York: Viking, 2009.

Beir, Robert L. *Roosevelt and the Holocaust.* With Brian Josepher. Fort Lee, NJ: Barricade Books, 2006.

Bentley, James. *Martin Niemöller, 1892–1984.* New York: Free Press, 1984.

Beorn, Waitman Wade. *Marching into Darkness: The Wehrmacht and the Holocaust in Belarus.* Cambridge, MA: Harvard University Press, 2014.

Berenbaum, Michael. *The World Must Know: The History of the Holocaust as Told in the United States Holocaust Memorial Museum.* Washington, DC: United States Holocaust Memorial Museum, 1993.

Blake, Robert, and William Roger Louis, eds. *Churchill: A Major New Assessment of His Life in Peace and War.* New York: Oxford University Press, 1993.

Blumenson, Martin. *Breakout and Pursuit: The U.S. Army in the European Theater.* Washington, DC: United States Army Center of Military History, 1961.

Bodson, Herman. *Downed Allied Airmen and Evasion of Capture: The Role of Local Resistance Networks in World War II.* Jefferson, NC: McFarland, 2001.

Bosch, William J. *Judgment on Nuremberg: American Attitudes toward the Major German War-Crime Trials.* Chapel Hill: University of North Carolina Press, 1970.

Braham, Randolph L. *The Destruction of Hungarian Jewry: A Documentary Account.* New York: Pro Arte, 1963.

———. *The Politics of Genocide: The Holocaust in Hungary.* Detroit: Wayne State University Press, 2000.

———, ed. *The Destruction of Romanian and Ukrainian Jews during the Antonescu Era.* Ann Arbor: University of Michigan Press, 2008.

Brandon, Ray, and Wendy Lower, eds. *The Shoah in Ukraine: History, Testimony, Memorialization.* Bloomington: Indiana University Press, 2009.

Brown, Anthony Cave. *Bodyguard of Lies.* Guildford, UK: Lyons Press, 1975.

Browning, Christopher R. *Ordinary Men: Reserve Police Battalion 101 and the Final Solution in Poland.* New York: HarperCollins, 1992.

Brunner, Joseph. "American Involvement in the Nuremburg War Crimes Trial Process." *Michigan Journal of History* 1, no. 4 (winter 2004): 2–6.

Butler, Rupert. *Legions of Death: The Nazi Enslavement of Eastern Europe.* London: Hamlyn Publications, 1983.

Buttar, Prit. *Between Giants: The Battle for the Baltics in World War II.* Oxford: Osprey Publishing, 2013.

Caracciolo, Nicola. *Uncertain Refuge: Italy and the Jews during the Holocaust.* Urbana: University of Illinois Press, 1995.

Carruthers, Bob, ed. *Hitler's Forgotten Armies: Combat in Norway and Finland.* Barnsley, UK: Pen and Sword, 2012

Center for Advanced Holocaust Studies. *Children and the Holocaust: Symposium Presentations.* Washington, DC: United States Holocaust Memorial Museum, 2004.

Chalamet, Christophe. *Revivalism and Social Christianity: The Prophetic Faith of Henri Nick and André Trocmé*. Eugene, OR: Pickwick Publications, 2013.

Charitan, Arnold. *Tenements*. New York: iUniverse, 2007.

Chuter, David. *War Crimes: Confronting Atrocity in the Modern World*. London: Lynn Rienner, 2003.

Cochrane, Arthur C. *The Church's Confession under Hitler*. Philadelphia: Westminster Press, 1962.

Cohen, Roger. *Soldiers and Slaves: American POWs Trapped by the Nazis' Final Gamble*. New York: Anchor Books, 2006.

Cohen, Susan. "Winter in Prague: The Humanitarian Mission of Doreen Warriner." *AJR Journal* 2, no. 8 (August 2011): 4–5.

Conot, Robert E. *Justice at Nuremberg*. New York: Harper & Row, 1983.

Cooke, Philip, and Ben H. Shepherd, eds. *Hitler's Europe Ablaze: Occupation, Resistance, and Rebellion during World War II*. New York: Skyhorse Publishing, 2014.

Cook-Sather, Alison, and John E. Moser. *Global Great Depression and the Coming of World War II*. New York: Paradigm Publishers, 2015.

Cooper, Lisa. *A Forgotten Land: Growing Up in the Jewish Pale; Based on the Recollections of Pearl Unikow Cooper*. Jerusalem: Urim Publications, 2013.

Cornelius, Deborah S. *Hungary in World War II: Caught in the Cauldron*. New York: Fordham University Press, 2011.

Crowe, David M. *The Holocaust: Roots, History, and Aftermath*. Philadelphia: Westview Press, 2008.

——. *Oskar Schindler: The Untold Account of His Life, Wartime Activities and the True Story behind the List*. New York: Westview Press, 2004.

Crowhurst, Patrick. *Hitler and Czechoslovakia in World War II: Domination and Retaliation*. London: I. B. Tauris, 2013.

Curilla, Wolfgang. *Der Judenmord in Polen und die deutsche Ordnungspolizei 1939–1945*. Paderborn, Ger.: Schöningh, 2010.

Curtis, Jim. "Escaping the Train from Auschwitz: Catholics and the Holocaust." *Catholic Medical Quarterly* 63, no. 3 (August 2013): 45–46.

Dafni, Reuven, and Yehudit Kleiman, eds. *Final Letters*. London: Weidenfeld & Nicholson, 1991.

Davies, Norman. *No Simple Victory: World War II in Europe, 1939–1945*. New York: Penguin Books, 2008.

Diamond, Hanna. *Fleeing Hitler: France 1940*. Oxford: Oxford University Press, 2007.

Dobschiner, Johanna-Ruth. *Selected to Live*. London: Hodder & Stoughton, 2006.

Downing, David. *The Nazi Death Camps*. Pleasantville, NY: World Almanac Library, 2006.

Draper, Allison Stark. *Pastor André Trocmé: Spiritual Leader of the French Village Le Chambon*. New York: Rosen Publishing, 2001.

Dumbadze, Alexander. *Bas Jan Ader: Death Is Elsewhere*. Chicago: University of Chicago Press, 2013.

Eby, Cecil D. *Hungary at War: Civilians and Soldiers in World War II*. University Park: Pennsylvania State University Press, 1998.

Edelheit, Hershel, and Abraham J. Edelheit. *A World in Turmoil: An Integrated Chronology of the Holocaust and World War II*. New York: Greenwood Publishing, 1991.

Edwards, Robert. *The Winter War: Russia's Invasion of Finland, 1939–40*. New York: Open Road, 2011.

Elson, Robert T. *Prelude to War*. New York: Time-Life Books, 1977.

Erickson, John. *The Road to Berlin*. Vol. 2 of *Stalin's War with Germany*. London: Orion Publishing, 1998.

Faber, David. *Munich 1938: Appeasement and World War II*. New York: Simon & Schuster, 2009.

Fabri, J. *L'abbé Joseph Peeters, curé de Comblain-au-Pont*. Liège: Catholic Intellectual Center of Belgium, 1957.

Fagen, Lewis. Oral History Interview. Oskar Schindler/Imperial War Museum Collection. Record Group 50.147-0003. United States Holocaust Memorial Museum.

Feingold, Henry L. *The Politics of Rescue: The Roosevelt Administration and the Holocaust, 1938–1945*. New Brunswick, NJ: Rutgers University Press, 1970.

Feng Shan Ho Collection. Center for Holocaust and Genocide Studies. University of Minnesota.

Fest, Joachim. *Inside Hitler's Bunker: The Last Days of the Third Reich*. New York: St. Martin's Press, 2004.

Files, Yvonne de Ridder. *The Quest for Freedom: A Story of Belgian Resistance in World War II*. Santa Barbara, CA: Fithian Press, 1991.

Foehr, Stephen. "Zealand: Heart and Soul of Denmark." *Islands: An International Magazine* 6, no. 2 (March/April 1986): 60–71.

Ford, Herbert. *Flee the Captor*. Hagerstown, MD: Southern Publishing, 1966.

Friedman, Philip. *Roads to Extinction: Essays on the Holocaust*. Lansing: University of Michigan Press, 1980.

Frojimovics, King, and Eva Kovacs. "Jews in a 'Judenrein' City: Hungarian Jewish Slave Laborers in Vienna (1944–1945)." *Hungarian Historical Review* 4, no. 3 (2015): 713–25.

Gaul, Oberst Walter. "The German Air Force, Luftwaffe and the Invasion of Normandy, 1944." Navy Department Archives. US Naval History and Heritage Command. www.history.navy.mil.

Gerlach, Wolfgang. *And the Witnesses Were Silent: The Confessing Church and the Persecution of the Jews*. Translated by Victoria J. Barnett. Lincoln: University of Nebraska Press, 2000.

Gerwarth, Robert. *Hitler's Hangman: The Life of Heydrich.* New Haven, CT: Yale University Press, 2011.

Gilbert, Martin. *The Holocaust: A History of the Jews of Europe during the Second World War.* New York: Henry Holt, 1985.

———. *The Righteous: The Unsung Heroes of the Holocaust.* New York: Henry Holt, 2002.

———. *The Second World War: A Complete History.* New York: Henry Holt, 1989.

"Gilleleje 1943." Eliane Attias, producer. Jewish Federation Council of Greater Los Angeles, 1970.

Gillot, François. "My Parents Were Gassed; A Manchegan Family Saved Me." www.d-day.tendanceouest.com.

Gladwell, Malcolm. *David and Goliath: Underdogs, Misfits, and the Art of Battling Giants.* New York: Little, Brown, 2013.

Glantz, David M. *Operation Barbarossa: Hitler's Invasion of Russia 1941.* London: History Group, 2009.

Goldberger, Leo. *The Rescue of the Danish Jews: Moral Courage under Stress.* New York: NYU Press, 1987.

Gordon, Sarah. *Hitler, Germans, and the "Jewish Question."* Princeton, NJ: Princeton University Press, 1984.

Gronowski, Simon. "Auschwitz and Forgiveness." Michelvanderburg.com.

———. *L'enfant du 20e convoi.* Liège, Belg.: Luc Pire, 2005.

Grose, Peter. *A Good Place to Hide: How One French Village Saved Thousands of Lives during World War II.* New York: Pegasus Books, 2015.

Guggenheimer, Heinrich W., ed. *Jerusalem Talmud.* New York: Walter De Gruyter, 2005.

Gutman, Israel, Sara Bender, Daniel Fraenkel, and Jacob Borut. *Lexikon der Gerechten unter den Völkern: Deutsche und Österreicher.* Göttingen, Ger.: Wallstein Verlag, 2005.

Gutman, Yisrael. *The Jews of Warsaw, 1939–1943: Ghetto, Underground, Revolt.* Bloomington: Indiana University Press, 1982.

Gutman, Yisrael, and Michael Berenbaum, eds. *Anatomy of the Auschwitz Death Camp.* Bloomington: Indiana University Press, 1994.

Haarr, Geirr H. *The German Invasion of Norway: April 1940.* Annapolis, MD: Naval Institute Press, 2009.

Hallie, Philip P. *Lest Innocent Blood Be Shed: The Story of the Village of Le Chambon and How Goodness Happened There.* New York: Harper & Row, 1994.

Ham, Marilynn. *A Mighty Fortress: Hymn Arrangements for Solo Piano.* Fort Lauderdale, FL: FJH Sacred Piano Library, 2003.

Hamilton, Richard F., and Holger H. Herwig, eds. *The Origins of World War I.* Cambridge: Cambridge University Press, 2003.

Hammel, Andrea, and Bea Lewkowicz, eds. *The Kindertransport in Britain, 1938–39: New Perspectives.* Amsterdam: Rodopi, 2012.

Hargittai, István. *Our Lives: Encounters of a Scientist.* Budapest: Akademiai Klado, 2004.

Hargreaves, Richard. *Blitzkrieg Unleashed: The German Invasion of Poland.* Mechanicsburg, PA: Stackpole Books, 2008.

Harris, Mark Jonathan, director. *Into the Arms of Strangers: Stories of the Kindertransport.* Motion picture. Warner Bros., 2000.

Hart, B. H. Liddell. *History of the Second World War.* New York: Da Capo Press, 1999.

Hartman, John Jacob, and Jacek Krochmal. *I Remember Every Day . . . : The Fates of the Jews of Przemyśl during World War II.* Przemyśl, Pol.: Towarzystwo Przyjaciół Nauk w Przemyślu, 2003.

Hastings, Max. *Armageddon: The Battle for Germany, 1944–1945.* New York: Vintage Books, 2005.

Hauben, William. *From the Flames: Miracles and Wonders of Survival.* New York: Writer's Club Press, 2000.

Havard, Henry. *Picturesque Holland: A Journey in the Provinces of Friesland, Groningen, Drenthe, Overyssel, Guelders and Limbourg.* London: Richard Bentley, 1876.

Henry, René. *L'Almanach de Notre Terroir.* Liège, Belg.: Dricol Editions, 1998.

Hibbert, Christopher. *Mussolini.* New York: St. Martin's Press, 2008.

Hilberg, Raul. *The Destruction of the European Jews.* New Haven, CT: Yale University Press, 2003.

Ho, Feng-Shan. *My Forty Years as a Diplomat.* Edited and translated by Monto Ho. Pittsburgh: Dorrance Publishing, 2010.

Ho, Manli. *Diplomat Rescuers and the Story of Feng Shan Ho.* Vancouver: Vancouver Holocaust Center, 1999.

Hodge, Deborah. *Rescuing the Children: The Story of the Kindertransport.* Plattsburgh, NY: Tundra Books, 2012.

Hoekema, Alle G. "Dutch Mennonites and German Jewish Refugee Children, 1938–1945." *Mennonite Quarterly Review* 87 (April 2013): 133–53.

Hoffmann, Peter. *The History of the German Resistance, 1933–1945.* Montreal: McGill-Queen's Press, 1977.

Hogan, David J., ed. *The Holocaust Chronicle: A History in Words and Pictures.* Lincolnwood, IL: Publications International, 2003.

"Interview with Paul F. Du Vivier." Foreign Affairs Oral History Collection. Manuscripts Division. Library of Congress.

Ioanid, Radu. *The Sword of the Archangel: Fascist Ideology in Romania.* Translated by Peter Heinegg. New York: Columbia University Press, 1990.

Irving, David. *Hitler's War.* New York: Viking, 1964.

Jackson, Julian. *France: The Dark Years, 1940–1944.* New York: Oxford University Press, 2001.

James, Pierre. *The Murderous Paradise: German Nationalism and the Holocaust.* Westport, CT: Greenwood Publishing, 2001.

Jensen, Mette, and Steven Jensen. *Denmark and the Holocaust.* Copenhagen: Kobenhaven Institute for International Studies, 2003.

Jones, Michael. *Total War: From Stalingrad to Berlin.* London: John Murray Publishing, 2011.

Junge, Traudl. *Until the Final Hour: Hitler's Last Secretary.* Edited by Melissa Müller. New York: Arcade Publishing, 2002.

Karski, Jan. *Story of a Secret State: My Report to the World.* Washington, DC: University of Georgetown Press, 2010.

Katyn Forest Massacre Collection. General Records of the Department of State. National Archives and Records Administration.

Kay, Billy. *The Scottish World: A Journey into the Scottish Diaspora.* Edinburgh: Mainstream Publishing, 2008.

Keneally, Thomas. *Searching for Schindler: A Memoir.* New York: Doubleday, 2007.

Kershaw, Alex. *The Envoy: The Epic Rescue of the Last Jews of Europe in the Desperate Closing Months of World War II.* Cambridge, MA: Da Capo Press, 2010.

Kershaw, Ian. *Hitler: A Biography.* New York: W. W. Norton, 1998.

Kline, John. "A Return to Stalag IX-A." Indianamilitary.org.

Kotarba, Ryszard. *A Historical Guide to the German Camp in Płaszów, 1942–1945.* Warsaw: Institute of National Remembrance, 2014.

Krakauer, Max. *Lights in Darkness.* Translated by Hans Martin Wuerth. Stuttgart, Ger.: Calwer Verlag, 2007.

Laffer, Dennis R. "The Jewish Trail of Tears: The Evian Conference of July 1938." Graduate thesis. University of South Florida, 2011.

Lampe, David. *Hitler's Savage Canary: A History of the Danish Resistance in World War II.* Barnsley, UK: Frontline Books, 2010.

Landos, Tom. "Tribute to the Rev. Hans Christen Mamen." *Capitol Words* 150, no. 53 (April 22, 2004): 610.

LaPlage, Jean-Denis, ed. *An Illustrated Dictionary of the Third Reich.* Jefferson, NC: McFarland, 2014.

Lidegaard, Bo. *Countrymen: The Untold Story of How Denmark's Jews Escaped the Nazis.* New York: Alfred A. Knopf, 2013.

Longerich, Peter. *Heinrich Himmler.* New York: Oxford University Press, 2012.

Lower, Wendy. *Nazi Empire-Building and the Holocaust in Ukraine.* Chapel Hill: University of North Carolina Press, 2005.

Ludwig, Hartmut. *An der Seite der Entrechteten und Schwachen: Zur Geschichte des 'Büro Pfarrer Grüber' (1938 bis 1940) und der Ev. Hilfsstelle für ehemals Rasseverfolgte nach 1945.* Berlin: Logos Verlag, 2009.

MacDonald, Charles. *A Time for Trumpets: The Untold Story of the Battle of the Bulge.* London: Perennial, 1985.

MacDonogh, Giles. *1938: Hitler's Gamble.* New York: Basic Books, 2009.

Madritsch, Julius. *Menschen in Not!* Vienna, 1963.

―――. Oral History Interview. Oskar Schindler/Imperial War Museum Collection. Record Group 50.147-0011. United States Holocaust Memorial Museum.

Manvell, Roger, and Heinrich Fraenkel. *Heinrich Himmler: The Sinister Life of the Head of the SS and Gestapo.* London: Greenhill Books, 2007.

Martin, Russell. *Beethoven's Hair: An Extraordinary Historical Odyssey and a Scientific Mystery Solved.* New York: Broadway Books, 2000.

Mavrikis, Peter, ed. *History of World War II.* Vol. 1. London: Marshall Cavendish, 2005.

Mazower, Mark. *Inside Hitler's Greece: The Experience of Occupation, 1941–44.* New Haven, CT: Yale University Press, 1993.

Mendelsohn, Ezra, ed. *Jews and Other Ethnic Groups in a Multi-Ethnic World.* Vol. 3 of *Studies in Contemporary Jewry.* New York: Oxford University Press, 1987.

Mendes-Flohr, Paul, and Jehuda Reinharz, eds. *The Jew in the Modern World: A Documentary History.* London: Oxford University Press, 1995.

Metaxas, Eric. *Bonhoeffer: Pastor, Martyr, Prophet, Spy.* Nashville: Thomas Nelson, 2010.

Michman, Dan, ed. *Belgium and the Holocaust: Jews, Belgians, Germans.* Jerusalem: Daf-Noy Press, 1998.

Milano, Vince, and Bruce Conner. *Normandiefront: D-Day to St. Lô through German Eyes.* Stroud, UK: Spellmount Press, 2011.

Moulin, Pierre. *Dachau, Holocaust and US Samurais: Nisei Soldiers First in Dachau?* Bloomington, IN: Authorhouse, 2007.

"Mrs. Geertruida Wijsmuller-Meijer." *AJR Information* 33, no. 11 (November 1978): 11.

Murray, Williamson, and Allan R. Millett. *A War to Be Won: Fighting the Second World War.* Cambridge, MA: Harvard University Press, 2000.

Neitzel, Sönke, and Harald Welzer. *Soldiers: German POWs on Fighting, Killing, and Dying.* New York: Alfred A. Knopf, 2012.

Nelken, Regina. Testimony. Official Transcript of the Trial of Amon Goeth, Holocaust Education and Research Archive Team. www.HolocaustResearch Project.org.

Norris, Margot. *Writing War in the Twentieth Century.* Charlottesville: University of Virginia Press, 2000.

"October 1943: The Rescue of the Danish Jews from Annihilation." Archives. Museum of Danish Resistance. Copenhagen.

O'Donnell, James P. *The Bunker: The History of the Reich Chancellery Groups.* New York: Da Capo, 1978.

Offen, Bernard. *My Hometown Concentration Camp: A Survivor's Account of Life in the Kraków Ghetto and Płaszów Concentration Camp.* With Norman G. Jacobs. Portland, OR: Vallentine Mitchell, 2008.

"Olga Fierzova and Premysl Pitter." Displaced Persons/Return to Life. United States Holocaust Memorial Museum. www.ushmm.org.

O'Neil, Robin. *Oskar Schindler: Stepping Stone to Life.* Salisbury, UK: Susaneking, 2007.

Otto and Gertrud Morike Collection. Landeskirchliches Archiv. Stuttgart, Germany.

Paczkowski, Andrzej. *The Spring Will Be Ours: Poland and the Poles from Occupation to Freedom.* University Park: Pennsylvania State University Press, 1985.

Paldiel, Mordecai. *Churches and the Holocaust: Unholy Teaching, Good Samaritans and Reconciliation.* Jersey City, NJ: KTAV Publishing, 2006.

———. *Diplomat Heroes of the Holocaust.* Jersey City, NJ: KTAV Publishing, 2007.

———. *The Righteous Among the Nations: Rescuers of Jews during the Holocaust.* New York: HarperCollins, 2007.

Powaski, Ronald E. *Lightning War: Blitzkrieg in the West, 1940.* Edison, NJ: Castle Books, 2006.

Presser, Jacob. *Ashes in the Wind: The Destruction of Dutch Jewry.* Detroit: Wayne State University Press, 1982.

"The Program for the Complete Elimination of Jewry." *Nazi Conspiracy and Aggression.* Vol. 1. Washington, DC: US Government Printing Office, 1948.

Rabben, Linda. *Give Refuge to the Stranger: The Past, Present, and Future of Sanctuary.* Walnut Creek, CA: Left Coast Press, 2011.

Raischl, Josef, and Andre Cirino. *Three Heroes of Assisi in World War II.* Phoenix, AZ: Vesuvius Press, 2014.

Rash, Felicity J. *The Language of Violence: Hitler's "Mein Kampf."* New York: Peter Lang Publishing, 2006.

Redlich, Fritz. *Hitler: Diagnosis of a Destructive Prophet.* New York: Oxford University Press, 2000.

Reitlinger, Gerald. *The SS: Alibi of a Nation, 1922–1945.* New York: Viking Press, 1957.

Rich, Elaine Sommers, ed. *Breaking Bread Together.* Eugene, OR: Wipf and Stock, 2007.

Rittner, Carol, and Sondra Myers, eds. *The Courage to Care.* New York: New York University Press, 1986.

Rosenfeld, Alvin H., ed. *The Writer Uprooted: Contemporary Jewish Exile Literature.* Bloomington: Indiana University Press, 2008.

Rothfels, Hans. *The German Opposition to Hitler.* London: Oswald Wolff, 1961.

Rozett, Robert, and Shmuel Spector, eds. *Encyclopedia of the Holocaust.* London: Routledge Publishing, 2000.

Ryan, Cornelius. *The Longest Day: June 6, 1944.* New York: Simon & Schuster, 1959.

Sachs, Ruth Hanna. *Coming Together*. Vol. 1 of *White Rose History*. Lehi, UT: Exclamation! Publishing, 2002.

Sakowicz, Kazimierz. *Ponary Diary, 1941–1943: A Bystander's Account of a Mass Murder*. Edited by Yitzhak Arad. Translated by Laurence Weinbaum. New Haven, CT: Yale University Press, 2005.

Sauvage, Pierre. "Ten Questions about Righteous Conduct in Le Chambon and Elsewhere during the Holocaust." US Holocaust Memorial Council Conference, Elie Wiesel, chairman. Washington, DC, September 19, 1984.

————, director. *Weapons of the Spirit*. Chambon Foundation.

Anton Schmid Collection. Shoah Resource Center. International School for Holocaust Studies.

Schreiber, Marion. *The Twentieth Train: The True Story of the Ambush of the Death Train to Auschwitz*. New York: Grove Press, 2000.

Shirer, William L. *Berlin Diary: The Journal of a Foreign Correspondent, 1934–1941*. New York: Alfred A. Knopf, 1941.

————. *The Rise and Fall of the Third Reich: A History of Nazi Germany*. New York: Simon & Schuster, 1960.

Shwartz, Betzal, ed. *The Book of Kobrin: The Scroll of Life and Destruction*. Translated by Nilli Avidan and Avner Perry. San Francisco: Holocaust Center of Northern California, 1992.

Simon, Andrea. *Bashert: A Granddaughter's Holocaust Quest*. Jackson: University Press of Mississippi, 2002.

Simpson, William C. *A Vatican Lifeline: Allied Fugitives, Aided by the Italian Resistance, Foil the Gestapo in Nazi-Occupied Rome, 1944*. London: Pen and Sword, 1995.

Smelser, Ronald, and Rainer Zitelmann, eds. *The Nazi Elite*. New York: NYU Press, 1993.

Smith, Lynley. *From Matron to Martyr: One Woman's Ultimate Sacrifice for the Jews*. Mustang, OK: Tate Publishing, 2012.

Smith, Michael. *Foley: The Spy Who Saved 10,000 Jews*. London: Hodder & Stoughton, 1999.

Snyder, Timothy. *Bloodlands: Europe between Hitler and Stalin*. New York: Basic Books, 2010.

Spector, Shmuel, and Geoffrey Wigoder, eds. *The Encyclopedia of Jewish Life before and during the Holocaust*. New York: NYU Press, 2001.

Spicer, Kevin P., ed. *Antisemitism, Christian Ambivalence and the Holocaust*. Bloomington: Indiana University Press, 2007.

Stackelberg, Roderick, and Sally A. Winkle, eds. *The Nazi Germany Sourcebook: An Anthology of Texts*. New York: Routledge, 2002.

Stahel, David. *Operation Barbarossa and Germany's Defeat in the East*. Cambridge: Cambridge University Press, 2009.

Steinweis, Alan E. *Kristallnacht 1938*. Cambridge, MA: Harvard University Press, 2009.

Stephens, Don. *War and Grace: Short Biographies from the World Wars.* Darlington, UK: EP Books, 2005.

Stepkova, Teresa. "Premysl Pitter." www.holocaust.cz.

Stroud, Dean G., ed. *Preaching in Hitler's Shadow: Sermons of Resistance in the Third Reich.* Grand Rapids, MI: William B. Eerdmans, 2013.

Taylor, Jay. *The Generalissimo: Chiang Kai-shek and the Struggle for Modern China.* Cambridge, MA: Harvard University Press, 2009.

ten Boom, Corrie. *The Hiding Place: The Triumphant True Story of Corrie ten Boom.* With John Sherrill and Elizabeth Sherrill. Old Tappan, NJ: Fleming H. Revell, 1971.

———. *Tramp for the Lord.* With Jamie Buckingham. Grand Rapids, MI: Fleming H. Revell, 1974.

———. *In My Father's House: The Years Before the Hiding Place.* With C. C. Carlson. Old Tappan, NJ: Fleming H. Revell, 1976.

"Testimony of Heinrich Grueber." Adolf Eichmann Trial. Session 42, 5 May 1961. Adolf Eichmann Trial Collection. Steven Spielberg Film and Video Archives. United States Holocaust Memorial Museum.

"Testimony of Otto Ohlendorf." Nuremberg Trials. National Archives and Records Administration.

Thomas, Gordon. *The Pope's Jews: The Vatican's Secret Plan to Save Jews from the Nazis.* New York: St. Martin's Press, 2012.

Toland, John. *Adolf Hitler: The Definitive Biography.* New York: Doubleday, 1976.

Tortzen, Christian. *Gilleleje, oktober 1943: Under jødernes flugt for nazismen.* Copenhagen: Fremad, 1970.

Trevor-Roper, Hugh. *The Last Days of Hitler.* Chicago: University of Chicago Press, 1992.

"The Trial of Adolf Eichmann." Session 41, part 3. Nizkor Project. Nizkor.org.

"The Trial of Amon Goeth." Part 3, 26 September 1946. Holocaust Education and Archive Research Team. www.holocaustresearchproject.org.

Trocmé, André. *Jesus and the Non-Violent Revolution.* Rifton, NY: Plough Publishing House, 2011.

André Trocmé and Magda Trocmé Papers. Swarthmore College Peace Collection.

Unruh, John David. *In the Name of Christ: A History of the Mennonite Central Committee and Its Service, 1920–1951.* Scottsdale, AZ: Herald Publishing, 1952.

Vajda, Tibor Timothy. *In the Whirlwind of History: Struggle On and Keep the Faith.* New York: iUniverse, 2005.

van Liempt, Ad. *Hitler's Bounty Hunters: The Betrayal of the Jews.* Oxford: Berg, 2005.

Veranneman, Jean-Michel. *Belgium in the Second World War.* Barnsley, UK: Pen and Sword, 2014.

Vickers, Hugo. *Alice: Princess Andrew of Greece*. New York: St. Martin's Press, 2002.

Wachsmann, Nikolaus. *KL: A History of the Nazi Concentration Camps*. New York: Farrar, Straus & Giroux, 2015.

Walters, Guy. *Hunting Evil: The Nazi War Criminals Who Escaped and the Quest to Bring Them to Justice*. New York: Broadway Books, 2009.

Wapshott, Nicholas. *The Sphinx: Franklin Roosevelt, the Isolationists, and the Road to World War II*. New York: W. W. Norton, 2015.

Warmbrunn, Werner. *The Dutch under German Occupation*. Stanford, CA: Stanford University Press, 1972.

Warriner, Doreen. "Winter in Prague." *Slavonic and East European Review* 62, no. 2 (April 1984): 209–40.

Wasserstein, Bernard. *The Ambiguity of Virtue: Gertrude van Tijn and the Fate of the Dutch Jews*. Cambridge, MA: Harvard University Press, 2014.

Weinberg, Gerhard L. *A World at Arms: A Global History of World War II*. Cambridge: Cambridge University Press, 1994.

Weintraub, Stanley. *11 Days in December: Christmas at the Bulge, 1944*. New York: New American Library, 2006.

Wernick, Robert. *Blitzkrieg*. New York: Time-Life, 1977.

Wette, Wolfram. *Feldwebel Anton Schmid: Ein Held der Humanität*. Frankfurt, Ger.: S. Fischer, 2003.

———. *The Wehrmacht: History, Myth, Reality*. Translated by Deborah Lucas Schneider. Cambridge, MA: Harvard University Press, 2006.

Whitlock, Flint. *Given Up for Dead: American GIs in the Nazi Concentration Camp at Berga*. New York: Basic Books, 2005.

Wiesenthal, Simon. *The Murderers among Us: The Simon Wiesenthal Memoirs*. Edited by Joseph Wechsberg. New York: McGraw-Hill, 1967.

Wijsmuller-Meijer, Truus. *Geen tijd voor tranen*. Amsterdam: P. N. van Kampen, 1964.

Williams, Althea. "A Child in Time: Surviving Auschwitz." *History Today* 6, no. 4 (April 2013): 46–47.

Wilt, Alan F. *War from the Top: German and British Military Decision Making during World War II*. Bloomington: Indiana University Press, 1990.

Winstone, Martin. *The Holocaust Sites of Europe: An Historic Guide*. London: I. B. Tauris, 2010.

Wood, E. Thomas, and Stanislaw M. Jankowski. *Karski: How One Man Tried to Stop the Holocaust*. Hoboken, NJ: John Wiley & Sons, 1994.

Woolfson, Shivaun. *Holocaust Legacy in Post-Soviet Lithuania: People, Places and Objects*. London: Bloomsbury Publishing, 2014.

Wuerth, Hans M. "During Holocaust, Jews Were Helped by Righteous Gentiles." *Morning Call*, January 26, 2013.

Yahil, Leni. *The Rescue of Danish Jewry: Test of a Democracy.* Philadelphia: Jewish Publication Society of America, 1969.

Yee, Edmond. *The Soaring Crane: Stories of Asian Lutherans in North America.* Minneapolis: Ausburg Fortress, 1998.

Young, Justin. "Andre Trocme and Le Chambon: The Preciousness of Human Life." Unpublished thesis. University of California–Santa Barbara, 2005.

Zabarko, Boris, ed. *Holocaust in the Ukraine.* Portland, OR: Vallentine Mitchell, 2005.

Zuckerman, Larry. *The Rape of Belgium: The Untold Story of World War I.* New York: New York University Press, 2004.

INDEX

Note: Page numbers in *italics* indicate photographs.

ABOUT THE AUTHOR

HISTORIAN ROD GRAGG is a former news journalist. He is the author of more than twenty books on topics in American history, and his works have won various awards. He and his family live in South Carolina, where he serves as director of the CresCom Bank Center for Military & Veterans Studies at Coastal Carolina University.